DEFIANCE IN THE FAMILY

DEFIANCE IN THE FAMILY

Finding Hope in Therapy

David V. Keith
Gary M. Connell
Linda C. Connell

Routledge
Taylor & Francis Group
New York London

First published by BRUNNER/MAZEL Philadelphia and London

This edition published 2013 by Routledge

Routledge
Taylor & Francis Group
711 Third Avenue
New York, NY 10017

Routledge
Taylor & Francis Group
27 Church Road
Hove, East Sussex BN3 2FA

First issued in paperback 2014

Routledge is an imprint of the Taylor & Francis Group, an informa business

DEFIANCE IN THE FAMILY: Finding Hope in Therapy

Cover design by Howell Burnell.

A CIP catalog record for this book is available from the British Library.

Library of Congress Cataloging-in-Publication Data
Keith, David V.
Defiance in the family : finding hope in therapy / David V. Keith, Gary M. Connell, Linda C. Connell.
p. cm.
Includes index.
ISBN 1-58391-004-2 (alk. paper)
1. Oppositional defiant disorder in children—Treatment. 2. Oppositional defiant disorder in adolescence—Treatment. 3. Ecological family therapy. 4. Oppositional defiant disorder in children—Treatment—Case studies. 5. Oppositional defiant disorder in adolescence—Treatment—Case studies. 6. Ecological family therapy—Case studies. I. Connel, Gary M. II. Connell, Linda C. III. Title.

RJ506.066 K44 2000
618.92'89156—dc21

00-052947

ISBN 13: 978-1-58391-004-7 (hbk)
ISBN 13: 978-0-415-76331-8 (pbk)

Dedication

This book is dedicated to Noel Keith and to those delightful people we still refer to as our children. They were just defiant enough and gave us numerous second chances for growth.

Peter, Rosalind, Douglas, and Gregory Keith
Christian and Arin Connell

Contents

Acknowledgments

We want to acknowledge the help of the family whose members the reader meets in the transcripts. We did not choose them because they fit our formulations, but because they were so rambunctiously defiant and frustrating to work with. We had written the first section of the book before engaging with them in therapy. It was surprising how well they fit the model we were developing for working with the problem of defiance. Our work with them deepened our understanding of the interaction of the family process, defiant behavior, and the therapeutic process. This was real therapy for these family members. They shared their lives and their pain and were a very important part of the project.

William Bumberry and Noel Keith are a significant part of anything we write; they have intimate knowledge of our thinking and our work. When we were trying to formulate something or give shape to an ambiguous process, we would bring it to them, and they would helpfully heat it in their forges and shape the idea so as to make it useful. The spirit of Carl Whitaker was also present at the forge; he is in the background of anything we write. He was our model for being an experiential learner. Our friends William Bumberry, PhD, David Kaye, MD, and Russel Haber, PhD, helped us with detailed reading of the manuscript and provided needed suggestions and encouragement. Christian Connell, PhD and Jennifer Connell, MSW transcribed the interviews and gave technical assistance to the computer-inept authors. Katherine Mortimer and Tim Julet at Taylor & Francis gave professional guidance in bringing our experience into a book. Katherine encouraged our efforts and helped us voice our ideas. It has been an enriching process for us. We hope we have made it possible for the reader to share in that enrichment.

Introduction

This book describes the relationship between health and defiance in families and emphasizes how family therapy can repair relationships disrupted by defiance. While it is written with therapists in mind, we hope the book will also be useful to families, both in understanding defiance and in understanding the therapeutic process in family therapy. The ideas in this book are based on our model for looking at human experience one which is derived from clinical experience and guided by a systems orientation or epistemology.

Our thinking and clinical work are based on an ecosystemic thinking pattern. We are not talking about the *Diagnostic and Statistical Manual of Mental Disorders*, Fourth Edition, of the American Psychiatric Association (APA, 1994), diagnostic category of oppositional defiant disorder or any other formal way of configuring pathology. The DSM series represents a way of looking at human experience from a model based on linear thinking, the dominant thinking pattern in our culture and is a retreat from an ecosystemic orientation. The ecosystemic viewpoint can be confusing at times, because it acknowledges the world of human experience as an unsolvable labyrinth. An ecosystemic orientation makes us aware of the endless ambiguity inherent in human experience. It helps us appreciate and take pleasure in the ambiguity of living.

Defiance potentially plays a crucial role in all relationship parameters, inside the family and between the family and the community. Defiance is ubiquitous and leads to health or destruction. It is part of the dynamics of a healthy marriage, especially when rules are being renegotiated. While defiant behavior is painful, burdensome, and paralyzing, we want to show that it can be exhilarating and rejuvenating. Defiant behavior raises the level of ambiguity about living and leads families into therapy. The conventional therapeutic response attempts to modify the defiant behavior to bring about a sounder social adaptation. However, what is crucial is not the behavior itself, but the context of the behavior and the responses it stimulates. Family therapists are uniquely suited to deal with defiance, but they must work hard to maintain their role as therapists and not be co-opted into becoming educators, investigators, or probation officers.

From our perspective, colored by existential and systemic thinking, defiance is a way of protecting and preserving the inner Self (Soul), in the face of perceived threat, from being ignored, forced into a system of values it does not trust or honor, treated like an object, either admired or despised, or double bound into nonexistence. Obviously, defiance has both constructive and destructive components. This book does not discuss extremes of defiance or antisocial behavior. Instead, it discusses families in which defiance is problematic but workable within the context of our therapeutic philosophy. Defiance can be so extreme that it results in an irreversible situation, in which the child is removed and the community takes over. Such families are beyond the scope of the book.

In Section 1, we describe our model for how families work and how defiance arises out of family interactions. We encourage you to deconstruct and reconstruct it to fit your own type of therapy. A clinical model is an atheoretical model, a model for having a model based on the practitioner's experience. We assume each therapist, like every family, has an implicit model for family relationships and how they work. To go further, it is crucial in experiential therapy that the therapist have a model. In the therapeutic interaction, the models are *parallel* to one another, but the therapist's model is more *explicit*, more accessible.

Section II offers a clinical application of our model with detailed discussion of therapeutic interventions. Two chapters contain transcripts of interviews. They are designed to give therapists some sense of the methods of working with defiance, within a family context, to support the development and overall health of the *person* and the *family*. Our philosophy is that family therapy works to rejuvenate the family "we" so its members can deal with the community and each other on their own. In the process, the therapist temporarily takes on the role of the defiant family member.

Throughout our writing we stumbled over the use of the word "children" to refer to adolescents. We do not mean to be indiscriminate in our use of the same term to refer to two developmentally distinct groups. Children are the progeny of their parents. Therefore, regardless of their age, they are in some sense children. We have used the word "children" as a way to distinguish between the generations. Sometimes the "child" is an "adolescent" with muscles and a goatee.

As experiential learners we take to heart what Norman O. Brown (1966) said, "Meaning is new, or not at all." And, "The God Delphi, who always spoke the truth, never gave a straight answer, in the upright Protestant way; he always spoke in riddles, in parables; ambiguities, temptations; that hearing they might not hear and not understand. . . . The real deceivers are the literalists, who say I cannot tell a lie, or *hypotheses non fingo*" (I deal entirely with facts).

1

Defiance in Families:

Rebellion in the Name of Health

We are bombarded daily by examples of defiant children and adolescents out of control, killing themselves, their parents, or each other. The gruesome stories turn into cultural pornography for the media. The problem of defiance is all around us, in all social classes, and in every school and neighborhood. It is reaching epidemic proportions. Many of society's responses to defiance only stimulate more defiance. For example, the impulse to punish, exclude, or enact zero-tolerance policies may be an error that adds to the problem. In this book, we work with the idea that family therapy is a way to detoxify and to undermine the alienation that results from defiance. However, this is not a simple solution. It is a solution that takes more energy than punishment and more time and investment than medication, but we believe the change that comes from therapeutic work with families is more enduring.

We have many ways of distressing our intimates, especially children and spouses. One way is by making them responsible for carrying *our* hopes for the future. Another, more dangerous way is by identifying in them what we fear most in ourselves, then acting as though it has nothing to do with us. In this book we focus primarily on defiance in parent-child relationships, but much of what we say can be transposed to dealing with defiance in marital relationships as well.

Defiant adolescents and oppositional children are demonized in our culture. How do we deal with demons? We provide structure and discipline so that they will stop being demons and become more angelic. When structure and discipline work, the result is very pleasing. We are not about to worry about the angels. We worry about what to do when discipline only makes the demons more defiant. Our culture, looking backwards to some fantasied era, follows simple principles. If children don't behave, we extrude them, diagnose them, or medicate them. We kick them out of the school, the family, and the inpatient unit until they learn to behave. The prevailing thinking is that those demons need "counseling." "Send him to the counselor! Let's get to the bottom of this!" The counselor says, "This kid doesn't want to be here, so how can I help him?" Now what? We favor simple solutions when they work, but what about when they don't work? It is possible that many of our solutions become part of the problem. "Spare the rod and spoil the child" is a solution, but don't forget: use the rod and embitter the child; use the rod and wound the child.

In this book, we look at defiance as a byproduct of family interactions and, simultaneously, a byproduct of the family's interaction with the culture. The family serves several contradictory purposes. It teaches its members, especially children, to adapt to the culture, it shields its members from the culture, and it teaches its members when not to adapt to the culture. More helpful than demonizing the defiant child's family and throwing the group into a human-sized wastebasket, is working to help families repair problems that lead to defiance.

When the parent, the school, or counselor says, "He *chooses* to do these defiant things. He has to start making the right *choices*, or we are going to kick him out," we respectfully disagree. Choices are part of a pattern that includes irritated-to-outraged adults. Children's choices are heavily shaped by the context in which they live. The therapeutic process looks at the culturally invisible parts of the pattern that are embedded in how the family operates.

WHAT IS DEFIANCE?

At the outset, let's look more deeply at this phenomenon called *defiance*. Defiance is "bold resistance to an opposing force or authority; a deliberately provocative behavior or attitude." But if we go further, to the etymology of the word, we find it implies a renunciation of faith in, or alliance or amity with. It represents a declaration of hostility against something. Defiance is a result of a collapse of *fealty*. Fealty is the duty and loyalty owed by a vassal or tenant to his feudal lord, or of a dependent person to their caretaker. Fealty refers to faith, loyalty, and fidelity; it is synonymous with allegiance.

What we find fascinating, is that defiance comes from the same etymological root as *faith* and *fealty*; they are part of the same *mater eternus*. If we look for defiance in the etymological dictionary, we are referred to *defy* (Partridge, 1966). Quoting loosely, we find; "to renounce a sworn faith, hence to remove one's confidence from, to provoke or defy" (Partridge, 1966). Then, surprisingly, we are referred to *fidelity* and *fait, faith, faithful, fidelity, fealty, federal, federate, federation. . . . fiancé, fiancée, confidant, confident, confidential*. These are all words that have to do with trust and unity. Then the ground shifts slightly to *diffident* and *diffidence*, which imply hesitance or a lack of self-confidence. Finally, we arrive at *defy, defiant, defiance*. Continuing leads to extremes; *infidel, infidelity, perfidious, perfidy*, having the implication of being disloyal and without faith. What is important in the linguistics of experience is that faith and defiance are linked. Defiance emerges when faith is compromised. But we must emphasize that this collapse and reconstruction of faith and fealty is an inevitable component of family living. We believe that where there is caring, all pathology is sharing or repairing. But if the origins of the defiant behavior (collapse of fealty) are not considered and the process continues, it becomes treacherous and perfidious, and the defiant one is morphed into an extruded infidel.

The family is a metaphorical forest of personal growth. That is to say, the complexity of any family is immeasurable and poetic. In order to know what is going on in a family, it is necessary to enter the family. The interior is much like a forest. The family is the arena for loss of faith and bold resistance, the collapse of fealty we call defiance. Defiance is disruptive and destructive; it urges a suppressing response. Defiance is a call for repair and, while harshness is sometimes required, the salve of caring is always necessary. What is important is that faith and defiance are linked. Defiance emerges when faith is compromised. We underscore that this collapse and reconstruction of fealty is an inevitable component of family living. If the origins of defiant behavior are not considered and the process continues, a three-generational battle of good versus evil results.

Defiance is a dance, but it is not one person dancing alone. Defiance is part of a multiple-person behavior system. In extreme situations, the defiant one ends up in a parallel universe that has very different values from those held by the other family members. When statements are made about the need for a child to make the right choices, it is important to consider the fact that he is making choices based on experiential coordinates adults seldom comprehend. Children live in a parallel universe. Adults who try to enter by recalling their own growing up, still don't approximate what children are experiencing. This book provides a perspective for thinking about defiance and how therapists and parents respond to it. The more ways we have of looking at a complex problem like defiance, the better able we are to understand how to engage it.

Defiance does not just appear. Rather, it represents a response to a disruption of faith, a collapse of fealty somewhere in the family. There is a deterioration of the trust between child and parents necessary to guarantee an environment of self-realization for all members. From an existential view, defiance refers to a situation where the *I* is not respected. Defiance is part of a correcting system; it is activated in order to provide correction but is easily distorted or overamplified when there is poor response. The response may be overly repressive at one extreme, or nonexistent at the other.

There is a capacity for defiance in all of us. This fight or flight reaction is an instinctual response. When an individual's or system's integrity or dignity is threatened and when that threat is persistent or overwhelming, defiance protects the threatened boundaries. The threat may be real or perceived and may come from any authority figure, such as a parent or teacher. Families with younger children usually experience concern or discomfort around the child's behavior and seek help or advice. In adolescence this behavior requires attention, not only because of family conflict, but as a result of complaints from other systems (e.g., the school). The outside systems pressure the family to seek help by threatening sanctions against the child or family, such as expulsion from school. When outside systems mandate referral, families may enter therapy angry and resistant. The therapeutic endeavor is to understand what purpose defiance serves by getting to the underlying dynamics: the fear of extrusion and the loss of faith. It is useful to keep in mind, however, that defiance begins as a self-protective function to avoid pain and to restore dignity or integrity.

HEALTHY FAMILIES

Healthy families have a dynamic stability we think of as "normally crazy." Growth requires imbalance and takes place both within individual family members and within the family as a whole. The family system allows for and, in fact, encourages and supports efforts toward growth. Growth is not an even process; it can be chaotic and uncomfortable under the best circumstances, especially when the growing is being done by an adolescent. Growth pressures families. When parent says, "We feel so crazy," a therapist might respond, "If you don't feel crazy, you are probably not engaged." Children and parents seldom follow the developmental trajectories found in books. Family developmental literature provides a rough map for understanding family life. It describes commonalties among families, tasks requiring mastery at various stages, and predictable crises families encounter as they mature. But defiance is not likely to be viewed as a component of normal development. In most linear frameworks, defiance is viewed as pathological.

Defiance is an interaction, a multi-person dance. However, this perspective is not held by those seeking therapy or by the community referring families for treatment. In healthy families there is a robust dialectical tension between the individual and the group. This spirited dance adds to the liveliness of the family through respect for and enjoyment of differences. The capacity for differentiation paradoxically increases the richness of intimacy. However, experience has taught us that this spirited dance is an essential component of growth and development; it occurs in all families and all individuals. In fact, it actually serves an important function in the preservation of family unity. Healthy families are able to acknowledge and respect the uniqueness of each generation. Said differently, and this is an important theme of the book, *the older generation is able to learn from the younger generation, even to accept parenting from the younger generation*, either for fun or out of necessity, such as during periods of illness or distress. Part of the energy for family health comes from the endless dialectic of differentiation and engagement, individuation and togetherness. The dialectics come to resolution through the recognition of family loyalty and family identity when fealty is intact. The healthy family may have lusty heated battles over school, alcohol use, or sex, but the next day all are there for dinner. Tension is acknowledged, but not paralyzing.

The toddler who has a tantrum because he would rather watch television than eat supper is being defiant. He is letting his parents know he is not happy with their plan for him. This is healthy behavior. The parents know how to pressure for compliance and, simultaneously, to enjoy and respect the energy of difference. The parent allows the child an opportunity to have an opposing viewpoint. Through these efforts, the child learns how to belong, how to get needs met, and ways of relating when displeased. Through honest negotiations, deep emotional investment, and modeling, the parent teaches the child to express himself, but more crucially to *be* a self.

A MODEL FOR FAMILY ORGANIZATION

A healthy family is organized in the form of a hierarchy, much like an army. This metaphorical army has no interest in obliterating anyone. Its mission is to fight for and support health. The parents are the commanding officers of the army. Both are five-star generals. The children are the privates and sergeants who gradually work their way up to junior officer status. One five-star general cannot boss the other five-star general around; they are peers. Rank has its privilege. The generals have the right to make unilateral decisions without consulting the soldiers. Rank also has its responsibility, and the generals are responsible for the troops' morale. When fealty is intact, morale is robust. The health of the army, both as a group and as individuals, is rooted in the group's spirit. Dissension increases when morale is poor and *I*-oriented behavior is viewed as defiance. That's when fealty collapses. Evidence of good morale is seen in the individual member's right to belong or individuate on their own initiative without being demonized. The *private style* of family members is respected without counter-pressure or bitter resignation. Private style has to do with the freedom to be an *I*, and to experiment with lifestyle.

This component of family living, respect for private style, depends upon the maturity of the parents. Adding to the complexity of this role is a requirement for the parents to protect children from the culture's endless coercion to emulate icons that are dramatically different from the family. Parents thus have the responsibility for simultaneously teaching children to adapt to the culture and to have the ability to be countercultural.

Changes in society over the past 25 years have had profound effects on family life. Many of these effects are toxic, but *culturally invisible*. Cultural invisibility has the implication that these behavior patterns are so much a part of the way we live, we don't perceive the pressure they impose. Those who question them are seen as wrong or inappropriate. Examples include the community's access to the family interior in the name of abuse prevention and the precipitous expansion of the use of medication to manage behavior. Many families are demoralized, overwhelmed, and stressed beyond imagination. The many-faceted monstrosity we call "the media" bombards us with fictional characters that are surreal models for living. Advertisement invades our homes in ways that promote dissatisfaction with accomplishments and the trappings of daily life. Parents feel inadequate to provide the latest gadgets for their children. Despite wanting the best for them, parents worry they aren't providing all their children need. Indeed, parents want a better life for their children. The culture of experts imposes standards for development and education that serve institutional more than personal needs. In the guise of caring, parents have expectations, largely unconscious, for their children that impose immense pressure on the next generation's formulae for happiness and satisfaction which have eluded most parents themselves.

Our values and goals regarding family life are challenged and disrupted. In an effort to live the "good life," we lose sight of the joys of relationships and the intrinsic value of work and creativity. Daily expectations of work and success compete with family life; time and money dominate. Parents find little support, economically or philosophically, from their government or corporate America. More children than ever live in poverty, attend inadequate schools, receive poor health care, are falling behind academically, and experience divorce, violence, and unpredictability. Children are often left to their own devices to make sense of the world because parents are too busy pursuing a lifestyle that promises happiness, leisure, and freedom, but often results in debt, despair, and overwork. The intrinsic worth of people, relationships, learning, and work is diminished in relation to this view of life as only a means to something else, most likely unattainable. The roadblocks for families are omnipresent and contribute to increased defiance, between the family and the community, and within the family.

The biopsychosystemic ecology of the family includes mother, father, brother, sister, sibling subgroup, the marriage, and the families of origin. A healthy family has a three-to-four generation in-the-head family they can use as a reference library for making decisions about how to live. One goal of the therapeutic process is to develop a sense of connection in the immediate family to its past generations. The effect of doing this expands the context of the child's defiance, so that it becomes part of the bigger family picture. The initial family history attends to both the past and present. It considers not only facts, but also the symbolic and process components of historical events. For example, in an initial history a therapist learned that mother's parents divorced when she was 14 years old. The therapist asked, "What happened to the family after they split up? Do you think that had anything to do with you getting pregnant the next year?" There is often a connection between stressful events in family life.

As emphasized later in the book, the conjoint, multi-person, multi-generational, context-oriented family history is a powerful tool for shedding light on the family and its members perceptions and building a foundation for development. We learn about a family through the stories it tells, both individually and collectively. A family's history is made up of a complex and odd mixture of facts and symbolic events, most easily conveyed through stories. Family facts are malleable, shaped by what members fear, hope for, see, and can't see when they look in the mirror.

We are not just looking at families; we are looking at families in relation to a therapeutic process. At the first meeting with a family, we ask what the members are looking for from therapy. This is part of encouraging them to give up the delusion that we, or any experts, know what is best for them. We coach them to be in charge of themselves, a mature form of defiance. Usually a therapy project begins as an effort to fix a family problem, but inevitably, the problem appears rooted in family systemic tangles, which need attention (e.g., father's dishonesty or mother's self-righteous rage). How have they tried to fix things so far? Are the parents emotionally and physically available to each other and to the children? Can they be a team or do they defeat each other's attempts at parenting? How honest and in-depth can parents stand to be? These are all questions we believe families benefit from discussing in an initial assessment.

FAMILY THERAPY AND DEFIANCE

Why do families come for therapy? They come in frustration edged with confusion, stimulated by their own or someone else's anxiety. One or more of the following issues is often identified: (a) The parents' fantasies about their child's future are too disturbing, (b) They are attempting to fix something and the child stays the same, (c) They are trying not to notice how serious a problem has become, but an outside agent (e.g., the court or school), has insisted they do something about what is wrong.

When defiant families enter therapy they display erratic and complex processes, related to a blend of anxiety and fear about when and what to expose about themselves. Patterns in such families are similar, even when they come from different socioeconomic contexts. They may be added by therapists, executives, ministers, or laborers; they may be overly represented in lower socioeconomic groups. Although defiance is not unique to any particular status, it may be more desperate in families with lower socioeconomic status and fewer resources. Defiance, especially in the younger generation, is a shield for desperation. Families with few resources often come to the attention of the community due to an inability to cover up their problems or to deflect the community's interest. Defiant families frequently exclude or dampen intimacy, role flexibility, creativity, problem solving, and personal self-confidence. When the family spirit is thus diminished, defiance may appear in one or more family members. The range of symptoms in the adolescent includes the usual signs: being mouthy, staying out all night, coming home drunk, abusing drugs, or failing in school.

What is frequently missing in many family evaluations is an appreciation for and the freedom to attend to the context of each person's behavior. We assume that there is a broader context, both real and symbolic, and that the upsetting behavior is related to this context. Defiance is an attempt to bring a larger problem into awareness. The larger problem, the pain behind the pain, may be parental conflict, marital dissatisfaction, child maltreatment, parental rages, a crisis in a grandparent's life, phobias, the proximity of death, or any host of systemic problems. The larger problem is embedded in the family life cycle across generations.

Each family, like each individual, has an identity. This identity is complex and accessible, both in direct and indirect ways. Identity emerges out of a mixture of historical facts, family stories, metaphorical reality, and behavior patterns. One family member cannot describe a whole family. He can only describe his fantasy about the family. For example, mother may be frantic about her son's behavior. Father normalizes the son's behavior and insists mother is crazy because her parents were so puritanical. It is crucial to have the whole family present for the first interview in order to obtain the kind of history which is necessary at the beginning of the therapeutic project. The first interview can only be conducted once.

When family image and identity are challenged, family members inevitably become defiant. Families who have a history of handling distress in their past, are more likely to self-correct with family support, energy, and honesty when they encounter distress sufficient to challenge their present way of approaching life. Some families are chronically intergenerationally defiant; defiance is a core component of their identity, they have more difficulty self-correcting, and they run the risk of organizing their lives around defiance. For example, an adolescent upset his mother and the school because he liked to stay out late, would not do homework, and was always getting in fights. He and his mother were at the initial interview. The father lived out of town. As the therapist talked with the mother and son, he pointed out, "The school said in their report that you have been getting in fights." And the boy replied, "No, I assault people." When questioned further, he explained the difference between getting in fights and assaulting people. Later in the interview the therapist learned father was a Vietnam veteran with posttraumatic stress disorder and a bad temper. He was discharged from the military for assaulting an officer. Thus, assault is part of the fabric of the adolescent's identity, his identification with his lost father. This identification is, on some level, his effort to save his father and to give meaning to his father's life.

Family image and family identity are not the same. Image is more conscious and describes the "who-they-think-they-are" or the "who-they-intend-to-be." It emphasizes positive, desirable features. Identity, on the other hand, is rooted in the unconscious. It is made up of the totality of experience and is less accessible. It is most accessible through primary process reflection by a multi-generational group and can include broken dreams, unacknowledged acts of cowardice, or secret rages. When a therapist comments on parenting, he may be challenging both image and identity.

THE ETIOLOGY OF DEFIANCE

It is important to note that there is always pain behind the pain of defiance. The therapist needs to gain awareness of what that deeper pain is and how it relates to the present dilemmas. The world of background pain is not a world of concrete reality; it has the emotionally ambiguous quality of a dream world and its meaning is implicitly symbolic at multiple levels. It is a world that disappears in the bright light of reason. The crucial question is this: if defiance is the result of a collapse of fealty, what is the pain behind the pain that produced this collapse? The pain may be in a story, but more likely, the pain is in the process, in the living patterns. However, the family is not able to see it and may not be glad to hear what the therapist's intuition apprehends. Concrete conclusions presented by a parent or therapist are usually an error.

A therapist is first told about, and then sees evidence of, defiant behavior. In the following paragraphs we delineate some of the conditions that stimulate and perpetuate defiance. The family is not likely to define these problems. A therapist initially may not see them. Some of what we are talking about depends on intuition, which is based on the residual of a therapist's experience in relation to the family's story. The following descriptions are meant to help the therapist see into the family system to identify the underlying pain.

1. The unconscious problem of broken faith becomes rigidly fixed and severe when conflict is based on something symbolic in the family's background. There is an unacknowledged symbolic process or catastrophe fantasy. For example, a fear of craziness may be based on the fact that a family member, a generation back, was hospitalized and diagnosed as schizophrenic. Therefore, in the family mythology someone else is supposed to be schizophrenic. Perhaps father is 38 years old, his father died at age 39. Thus, father may have the fantasy he will soon die. Mother's parents divorced after 14 years of marriage. She may anticipate that her husband is going to leave her. High-voltage ambiguous facts feed the family's fantasy life, create hidden phobias, and guide their decisionmaking and values. These fragments are not conscious enough to be included in the initial history. The result is overcaution related to a fear that the catastrophe will occur again.

For example, the Bensons were referred with their son Joe, an oppositional 13-year-old. When Joe was 4 years old, his mother was hospitalized for 5 months during a pregnancy which produced a baby who died 8 days after birth. There were some stories about Joe's surprising sadness over the death a year later. Symbolically, this was an emotionally powerful period in the family's life, yet they were matter-of-fact about it. The parents underestimated the importance of this daughter's death to Joe and to themselves. They underestimated the pain Joe was in over his behavior problems. This situation produced a circle of defiance. He was in pain and resisted pressure; more power was brought to bear and he became defiant. When mother wept as she recalled the death of the baby, father became irritable with Joe. In this case, fealty was weakened by deep, but unacknowledged, emotion.

2. Mother or father has an unconscious and unacknowledged, but insatiable, emotional hunger. Both of the following patterns are symptomatic: (a) Mother attempts to manage all things in the family with her overmothering. (b) Father is emotionally distant and does not believe in counseling. His problem

with counseling is that it exposes his hunger. As long as his hunger remains unacknowledged and unnamed, it need not be felt. One corrective response from a therapist would be to mother the parent, but mothering is best done in the family context. Family therapists should beware of this situation. They are often seduced into doing individual therapy with the fantasy of a pseudo-peer relationship with a pseudo-grown-up. Hunger is a family problem. The hunger referred to is not easily acknowledged; efforts to gratify it may be received with hostility. It is painful to learn about it. Thus, a mother may be very loving with her children, but not be able to accept love from anyone. This interferes with healthy relatedness. If mother's hunger is exposed, father feels responsible, however, he responds with hostility. There are many men who become abusive when a woman they love is in pain.

3. A political position or a diagnostic entity takes precedence over personhood. The family or someone in the family may have a commitment to a political or religious position which amplifies the rigidity in their personal living, such as born-again Christianity, feminism, antifeminism, or addiction recovery. Life may also be organized around a diagnosis. For example, father has obsessive-compulsive disorder, mother has fibromyalgia, or Bobby has attention-deficit disorder. We are not implying that these views are inherently wrong, but when a rigid commitment comes between the persons in a family so that it takes precedence over personal living, it represents a collapse of fealty. In one family, the parents had gone into the Amway business. The son and daughter experienced this as a "thought control system" that interfered with the parents' spontaneity. This is an example of a belief system taking precedence over personhood. The children reacted with a concert of acting-out behaviors, defying the "positive" values of the new language. Life for this family had been postponed until the future date when they would reach a predetermined goal and magically achieve a trouble-free, affluent lifestyle.

4. The family does not know how to play. Its members lack an ability to pretend or to be amused by themselves. Concrete thinking and the absence of imagination are cultural symptoms of not knowing how to play. Any political or religious position, as noted above, can have the same effect of concretizing values and interfering with the spontaneity that health requires.

5. The family is unable to stop playing. This is the flip side of the above dynamic. Such a family has a playful quality, perhaps too playful. There is no "off" switch to its playfulness. A witty remark is always required, thus, no one or nothing is taken seriously. The attitude of this family is, "Don't worry, they will grow out of it. I got in trouble too, no big deal!" The children's behavior demands maturity from the parents, but, because all is trivial, no one is able to take and hold a position.

6. Intimacy is viewed as compromising integrity. Some families have a limited capacity for intimacy and consider showing love a weakness. While they believe intimacy collapses individuation, we believe individuation is not possible when there is no intimacy. Unusual integrity in the parent results in more defiance in the children. This is a common characteristic of a defiant family, in

which their shared anger at the community is the bond that unites them. However, intimacy between persons is absent from the family, as if they are phobic of intimacy. On another level, a well-organized family may acknowledge their love for one another, but be stiff and duty bound. "He knows I love him. I don't have to tell him." This statement represents the *fact* of loving, based on the biological linkage through the children and the long-term relationship. It is different from the *feeling* of being loved.

7. The parents are unbending or unyielding. They are committed to consistency. There is too much *no* not enough *yes* or negotiation that allows new experiences or leads to changing perceptions. The member who says "no" is always correct. Obviously, if you don't do anything, you won't make mistakes. If you don't spend money, you won't go broke. "Yes" is taking a chance. Any attempt to live risks getting it wrong. Getting it wrong is not the same as death. Emerson told us that consistency is the hobgoblin of small minds. A common dynamic emerges when adolescents begin to individuate from the family. Parents have the fantasy that if they keep a tight rein on the child, life will be smoother, when in fact the tight rein leads to more bucking. Adolescent defiance begins as a healthy part of development. While it is important to notice naughty behavior, it is not always necessary to do something about it. "Peek-a-boo, I see you," is good enough. It lets the adolescent know the parents are watching. Ignoring is one of the worst parental sins. Usually the parent is attempting to ignore something they believe they can do nothing about.

8. The parents were parentified in their family of origin. These parents acted as though they were 50 years old since the age of 5, and they have been parents for so long that they are "biologically" unable to do anything wrong. For example, in a moment of insight, in the fifth interview, the father of an angry defiant son surprised the therapist when he began to weep as he recalled a mischievous event from his own early adolescence. His teacher had said, "William, you wouldn't do that. You don't do things like that." Father complained that he was so good, he could not get any credit for misbehaving. The dynamic here is that he is covertly defiant but lacks the courage to do what his son does. His weeping was hard to figure out. The therapist suggested to the father, both tenderly and playfully, "Your son might feel better if you got a tattoo."

9. Family image takes precedence over family spirit. These families do the right thing, belong to the right groups, are well respected in the community, but when they appear for therapy the only family member who appears alive is the defiant child. This child will not settle for the plastic existence of the rest of the family, making explicit the duplicitous nature of the family. From the outside, they are an appealing successful family by all standards. Internally, they are disconnected and remain together only to support an image. The community may force this image on the family when it has "VIP" status (e.g., pastor, police officer, teacher, physician). The family may be cornered by the way they are seen. Thus the defiant child may be attempting to free the parents from the demands of their reputation.

10. The family is isolated. This isolation may be due to chronic illness,

alcoholism, poor resources, family violence, or shame. Isolation may also result from "VIP" status. The isolation is both protective and problematic. Their commitment to isolation makes it difficult for them to form a bond with a therapist. Entering a therapeutic alliance undermines the basis of their bond and simultaneously makes them aware of the lack of internal personal intimacy.

Families do not offer these etiological components when they talk about their concerns, nor do they agree if they are defined as a problem. This is where professionalism based on clinical experience becomes so important. These features are components of our model of how defiant families work, based on our experience. The therapist must be alert to the process dynamics to get a clearer sense of the terrain. At its simplest, this might be called reframing or deconstruction. Awareness of how these families interact, not only with each other but also with the community, gives the therapist a clearer sense of the function the defiance serves. Underlying dynamics become clear as the therapist gets to know the families better. As engagement increases, the therapist's view may change differently. However, involvement also complicates the ability to comment effectively by interfering with objectivity. Family symptoms interfere with the development of healthy coping strategies. A defiant family is often defined by pathology that polarizes family members from the community. Pathology can also be used to extrapolate backwards. For example, an angry child suggests a history of abuse. Overrigid parenting may be the result of chaotic life in the previous generation.

THE PARENTS' ROLE IN DEFIANCE

Talking about parenting and parents can be painful. One tender spot is the matter of guilt and projected blame. But one of the most sensitive issues is the interaction of parenting and gender. Our way of looking at families may seem too traditional. The traditional model of a family is our departure point and the template we use to organize our discussion. The following observations have the limited validity of our clinical observation. Gender roles have been and continue to be in a healthy state of flux. Nevertheless, because women bear children they also tend to become mothers, and whatever the basis, genetic or social, women do a better job of mothering. A critical by-product of industrialized society is that children are bonded more closely to mothers while fathers are alienated from the family. On a positive note, men who grow up close to their mothers are likely to have nurturing qualities which contribute to the richness of family life. Men nurture, interact with, and rear children competently, but differently from women; not worse, not better, but differently (Pruett, 1997). The following section suggests that there are gender-related parenting patterns which contribute to defiance.

Very simply, fathers often interfere with fealty through noninvolvement and/or abusive, disconfirming behavior. Mothers tend toward symbiotic overinvolvement. When the bond of love (sometimes called "marriage") between parents is weakened or becomes poisonous, the resulting parental-role structure becomes distorted. Children monitor the emotional status of each parent as well as the relationship between the parents. When the marital relationship is weakened or distressing, the child loses faith and symptoms result.

Stimulating Defiance: Father's Role

Margaret Mead said that fathers are biological accidents: they are needed for conception and then become unnecessary. But fathers have a psychological role which is to help mothers and children disengage from the intoxicating pull of the "paradise" of the mother-child relationship. Fathers are important as a presence, and while they can be nurturing and caring, their relationship with children is qualitatively different.

The caring father's presence interrupts the symbiotic relatedness between mother and child, allowing it to be less demanding. Mother and child begin as one. During pregnancy and in infancy this symbiotic relationship is essential for survival. The birth of a baby inevitably stimulates a mother's maturity. If the mother's self is fragmented, the new baby may provide healing benefit for the mother and her self-esteem. However, as the baby grows and begins to individuate, the mother's fragmented self may be reexposed, especially if other intimate relationships with her husband, female friends, or mother are absent or toxic. In such cases, an unconscious mother-child pact emerges which interferes with change in the relationship between baby and mother.

The father represents an alternative reality to that of the mother. Although our long-term monotheistic proclivities suggest an implicit hunger for a unified reality, we live in a metaphorical reality of multiple meanings with no certain ground. This reality is the multi-generational culture of each family background. In healthy families, the father has a strong presence and involvement with his children. Role flexibility allows him to function as a mother when necessary. The father interacts with his children in a manner that stimulates and activates them. He approaches the child more playfully, providing novel interactions. This interaction is in stark contrast to the mother's soothing, calming tone. Fathers, like mothers, probably learn most about parenting and intimate relating from their own mothers. According to Chodorow (1978), the early relationship with the mother generates a basic relational stance and creates the potential for healthy parenting in anyone who has been mothered adequately and desires to recreate such a relationship.

It is of fundamental importance for the therapist to be able to comment on father's behavior. His involvement, or lack of involvement, his uptightness or irritability, his loneliness, and his emotional hunger are key ingredients to family dynamics. In a defiant family, the father is typically absent, physically or emotionally. This absence may be in the service of the family's well-being, such as with the need to make a living. But the absence is often a form of *culturally invisible pathology*. Culturally invisible pathology involves behavior patterns supported by the culture which create trouble in relationships, such as dedication to career and getting ahead. In this type of absence, the father's emotional resources are unavailable because they are depleted in other arenas. A father creates tension for the rest of the family when he is preoccupied with family finances, job responsibilities, or any other situation that interferes with physical and emotional availability.

If the game of chess is modeled on a war between families, the goal of the game is to protect the king (father). It is easy to underestimate the importance of this dynamic in how a family works. The father may enhance family unity by enjoying the family's efforts to protect and resuscitate him. He detracts from it when he ignores their caring or refuses their help. The underside of men's psychology reveals self-loathing. This unacknowledged pain places incredible burdens on their intimates. Some fathers end up in the wrong generation, for example, when they are treated like one of the children. This situation may be induced by the father's or the mother's infantile needs. He may trick her into being his mother and then complain about it. On the other hand, she may be incapable of peer relatedness and may overmother out of fear of her own infantile need.

In the therapist's office, the father may complain about his position outside the family. He may be an outsider for numerous reasons. These may include having turned his back on the family, having been left out and electing to stay out, trying to regain entry only to find the door locked, or staying away because of fear of the mother. The latter can be true even with an abusive father. The family may complain about his absence, but when he tries to be involved it does not work out well. In cases in which his role is ambiguous, he may arrive, offer advice, seem concerned, but fade out abruptly or without comment, leaving the family in the mother's hands.The image of concern he has created may be without substance. The father's behavior generates a collapse of fealty.

A father may be absent because he fears becoming too emotional or enraged. He becomes a more serious problem when he is abusive to anyone in the family. A child may take on the role of a "knight in shining armor" as a way of protecting the mother from such abuse. Too often the armor is based on fantasy and does not protect against injury. The father's rage may become a problem. While marriage begins as a relationship between peers, peer relationships remain dynamic and unstable. Relationships with a generation gap are more stable and less dynamic. Thus, in the interest of stability, a generation gap often develops in marriage. Wife becomes mother and husband becomes little boy. Little boys are grandiose at points in their development. When the husband is abusive, he is not acting the role of a peer or parent, but that of a little boy punishing his big mother for belittling him.

It is essential to pay attention to the relational conditions in the family that activate defiant behavior in children. These are situations the therapist must acknowledge because the family members are too intimately involved in the process or are too anxious, threatened, and defensive to be able to point them out. They are only able to define the problem in concrete terms, usually focusing on the defiant child's behavior.

The therapist should encourage the father's involvement in therapy as early as possible. The father's patienthood may create discomfort for himself and for his family, but the family's prognosis improves when he can become a patient. When he is not involved in therapy, the likelihood of improvement decreases. The father is often on the periphery of the family, and good at making excuses not to be involved. He is either too busy, has important business matters, or the time is inconvenient. If the father is involved in treatment, it is more likely to progress. His absence or disparaging noninvolvement is a symptom of a collapse of fealty.

Stimulating Defiance: Mother's Role

The dynamic here is complex. The father tends to stay in the background. He is much better at seeming innocent and adroit at avoiding responsibility or being recalcitrant. In contrast, the mother tends to be more emotionally and physically available. She is engaged in the therapeutic process, but often feels as though the therapist is blaming her. The recommended correction is to put pressure on fathers in the beginning. Essentially the father's sins are harder to define because they take the form of what he does not do, they are sins of omission. On the other hand, the mother's sins have to do with her involvement in efforts to fix things. When we describe pathology, it is easier to talk about what someone is doing, as opposed to what someone is not doing.

The mother's is the emotional heart of the family. Despite attention paid to fathering over the last 20 years, the mother is still likely to be the primary caregiver, even when she has heavy responsibility for earning a living. She retains the job of maintaining the *quality* of family life and is responsible for child-rearing decisions. All too often mothers feel stretched to their limit, yet they can't stand to be benched. We all know too well the virtuous feelings that come from being overburdened.

The birth of a baby represents a quantum leap in the intimacy and complexity of living. There is deep mutuality in a relationship with an infant. A baby salves the mother's deepest wounds of loneliness and meaninglessness. But as the baby grows, the pain returns, and the small garden of paradise becomes the world-as-before. When the mother's "I" is not secure, it puts pressure on the baby who by simply *being* provides a feeling of being healed, a sense of wholeness and adequacy, and a decrease in pain for the mother. When a mother is anxious, the baby's upset demands she care for him, and when she is caring for him, her pain is lessened. This dynamic is present in all mother-child connections and presents itself in myriad ways. It is not inherently pathological, it just *is*. It becomes pathologic when it can't be outgrown. If a mother has been wounded in the past or present in an historically notable or symbolic way, this may contribute to pathology in the child. If the baby is cared for and loved by the father, and the father loves the mother, the mother is not so desperate for the baby to remain a baby. This is not a moral problem about being good or bad. It may look like a moral problem, however, because of the confusion created by parental guilt and disappointment in self or spouse. It becomes a psychological problem when the baby grows, and as the mother's anxiety goes up, she demands the baby remain a baby. This is not an intentional problem, but one that is the result of pain and represents a search for more health. Nevertheless, the child experiences the father's lack of involvement and the mother's resultant dependency as a corruption of family function, and he loses faith in the family's ability to help him grow up. This type of family relationship results in defiance (or depression, anorexia, or somatization) as a way to preserve the "I." The child senses he must grow up, even if it kills him.

Case Example: Symbolic Elements of Defiance. Brian was 12 years old, a spectacular basketball player, and a popular seventh grader. The middle of three children, he was viewed as having attention-deficit disorder because of minor acts of defiance at home and school. The pediatrician prescribed Ritalin, but it made him anxious and interfered with his sleep. After the medication was stopped, the sleep problem persisted. He became afraid of being anxious. A psychiatrist suggested Paxil, but the family refused, fearing it too might make him worse. Brian was then referred for therapy. The therapist wanted the whole family to attend, but father, a successful general surgeon, was against counseling for unclear reasons. The therapist's theory was the father feared he would discover his own hunger for intimacy. When the situation intensified, father grudgingly agreed to participate. During the first interview, they talked about the family in the present and symbolic past. They were a healthy, satisfied family. Brian was clearly the family star, except for his tendency toward mouthiness and his anxiety, which seemed incongruous with other aspects of his personality. Several crucial dynamics came to light during that interview. When Brian was born, mother's brother was ill with leukemia. When Brian was four months old, mother went to live with and care for her brother, who died when Brian was 10 months old. Mother admitted that breast-feeding Brian during that period "saved her life," by holding her together emotionally while she was caring for her dying brother. Breast-feeding calmed her and restored order to her world, which was disorganized by her isolation and the haunting presence of death. Father was in the early years of his medical practice and unable to offer solace. This may also be related to why he was reluctant to bring the family to therapy. He did not want to go back to acknowledge his anger or jealously during those months. During the interview Mother relived the pain of the past experience with her brother and son, yet she was radiant and relieved as she spoke of it. The therapist's impression was that reliving those sad, but sweetly intimate, moments was deeply comforting to her.

At the time of the interviews, mother was a newly certified teacher who was just beginning to work after 17 years of mothering. She was anxious, and her anxiety reactivated the old relationship program between herself and Brian. Father was a nice person, but emotionally impaired. He could not appreciate her distress and tended to dismiss it. His nonsubjective nature added to mother's anxiety and thus to Brian's. Father represented a non-subjective physical presence, but he was too realistic. Hopefully, this illustrates how the baby was a healing presence in the mother's life. Brian's attention deficit disorder can be seen as attentiveness to the family's emotional field and a secondary problem with paying attention to less crucial issues, e.g., math and social studies. Likewise, when mother was disturbed, the family's anxiety increased. Her caring for Brian, made *her* feel better and thus *he* felt better. In the meantime, father's ambivalence about himself and his self-loathing, masked by professional competence were reactivated.

This example gives a picture of the underlying dynamics of defiance. It shows how a son can be programmed by his experience as an infant to respond to his mother's emotional pain. His symptoms restore the mother as well as the bond between them. The therapeutic process helps by identifying these dynamics and giving them value. It may not erase the troubles, but it at least alters the anxiety surrounding them.

The family image can be a source of strength or a burden. One of the parents, sometimes both, creates and serves a family image. The children are forced into being temple acolytes. The spouse is cajoled into being the assistant priest. The situation can be culturally invisible and avoid a therapist's notice, especially when the values are conventional and desirable. It becomes dysfunctional when the image takes precedence over the needs of specific family members and forces distorted perceptions onto the children. The image is constructed out of past experiences and hopes for the future. In a healthy family, members participate in creating a public and private image that makes them proud. For instance, a family may be proud of its Irish heritage, and in that way the family creates a positive, but complex image to which all can relate. The healthy family is proud of its image, yet has the freedom to make light of it. In the defiant family there may be unacknowledged disparity between the public and private image, which creates problems for various family members, particularly adolescents who are overly sensitive to and concerned about appearances. When there is disparity between the image the family presents to the public and its internal world, problems involving defiance often develop.

Case Example: Disparate Images. Patty made a suicide attempt at age thirteen. Her referring doctor said she was the most depressed teenager he had ever seen. Patty's mother was attempting to maintain an image of social competence and correctness, and Patty couldn't stand it because her mother was so dishonest, masked by appealing manners and social sophistication. There was a powerful, but covert issue, in that Patty's parents had decided to divorce, but since they owned a big house and were unable to sell it, they continued to live together. Their separation was secret to the community. Additionally, Patty's mother was dishonest about her interactions with her daughter. Her mother was a strange person in the way she would redefine emotional situations involving her husband and her children. This duplicitous façade created tension and hence, a collapse of fealty. During the eighth session Patty complained about her mother's anger. Her mother, who remained composed, implied her daughter was making it up. At the next interview, Patty reported her mother slapped her while they were on the way home from the last session, accusing her of making her sound like a bad mother. The mother appeared indifferent to the daughter's report and deflected questions by the therapist; she did not even acknowledge the comment. Therapist to co-therapist: "It looks like there are some things Mrs. Smith doesn't want to know about." As therapy progressed, Patty's depression decreased. Her return to school went well, her depression remitted. At this point she became more than defiant. She had several episodes of telling off teachers who pressured her about getting into college and living up to her parents' expecations. This behavior was a startling departure from the repressed, depressed girl who had attempted suicide four months earlier. Therapy ended when the parents became frustrated by the therapist's disagreement with their treatment planning. A month after the last interview, the mother sent the therapist a tape of Patty's fourth birthday party. It was very touching to hear the cool, angry adolescent at age four being so sweet and attentive to her parents. The mother's note said, "I just wanted you to hear my *real* Patty, the one I want to get back." This is an important statement. The mother's fantasy is that the real Patty is four years old. The implication is that the thirteen-year-old Patty is unacceptable. In this way, the mother was attempting to induce regression and preserve the symbiosis. The mother believes that if Patty could be her four-year-old self, it would heal her (mother), but the unconscious wish violates the trust between parent and child. She was punishing Patty for growing up. She simply can't have her little girl back. As the image crumbled, Patty's depressive symptoms disappeared, Father became less repressed, and Mother became more openly angry with the therapist.

Defiant families have a wide range of characteristics. In the interest of increasing understanding and at the risk of being too concrete, we describe four types. Defiant families may be *egocentric, disenfranchised, apathetic*, or *over-burdened*. This list is not a definitive list, rather it provides a way to think about family patterns which lead to the possibility of defiance becoming a centrally organizing feature of the family. They have in common a collapse of fealty, and the defiance is an attempt to restore authentic family unity.

FAMILY SCENARIOS

Egocentric Family

Father was a successful businessman. Mother was a realtor. Their second son, a talented basketball player, was suspended from the team for drinking. Three days later, while he was supposed to be grounded, he went joy-riding in his mother's Mustang convertible. The weekend before he was to rejoin the basketball team, he missed his appointment with the drug counselor and stayed out all night. The family doctor referred them for therapy. When they called they hoped for individual therapy for their son because they had such full schedules. The message to the therapist was, "You take care of him. We'll pick him up when you're done." The defiance was primarily intrafamily, but they also defied efforts to encourage introspection. When the therapist asks such parents, "How do you think you contribute to your son's troubles?" he may be negatively perceived. This type of family appreciates impersonal interpretations such as, "He is clinically depressed." or "He may have a learning problem." The collapse of fealty is less apparent, because of the family's abundance of wealth and worldly success.

Disenfranchised Family

Father is a Vietnam veteran disabled by post-traumatic stress disorder (PTSD). Mother is a recovering alcoholic who thinks all doctors (and therapists) are useless. Their 13-year-old daughter, Desire, ran away from home and stayed with a friend's family for 2 weeks. The defiance is hottest inside the family, but the school counselor is concerned about the daughter. She can be troublesome, but the counselor likes her. This family is the most belligerent at the outset of therapy. Due to their chronic illnesses and the resultant disabilities, they are embedded in the bureaucratic system, which simultaneously torments and supports them. Desire is the family's hope for the future, however, her parents are scornful and punitive when she does what their unconscious urges.

Apathetic Family

Father is a high school social science teacher. Mother is a secretary in an insurance company. She is being treated with Paxil by the family doctor. The family star is their 16-year-old daughter. Their 14-year-old daughter, Megan, has come home with beer on her breath several times. Mother found a thong and a package of condoms in the back of Megan's drawer. The family is stable, but the marriage is dead. The self of each parent has gone to sleep. They are overdutiful and resigned. Megan's defiance is intrafamily—urging the parents to come back to life.

Overburdened Family

Marcia, 35 years old, is a single parent with limited financial support. She works too much. She never married the children's father and became a pariah to her family of origin. The children's father, who is chronically unemployed, has gone to another state and lives with his mother. J.R., age 15, is always angry with her, calls her a whore when she dates, and refuses to do chores around the house. Kristin, age 13, is mother's helper, but misses school frequently. Her children are mother's only true significant other. Here the loss of fealty is multiaxial. Mother is isolated with no support she can count on, except from the children. She has lost faith in herself. Although the children's misbehavior is upsetting to her, it also serves several functions. It directs their frustration on to her. Their anger and misbehavior make her rageful and her rage explosions interfere with her depression. They also function as orgasm-equivalents, resulting in temporary repair of her relationship with her son.

These forms of defiance are common. They appear frequently in therapists' offices. Their common bonds include the inability to experience the full range of emotions (e.g., laughter is absent, crying is considered stupid or illegal, serious or profound is queer); the inability to consider alternatives for living ("My way or the highway."); the inability to be self-owning ("Look what you made me do."); and intolerance for ambivalence about themselves. Family processes have little to do with educational level. They have more to do with maturity, tolerance for ambiguity, the capacity to be amused by the self, the capacity to be playful, and the capacity to self-regulate. Defiant families tend to be reactive, preplanned, highly charged emotionally, and overburdened. They live at the extremes. Living the same day over and over, they do not have new experiences. It is as if no one is at the helm of the ship—the ship is sailing itself. This can be a terrifying environment for children, who may be chastised if they attempt to take over. Unpredictability, chaos, and intense moods are the norm.

Case Example: Defiance Fends Off Sadness. The Jones family, an overburdened family, was referred for therapy due to Steve's outrageous behavior at home and school. Steve was 12 years old and in the seventh grade. In the preinterview phone call, the therapist learned he had been permanently suspended from middle school, and consequently attended an alternative school which held classes from 4:00–7:00 p.m. As preposterous as it sounded, Steve was about to be kicked out of a school for misfits! Father was a disengaged alcoholic who left when Steve was a baby. Steve had never met him. Mother and Steve attended the session. The 16-year-old sister boycotted the session, despite mother's attempt to bring her.

Mother was in tears when the session began, having reached the end of her rope. Steve was physically small and his demeanor belied the escapades his mother described. When asked what the family was like, mother said, "We're a wreck and have been since the divorce. The kids' father is a no-good alcoholic who provides zero support. We are barely making it. I work second shift. The only help I get is from my mother, and she's about had it. What can I say? We're just a mess." When it was Steve's turn to describe the family, he said, "I don't think we're that bad. I get into trouble, but it's not Mom's fault. My sister is in trouble too, but I get most of the blame. We used to do things together, then Mom got busy with work. She's never home, and when she is, she is either angry or worried."

The family portrait was not encouraging. Family resources were scarce and stretched to the limit. Family members appeared defeated and discouraged, particularly mother who, despite her best attempt, had failed to provide for her family the life she had hoped for. The family was a mess and she blamed herself. She was scared Steve would end up becoming a criminal now that he was in school with incorrigible teenagers. Steve, despite his preinterview billing and tough exterior, was tearful through most of the session. The therapist tried to get him to talk about his worries with no success. The therapist asked him to describe what would need to happen to mother to make her feel like him. He thought a few minutes then said, "Well, basically two things. First, your IQ would have to be lowered quite a bit and second, everyone in the world would hate you. That should do it." With this disclosure mother burst into tears. She had no idea how distressed her son was about himself.

This brief case illustrates the basis for defiance as a corrective measure—fending off despair and sadness. It is a pattern that replays in our offices over and over in varying forms. Behind defiance is pain that appears murky and bottomless. In the example above, therapeutic tactics included talking about the sister and pathologizing the father, with the intention of getting them to participate. It is helpful to find out if other adults are part of the family and, if so, to include them in the interview. Steve's defiance is a push for mother's health and mood to improve. If he is successful with her, it will also improve his own health.

THE IMPLICITLY DEFIANT SELF

From an existential perspective, defiance is seen as an effort to protect the inside self, the "I." Defiance also serves to make the self more robust. Discipline and limit setting teach children to adapt, but they also stimulate defiance by giving the self "muscles." Dealing with the "I" in the context of the family is an essential component of our therapeutic methods. It is essential to our thinking about how psychotherapy supports both individual and family development and overall health. The child's defiance or opposition is simultaneously an effort to preserve the self of the child and to bring into being the self of each parent.

What follows is an amusing, but astounding, example of defiance in the name of integrity in action. At breakfast one Saturday morning, Robbie, 18 months old, left about an inch of juice in his glass. His father said, "Robbie, you didn't finish your juice," and dumped it into the sink. Within a couple of minutes, Robbie approached his father and issued a baby command for "Juice!" "No," father answered, "you did not finish your juice, so you can't have anymore." About 20 minutes later, both parents were busy in the kitchen when Robbie reappeared from playing, went directly to his mother with his arm extended toward the glasses and reissued his command, "Juice!" She got a glass, poured some, and handed it to him. He drank the juice except for the last inch, climbed on a chair, poured it into the sink, and returned to playing. It was astounding. Where does a toddler learn this? Is it an instinctive part of the formation of self? This was an example of defiance in the interest of advocating for the self, an example of a political instinct for power dynamics evident beginning in infancy. The behavior becomes symptomatic when fealty collapses and those in power do not demonstrate sufficient caring, or maturity in how they go about caring for their children.

When sufficient caring is not demonstrated, the child becomes anxious and overwhelmed by his own impulses. The parent fails to provide an environment in which the child can experience competence. In one family the young mother was extremely punitive and harsh with her children. The children, ages 2 and 4, sat motionless during the session, fearful of her reprisal. They watched her every move. She described age-appropriate behavior as negative and unacceptable. The children had learned to curtail all such activities in her presence. This mother had failed to provide a nurturing environment where exploration could take place, thus stunting her children's curiosity and development. If it continues, this relational behavior pattern could lead to deepening apathy or depression, or it could break out into hyperactivity or oppositional defiance.

SUMMARY

In this chapter we have provided a broad survey of the territory of interest to us. We have discussed defiance both as an intrafamily process and a process between the family and the community. We have given an outline of what we regard as a model for healthy family functioning.

We define defiance as an effort to restore a demoralized family and an interactional process that begins with a collapse of fealty. While defiance begins as an effort at repair, it may lead to extrusion if the family does not receive assistance. We have used a number of examples to suggest how family therapy works with the problem of defiance.

The etiology of defiance is in the unconscious behavior patterns of the family. The professional therapist becomes a talking mirror to help the family locate the pain behind the pain. The therapeutic pattern we describe works to build a family team, while simultaneously augmenting the personhood of each member. This is not possible in traditional linear logic but only in the circular dynamics of the sometimes awkward paradigm which is gradually working its way into the global culture.

2

Parenting:
A Second Chance at Growth

This chapter is a discussion of parenting aimed at helping family therapists with the difficult job of working with this most elusive and reactive family segment, the parental subgroup. It is not about how to parent. *Parent* is a role that is deeply connected with personhood and identity. When the role is separated from the person, parental integrity is compromised. This leads to a collapse of fealty. Defiance is stimulated as a way for the child to protect her growth and to induce the parent to connect the role with their person.

The parent role is abundantly complex. Each parent is a person with a history that embodies the experiences of both the individual parent and the parent's family. So, if mother's grandfather committed suicide and the family went broke, those events shape her values even though she did not experience them. Family life may become organized around avoiding unstated fantasized catastrophes. The role blends life experience and fantasies with experiences from the parent's childhood they wish to foster in their children, as well as those they hope to prevent. It includes ideas from the culture, past and present, and a system of selecting what is good or bad. The role carries both hopes and phobias, some conscious, but most unconscious.

This role we refer to as parent is like a poorly integrated collage of past experiences and fantasies about the future. Some of the pieces include personal changes related to marrying, joining the spouse's family, and having children. These profound personal experiences force new awareness, so the parent may see herself from other perspectives, but most of the change occurs outside of consciousness. Most parents use a parenting template that includes a desire for their children to be more successful versions of themselves. They hope success will be accomplished more easily because of their efforts to shield them from pain and provide security. Despite parental love, children have their own agendas. Shielding them from pain doesn't work well. Our children fight us because our dreams of improvement, grafted onto our children, are grotesque delusions of what we wanted for ourselves, but never achieved. They may also be dreams instilled by our parents of what they wanted for us, which we in turn pass on to our children. Children are seen as the families' redemption.

Who we *are* and what we *do* as parents is largely unconscious. It is important to deepen awareness, so we are not too quick to simplify the process of parenting. The therapist gathers information about the components of this complex role by asking the parents to describe their multigenerational families of origin, to recall themselves at their children's ages, and to reflect on the nuclear families they grew up in. Discussing the multigenerational family history leads inevitably to wading in the symbolic world of the unconscious. Attention to what is unclear and unconscious is a crucial component of our therapeutic methodology. It is important to interview the parents about the families in which they grew up, but it is even more important to do consultation interviews with the families of origin to really experience a family's context.

PARENTAL MATURITY

Defiance is a response to the collapse of intergenerational fealty. A conflict in parenting styles is often part of the collapse of fealty. When there is conflict in parenting styles, but the parents are *personally mature*, the therapy process is often brief. In other situations that are more complex therapeutically, the parents may be *personally immature*, and attempt to cover their immaturity with parenting that is overrigid, overintentional, or overinvolved. In these cases, parental reactions are exaggerated and inflexible. The role of parent can easily become a substitute for personhood, in the same way the role of physician can become a substitute for personhood. Such substitution is tempting because it reduces personal vulnerability and ambiguity. A therapeutic task in this situation is to increase the maturity of the person of the parent by helping her grow up so the child can reside safely in the correct generation.

Characteristics of maturity include the following:

- The ability to embrace personal ambivalence. This is manifested in the ability to question oneself by examining one's motives in depth. It involves the ability to explain or acknowledge the things in life which cause great personal pain. It allows parents to express doubts about themselves. The immature person does not question herself or tolerate the ambiguous complexity of adult experience.
- Flexibility in roles. Parents are able to learn from their children or have fun being peers with them. There is the possibility of backing down in a hot fight with the second generation. While sitting in a large airport between flights, Dr. Owen watched a family walk down the concourse. The father was angry and scolding his two small children, ages 6 and 4. "What a boor," he thought. "The poor kids." Then about 10 minutes

later his opinion of the man changed when the same family passed by traveling in the opposite direction. The boorish father was doing a syncopated skip step, holding the hands of both children. The 4-year-old daughter was leading the skipping. This is a sample of role flexibility.
- The freedom to be silly, even with one's own family. This refers to the parents' ability to be playful, to enter an "as-if" theater at home. This "as-if" theater involves the ability to be amused at one's self. It suggests a certain resiliency in relationships which is crucial to helping children grow up. For example, a mother becomes aware she has been yelling at the children all day, then playfully begins issuing her demands as a singing soprano. This novel behavior by the mother disrupts the tension, and all end by laughing.
- Tolerance for ambiguity and complexity, or the ability to tolerate uncertainty. Families, particularly those with defiant children, fear uncertainty. They are tempted to adopt a quick solution because it provides relief from indecision. Mature parents know there are no easy answers to complex problems. They are able to continue searching for solutions in the face of adversity. Their ability to be creative remains intact. When their expectations are dashed, they may be devastated, but not defeated.

THE THERAPIST'S RELATIONSHIP TO PARENTS

Work with families is daunting because of the complex and compelling transference relationships families induce in therapists. Most therapists are likely to compensate for their strong emotional responses by being extra polite or reasonable, which interferes with the capacity for observation that is so crucial for the clinician. The result is an overly cautious attitude toward parents. Therapists family members know in fragmentary ways, but transference enables them to take a fragment and convert it into the whole person. Transference is intensified in any therapeutic situation, but the voltage increases when working with a marriage. It increases again when we add children and goes into the red zone when we combine marriage, children, and defiance.

There is something in our cultural patterns which seeks to protect parental innocence in clinical situations and to disconnect psychopathological disorders of childhood from interpersonal experience. We view this disconnecting pattern as iatrogenic. Why, when the parents are obviously immature, indifferent, or toxic do we find it necessary to pretend we think the problem might be a "chemical imbalance" in their child?

The following case conference is reviewed as an example of how to identify conflicts in the way child mental health practitioners formulate problems. The case involved the evaluation of an oppositional 5-year-old boy and his divorced mother. The discussion involved a biologically trained therapist who viewed pathology as existing in a child and taught parents how to be therapist aides. Conversely, the family therapist believed as the authors do, that the child's problem was a symptom of the family's way of functioning, and that it was necessary for parents to become patients.

The mother brought her son to the Child Psychiatry Clinic because of problems at home and at school. He would not do what his mother asked—he was extremely stubborn. He was beaten up regularly on the school bus. He would set up his extensive dinosaur collection in patterns on the living room floor and would not let them be moved. He insisted on sleeping in the family room. The mother wept when she talked about him. It was notable that there were ambiguous complications at birth, including a low Apgar. When he was 10 months old his parents divorced. Mother raised him alone, and she had an ambiguous relationship to his father.

What is the diagnosis? This case can be viewed from different perspectives depending on the therapist's paradigm. The biologically trained practitioner thought the child had a developmental disorder within the autistic spectrum and saw evidence of childhood schizophrenia. The systems practitioner viewed the history and symptoms similarly to the authors. The history suggested that the child was conceived and born into a world of marital distress and pain. A child who arrives in such a world, especially one who has an ambiguous birth problem, often takes on exaggerated importance in the parents' world. In this situation, the mother may have bonded to the baby in a way that reduced her distress and excluded the immature father, who was already ambivalent about the marital relationship. The symptom which upset the mother most was the child's omnipotent behavior. Omnipotence in a young child is a by-product of parental immaturity or incapacity and, if the parent's behavior is not engaged therapeutically, can be mistaken for autistic or psychotic behavior in the child. Thus the systems practitioner viewed the child's behavior as a relational problem involving the maturity of the parents. The discussion between the two therapists had to do with the location of the problem and whether it was innate. One practitioner suggested a DSM diagnosis and recommended classes for the parents. The systems practitioner argued that the parents' personal maturity needed attention, and suggested family therapy. Parenting classes, in his view, would probably not prove helpful without a therapeutic experience which adds to the parent's personal maturity.

The parental subgroup of the family poses a problem in working with children and adolescents. Our culture allows freedom to comment on the behavior of children, but not on the behavior of parents. A therapist is expected to accept parents' reports about their children as valid, objective information and to assume that they are good observers. Unfortunately, theses observations are based on parental fantasy, a fact which is not usually well tolerated within our culture. Caution is required so as not to blame parents, at least to their faces. In conventional patterns of child and adolescent clinical work, there is a tendency to treat the parents as treatment aides. If needs are identified in the parents, their treatment is likely to be moved to marital or individual therapy, and the children are excluded. We strongly suggest that the therapy be conducted with the whole family so that the presence of the children in the sessions can serve to catalyze the parents' growth.

Family and contextual risk factors are associated with child behavioral problems. Research indicates that poverty, parental psychopathology, marital discord, isolation, single parenthood, parental criminal history, substance abuse, overcrowding, large family size, poor housing, disadvantaged school systems, and depression are known risk factors for child behavior problems. Parents affected by these factors often have difficulty accurately monitoring, classifying, and responding to their children's behavior due in part to lack of positive social support. Risk factors are cumulative and interact with one another; a single risk factor is rarely problematic enough to create difficulty. On a positive note, protective factors such as easy temperament, intelligence, high self-efficacy, positive self-esteem, problem-solving skills, and family cohesiveness moderate risk factors and preclude the development of continued problems. Protective factors exist at both the community and family levels.

Parental practices may increase the risk for development of behavior problems. Practices that negatively influence child behavior include harsh or inconsistent discipline, poor parental supervision and monitoring, and a lack of acceptance, warmth, and attachment. Nonresponsive, insensitive parenting leads children to develop maladaptive patterns of emotional control and interpersonal communication. Overcontrolled and undercontrolled parenting can lead to behavioral symptoms in children. During normal individuation, children with overcontrolling parents have difficulty asserting control over their environment. Such parents dismiss the child's wants in favor of their own. In the reverse situation, children of laissez-faire parents may be unsocialized due to the lack of early parental limit setting. These children often find limit setting by authority figures intolerable. Parents who are unresponsive to a child's initiation do not provide increased opportunity for interaction. The child learns that either they will be ignored or they must increase their demand for attention.

Parents do have responsibility for the way their children are. They are responsible because they are involved. Acknowledging responsibility is different from blaming; to attribute blame has the implication of intention. Our view is that children react to and identify with pathological fragments in the parents, and part of the solution is for the parents to acknowledge those fragments so as to refute the theory that the children's behavior comes out of nowhere. In our pattern of family therapy the parents do this by entering the regressive experience of becoming a patient. When they are not available to do this, the likelihood of permanent injury and disability in the child increases as defiance becomes more fixed and destructive.

IS IT POSSIBLE WE GET THE CHILDREN WE NEED?

This is a question with no clear answer, except, "We think so." We get the children we need to help us grow up. But we know growing up has an aversive side. As discussed in a later chapter, children raise parents in the sense that they respond to the needs of parents, and push the parents' development. We do get the children we need, and the gratification is so implicitly profound that there is pressure from the parents to keep the children as children. The process is circular, thus obscure. Children will sacrifice everything in the name of preserving their own "I," while inducing the parents to grow up so that the children may grow more securely.

Parents are the child's first and most influential teachers. They are the providers of love, guidance, and protection. The teaching is profound, and may more appropriately be called programming. Initially, the infant pressures the family organization and teaches the parents through reciprocal interaction. Parents who are tuned into their infant quickly learn how to interact positively and comfort the child, thereby enhancing the frequency and significance of communication. This loving, person-to-person, reciprocal interaction increases the responsiveness between parent and child. The process of learning through mutual interaction, which increases stimulation between two beings, is a powerful experience. It has more in common with alchemy than with education. The result of this interaction is the creation of a strong mutual attachment that endures throughout life. It is this deep biopsychosystemic interaction which creates the basis for the loyalty we have termed fealty. Time, attention, and involvement are integral to the developing relationship. If your children are not driving you crazy, you are not involved enough. Keep in mind that all biological learning has aversive components.

The fascinating thing is that all kinds of parenting styles can be successful. We think the most crucial variable is maturity, including the capacity for silliness, loving, and even small doses of creative hatred. Single-parent families can be successful when the parent is mature and there is a supportive network to create an adequate parenting team. Observing the interaction between parents and children of all ages gives the therapist an idea of the quality of connection between the two. Parents who are responsive to the child's cooing and smiling indicate a positive connection. The mature parent can take delight in the child's growing skills, even when the child is difficult.

FAMILY PORTRAIT

Unconsciously, the family creates a self-portrait that may dominate their lives. The portrait is shown to the public, but is different from what goes on in the private interior of the family. A good child fits the image. A bad child contradicts the image and is extruded. A vividly pathologic example of the problem of image is a family of an alcoholic business man who is active in community affairs, coaches little league football, and is an officer of the Lion's club. In the confines of his own home, however, he is alcoholic and has been having an incestuous relationship with his 12-year-old daughter since she was 7 years old. Inside the family there is no metacommunication. There is a family rule which says members may not discuss relationships because it would upset father.

Less obviously pathologic is the abnormally normal family. This family characterizes itself as normal. Its members are inflexibly normal. Mother has a symbiotic relationship with the son. The marriage has little life in it as mother and father have developed a back-to-back relationship. Father is jealous of mother's relationship to their son, but would never acknowledge it. They are active in the community social scene and this community life is a substitute for personal intimacy.

Case Example: Changing the Portrait Hurts

Mother, father, and two sons, ages 13 and 10, went through a crisis related to father's severe anxiety which apparently resolved in two sessions. During the third interview the family was recounting a story of the 10-year-old son using bad language. Mother told the younger son to tell the therapist the story. The older son became embarrassed and insisted that his brother and mother not say the vulgar word. The therapist said to the 13-year-old, "Plug your ears." The young man insisted and began to cry, sobbing with his head in his hands. He was desperate to preserve the family image and he was burdened by responsibility. What an amazing pressure on the oldest son. This example provided a glimpse inside an abnormally normal family. The dynamics are complex and often disguised on a metalevel. The level of emotional involvement is fixed—neither more closeness nor more distance is permitted.

PROJECTIVE IDENTIFICATION

We should be careful what we pretend because we become what we pretend (Bateson & Bateson, 1987). Children are likely to become what parents pretend they are or, when there is too much excitement about them, the opposite of what is desired. Conscientious parents may pressure children to be what they were, even though the model does not work for the present. Parents want children to have their lives but without their parents' pain. All parents project onto their children. They see both positive and negative fragments of themselves in their children. By imposing their ideas and beliefs onto their children, parents can become locked into an adversarial relationship.

Parents use their children to fix their errors and to relieve their anxiety about the future. A mother may impose her fantasy on her daughter in hopes that the daughter will be more accomplished and beautiful. At times, when the daughter lives up to the fantasy, the mother becomes jealous and devastatingly critical. For example, Mary M's mother had manic-depressive illness. Fearful that she would be ill in the same way as her mother, Mary M. protected her own sense of well-being by diagnosing the disorder in her daughter. In another case, father imposed his athletic ambitions on his sons. In order to make sure his son did not fail as he did, the father overcoached him and forced him to participate. Thus, the way that parents view their children (i.e., their fantasies about their children), has a profound effect on the children's development.

THERAPEUTIC BLAMING: EVOKING THE PARENTS' PATIENTHOOD

Being ironic, of course, this section talks about evoking the latent patienthood of the parents. The seeds for this portion of the therapeutic process are sown in the initial interviewing process. When members are invitated to comment on all family relationships, including the parental/marital dyad. The following series of questions guides the interview process away from the identified patient and toward the subjective experience of the family:

- What kind of families did each parent come from?
- How did they free themselves from their own parents?
- Speaking of the family in the room, how did mother and father get together? Why did each select the other and not wait for someone better to come along?
- How did the parents learn to parent? For example, how did their parents handle parenting?
- Is there anyone who is glad that things are going so badly for you?

While it sounds a bit absurd, the last question frequently leads to uncovering important family dynamics. For example, father's parents were angry about his marriage. Thus, he may think that they are pleased at the trouble his son is putting him through.

These are the kinds of questions which enable the parents to have the experience of being a patient. They are not blaming questions. They ask, "Who are you? What is your inner world like?"

Case Example: The Personhood of the Father

Mr. B., a dignified, middle-aged executive, is not working after being downsized. Contemporary culture provides so many clever euphemisms for becoming a nonperson. He says he is not disturbed by it, yet appears injured. Something in his non-verbal behavior indicates his wound. The therapist comments, "It sounds like you have been wounded, but either don't know it or don't know how to show it." This is attending to the father's personhood, accusing him of being in pain, thus allowing him to become a patient. The family is in therapy because their daughter, a senior in high school, has become defiant. The onset of her defiant behavior coincided with his being downsized. The family does not see any significance in the time correspondence. At the next interview, the father said, "It feels to me like you are saying I am to blame for my daughter's behavior." The therapist replied, "I wish it was that simple. We used to blame the mothers all of the time, behind their backs of course, but that didn't help. We have tried accusing fathers of being uninvolved or too drunk, but that doesn't help much either. It's really a problem of the whole family—three generations. It is usually a problem of pain or too much compromise, or unacknowledged disappointment. In your case, I don't think I am blaming you for the problem, but I do believe that if you were more open about your upset, it would be a relief, both to your wife and your daughter. I think both are burdened by your feeling like a failure."

An interview that attends to the above information often produces affect from the parents. When it does, it makes a major difference and can result in dramatic behavior change. We have concern that therapy that focuses on effective parenting alone tends to substantiate the dissociation of role and person. In the case of defiance, we think of education itself as a pathogenic process, therapy examining the parents' personhood would be expected to be more effective.

The next clinical example concerns an impossibly defiant, but good-hearted, 15-year-old boy. Mother worships an image of past wealth and social entitlement. Her role as mother is disconnected from her personhood. In the process of caring for her elderly, dying mother, she becomes deeply suicidal, then experiences a jump in personal maturity. The case spans 40 interviews over 5 years.

Case Example: Fantasies of the Past

Mr. and Mrs. B. (ages 60 and 54, respectively), each in their second marriage, had a persistently defiant son, Luke. School failure led to his transfer to a private school where his defiant noncompliance further embarrassed his parents. He tried alcohol, marijuana, and running away. He got into fist fights with his father and a 30-year-old half brother. Mrs. B., an attractive, but sharp-tongued, pretentious woman, grew up in an overtly successful and nouveau riche family. Her executive father was a debonair, high-functioning alcoholic. She attended boarding school and went to a college for wealthy young women for two years before marrying a young man who had grown up in a similar manner. He was a wealthy, bright, alcoholic party boy. They had two daughters in 4 years of marriage. Her effort to get him into alcoholism treatment in 1961 turned out like Thurber's story, "The Unicorn in the Garden." She was hospitalized in a psychiatric unit for a "nervous breakdown." She was tough and resilient, however, and got out of the hospital and the marriage, then raised her daughters on her own with help from her widowed mother. When the girls were ages 15 and 17, she married Walt, a handsome, unsophisticated man who worked as supervisor of a large factory. Walt had come up through the blue-collar ranks, and modulated his roughneck past with fundamental Christianity. After 5 years of marriage, she decided she had made an error and had married beneath herself. She decided to make up for the error by raising Luke in the lost image to which she aspired. Her efforts became a stimulus for his persistent defiance.

In the first interview, before the therapist knew much of the history, she found herself angry at Mrs. B.'s supercilious attitude and impertinence toward her husband, who had a serious, intermittent dysphonia (there were moments when he would lose his voice). There had been no clear diagnosis from the otolaryngologist, but by the therapist's estimation, the symptom was the result of a failing attempt to avoid crying. He appeared to choke up frequently during the interview. Mrs.

B. was deeply entangled in all aspects of her son's life. Over the 5 years of the therapist's intermittent work with them, the therapist attempted to disrupt this overmothering. Mrs. B was convinced that her brand of well-intentioned, take-the-bull-by-the-horns intrusiveness would get her son to do her bidding. It did not work. The therapist had a somewhat antagonistic relationship with the mother, but of the three family members she became the most attached to the therapist. She did not change much until the 5th year of therapeutic involvement.

When Luke was age 20, Mrs. B.'s mother, at age 86, went to a nursing home. Mrs. B. was dissatisfied with the care her mother received there and brought her home. She was very pleased with Luke's relationship with her mother. As her mother's health failed, Mrs. B. became openly discouraged with herself and her own life. In a panic, she called one morning to come for an emergency visit. She came alone; she was suicidal. Her upset about her mother was similar to her upset about her son. Her mother's decline did not fit her image. About 30 minutes into the interview, the therapist said, tongue in cheek, "I suppose if you kill yourself, it will help your mother stay young, and if you die, she won't have to die for 20 more years." She looked at the therapist, puzzled. There was a short silence, then she said in a self-mocking tone of grand resignation, "So I feel suicidal. I don't *have* to kill myself. *You* can't stop me from killing myself. It *is* really up to me. (Pause) You know what? I think I am going to go on living. I would miss out on too much if I died now." In that moment, she became free of the fantasy that the therapist understood her and could fix her. She was also freed of her fantasy that her essential maternal goodness would enable her to understand and correct her son's behavior. It was as if she had been encased in an image which, in that moment, fragmented and fell from her. She left saying, "I don't know why, but I feel different. I have never felt this way before."

This is a good example of a mother substituting her fantasy of what the family image should be for her own personal reality. Her son did not change until she became a patient. There was no abrupt reversal but Luke, who by this time was age 20, began to have a more collaborative relationship with his parents and to find ways to fit into the cultural social structure. The change in her made for a change in him. As she individuated and became an "I," his defiance lessened.

The preceding case has a great deal to do with disrupting the mother role. When mothers get desperate, they may become less personal and more motherly, which neutralizes individuation and stimulates defiance and opposition in the next generation. Therapeutic "blaming" takes the form of engaging the parents, both as parents and as people. The therapeutic task is to expose the person behind the role. When the defiant children hear about the parents' pain or struggles, it often softens the them.

Case Example: Multigenerational Interview

In this next example the treatment reached an impasse. The therapist conducted a consultation interview with the father's parents and something happened which changed the son.

Jack M. was a 15-year-old boy referred by Family Court. He was on probation for vandalism. His parents were successful, wealthy partners in a large advertising firm. In the initial phone call, Mr. M. told the therapist that his son had been asked what he wanted in a father and could not give an answer. This left the father incredulous. The therapist wondered intuitively, but did not ask, what kind of trouble father had with his own father. As part of the initial history, the therapist learned that father grew up in a family where his father, a WWII Marine, held a number of jobs. He ran the house like a boot camp. In his present family, Jack, the second of two sons, was the family star, an outstanding swimmer with Olympic potential, and an honor student. He abruptly quit the high school swim team in his sophomore year. Shortly thereafter he drove to Daytona Beach, an 1800-mile trip, with a friend in a car "borrowed" without permission from the friend's grandfather. This was a difficult case. Jack had everything necessary to earn the diagnosis of oppositional defiant "sociopath" in the making.

During the course of treatment, Jack's misbehavior escalated. The thera pist recalled the father's remarks during the initial phone call reemphasized the initial suggestion that they bring in the father's parents for a consultation. Father finally agreed and arranged for his parents to attend. Grandfather, in his early 60's, was unemployed, but cocky. He bore a distant resemblance to Kirk Douglas. He boasted about himself as a young man. As the interview went on, he began talking about what a fool his son, the millionaire, was. He told a story of how his son bought a car at age 16. Father told him it was a mistake, and it would cost him. He made his son keep it in the garage until he could pay him for rent. The 44-year-old executive, now turned son, was clearly embarrassed as he listened, eyes downcast, face flushed. He had a fixed grin on his face and tears in his eyes. The situation was ironic to the therapist, as this unemployed, sneering, dissatisfied 64-year-old man mocked his successful son. At the next interview, when the therapist questioned Mr. M., suggesting it looked painful to be worked over by his father, Mr. M. said he was amused by his father's story. "No, it didn't hurt to hear the story" he replied. The therapist didn't believe him, of course, and said so.

Over the next month, family life improved dramatically. Jack went back to school and studying. He wasn't sure he wanted to rejoin the swim team. "What happened?" the therapist asked. "When I saw what my grandfather did to my dad, I thought, my dad had enough of being treated bad by his dad. I felt sorry for being so mean to him and decided to stop." The multigeneration interview forced father's patienthood into the open. Although father did not own his patienthood, the son saw it. That created change.

A GUIDE TO EXPERIENTIAL PARENTING

The following ideas about parenting come out of our work with families. These comments reflect our assumptions about how to parent in a way that contributes to health. The list is available for addition, deletion, or revision. We never imply that parenting is easy. The growth that comes from parenting is aversive and painful—it is also delicious and richly rewarding. The following paragraphs reflect the language we use in the therapy room. It is sometimes flavored with irony and often amplified to capture attention or force a reaction.

1. "Your children are not your children. They are sons and daughters of life longing for itself. And though they are with you, yet they belong not to you. You may house their bodies, but not their souls, for their souls dwell in the house of the tomorrow which you cannot visit, even in your dreams (Gibran, 1923)." This is a painful truth, that is often overlooked. Although their pain feels like the parents' pain and their joys feel like the parents' joys, children's lives gradually become their own.

2. Parents have until children reach age 13 to hammer them into shape, using a rubber hammer, of course. After age 13, the parents become an anvil and the children hammer on them. At that point, the parents' job is to be a good anvil. An anvil "rings" when hit, but does not hit back against the hammer's blows. The anvil is a model for integrity in this situation. Regardless of what happens, it does not change shape or move. The point is that discipline and structure are most valuable before age 13. Children at that age have the ability, if necessary, to take care of themselves. Beyond that age, parents need to trust that they have provided the essentials to teach children right from wrong. This does not mean that children will always make the right choice, only that the teaching has been adequate. The rest is largely up to the adolescent.

3. The defiant, underachieving child may be demoralized. She may be fighting the sense that anyone understands her. The adult fantasy of such understanding and the diagnostic formulation provided by the clinic or school can be depersonalizing. In addition, persistent efforts at guiding the child can be demoralizing. The result for the child is the depressing feeling of being a nobody. Parents, therapists, and teachers need to face the fact that they do not fully understand children, especially adolescents, who probably live in a parallel universe. When a child has passed age 13 or so, the attempt to hammer her into shape, to change her with harshness, may break or humiliate her in a way that leaves permanent injury. It becomes necessary for the parent to accept that if they disappeared at that point, the child could make it on her own. Parents can be very helpful, but they are not essential. The parents' job, especially with adolescents, is to stay balanced and centered so they can retreat or advance from any position of interaction without losing equilibrium. Essentially they must maintain their integrity. While parents need to pay attention to what they believe is right, they also need to acknowledge and attend to their own pain, including their disappointment in themselves or their spouse. If the adolescents know about their parents' struggles, it is easier for them to listen to the parents' concerns.

4. A crucial guideline in healthy parenting is to emphasize *creativity* not *consistency*. Being a parent is like being a football coach. If a coach runs the same play over and over, in the name of consistency, the opponent will figure it out, adjust, and neutralize the game plan. Parents should feel free to be unpre-

dictable. Although consistency and harshness are sometimes important, they are problematic when energized by sadism.

5. Too much help can interfere with a child's emerging ability to integrate her own experience. Allowing her to struggle may be more helpful. For example, in this book, we are fond of introducing, tongue in cheek, the idea that every child ought to flunk at least one course in high school, so that both the child and the parents can learn that failing a class and death are not the same. The fear of fantasy of failure can be more paralyzing than the experience itself. Failure is a very important teacher. It turns out life does provide second (and more) chances.

6. Parentified children find it difficult to be treated like children. Once a child has had responsibility for herself or for her parents, it is difficult and perhaps wrong, to force her back into the role of obedient child. Parents need to respect a child's individuality. Some children are forced to grow up quickly by reason of disruptive experiences in the family. Examples include, an oldest child taking over part of the parenting when a parent has an extended illness; a child being sent to boarding school for a year; and a child supporting a parent through a prolonged postdivorce depression. These children have had the responsibility of officers and it induces undue pain and defiance if they are made to function as if they are privates again. It is important for parents to respect their initiative, even if they disagree with it and to acknowledge their dignity. Through their experiences these children have gained fragments of maturity.

7. When a child reaches age 15, it is important for her to find a role model outside the family to help her decide how to go about being a person. When a relationship with a role model is mutually rewarding we call it mentoring. A mentor helps to guide the adolescent into the world apart from the family. Mentors can be an asset to children from single-parent families by providing time and feedback within a close relationship. As one defiant 17-year-old said, "I've never had an adult that cared about me, no one who worried about me or wondered where I was. Do you think having a mom or dad who loved me would have made any difference?"

8. Parentectomy, the removal of child from the parent, is an illusion-based solution. Separating the parent from a child of almost any age is like the fantasy of the patient with a headache who thinks, "If only I could drill a whole in my head, I could let out the pain." This theoretical solution, if acted upon, would only create new problems. When a family has had previous therapy that did not work and members are hinting that the situation is hopeless, we suggest that a therapeutic separation could be helpful. Because it is complicated to turn a child over to a community agency, we usually suggest that the parents find someone in the family to take over for a while. Grandparents are usually very helpful. It is unusual for a child to continue the same behavior pattern while in the care of someone else. Of course there are exceptions to any situation. If a brain abscess *is* actually causing the pain, it is necessary to drill a hole in the head.

9. Parents can't be successful until they learn to enjoy being hated by their children. The ability to enjoy being hated depends upon a secure separation between the generations. It is difficult for parents to enjoy being hated by their

children, if the children are the most significant others. Hate is a strong word that provokes strong reactions. Yet in healthy intimacy, the amount of love is matched by the amount of hatred. Hate is based on the depth of disappointment that only those who we deeply love can stimulate. Thus, hatred is connected to investment. Healthy hatred occurs in flashes, rather than as a steady state. Viewed as a subjective experience requiring no action, hate may actually be an alternate form of defiance. It says, "I am not you." If a parent is honest she will be aware of the intense flashes of hatred she may feel for her children. When a 3-year-old says, "I hate you," we think the best response is, " I hate you, too, but don't worry about it. I'll feel better this afternoon."

10. Parents can't win, but they can choose their way of losing—the strict way or the lenient way. The easiest way to fail as a parent is by not caring. The job is defined by a series of dynamic dialectics. A parent can be too much of anything—too tough, too tender, too strict, too lenient, too cynical, too hopeful, too encouraging, too moralistic, too decisive, or too ambivalent. If the parent gets locked into one position, the young person is more likely to feel cornered.

11. Parents should remember that childhood is a nightmare. It is easy to underestimate the amount of pressure children in our culture experience. The pain a scapegoat feels is always underestimated, whether the scapegoat's demeanor is hostile, apathetic, or comical.

12. It is crucial that a parent be a presence in their child's life. It is interesting to note that adolescents, regardless of their behavior, can become very upset when a parent changes her role. So, the black-clad, sneering, arrogant teenage gangster, who is never at home, complains that her mother is never home. It is as if, in order for them to do their growing up, children need to have a secure *someone* in place. This issue is illustrated clearly in the midphase clinical chapter. *Being* a calm presence seems to be more important than what the parent *does*.

13. The common parental wish, "All I want is for her to be happy," is a veiled curse. It really means giving the child an impossible task. No one is completely happy. Life is hellish. While we have no choice whether we will suffer, we do have some choice as to how to cope with suffering. This is a more realistic wish for parents to have for their children.

14. Parents are role models. Children develop in reaction to, and by identification with, their parents. Parents who want their children to talk to them about themselves should share themselves with their children. This is modeling. Asking them questions models interrogation, and that frequently results in them learning how to avoid answering questions. When parents are upset with their children, they are always part of the problem and the failure to wonder how is pathological. Self-righteousness is symptomatic of single-mindedness, which is problematic. The next two ideas are similar in that they address the relationship between the parents.

15. A "united front" is important with younger children, who benefit from knowing their parents cannot be divided. These children benefit from being defeated by the parents' honest unity. The same is true for adolescents, of course,

but the problem becomes more complex at this stage. When dealing with adolescents, parents need to have the maturity and freedom to disagree about the child. This is tricky territory for parents. One parent cannot parent the other parent's parenting. The rule goes as follows, "I must ask myself if she loves the children as much as I do. If the answer is yes, then whatever she does she does out of her love of the children, and I should not interfere with it." This rule produces problems when the unity is based on dishonesty.

16. One parent cannot parent the other's parenting. This issue is related to the one above, except that it has to do with one parent assuming they have the prerogative to instruct their spouse about how to parent. If the father is the mother's supervisor, that makes her his daughter. A parent who has questions about the partner's parenting methods must consider whether the partner has the child's best interest in mind before intervening. For example, a 16-year-old daughter has been defiant with her mother and the conflict between them is frequent. Mother views her daughter as manipulative and endlessly second-guesses her. Father does not see not see the situation in the same way. He feels crazy when his wife is agitated about their daughter and wants him to do something about it. When he agrees with his wife, he feels dishonest. He needs to make his position clear by saying, "I don't agree with you. I just don't see it that way. I feel dishonest when I operate as if it is true."

17. Parents do not represent the school or the police force. When community agencies become involved, parents need to find a way to advocate for their children. There are many who will urge punishment, but no one is able to love children like their parents, and no one can match the parents' lifetime commitment or investment. They have something unique to offer the children.

Public education is a powerful and implicit part of our culture. The public school system assumes the freedom to make decisions about what is best for students, although it does not always know what is best for children or families. School officials know what is best for schools. There are times when parents have to make a choices about whose side they are on. Are they for the school, or are they for their children? The school system can be helpful in some difficult situations, but it can also be toxic and react with little insight. Parents need to be informed rather than accept blindly a school policy or diagnosis about how to handle their difficult child.

The next paragraphs provide a clinical application for some of the above guidelines. The clearest way for parents to fail is by not caring. But the burden of caring is to be caught in an endless series of dialectics. It is possible to be too resentful or too forgiving, too decisive or too indecisive, too strict or too lenient, or too soft or too tough. The behavior of oppositional or defiant children exposes differences between the parents' styles. One of the commonest is the question of being too tough or too soft. The therapist needs to remain a mature coach without not jumping into the fray with her own fantasies of what is best for any given family. The following comments offer ways to think about the too tough/too soft issue, but are not designed to provide a resolution.

Tough is different from abusive. Soft may be loving, or it may be a cover for panic. A spanking is not abuse. "Spanking is bad" is a fantasy. "Spanking is necessary" is a fantasy. The crucial question above, "Does she love the children as much as I do?" is important in dealing with defiance. If left unacknowledged, and one parent assumes that they care more than their partner does, or that their partner is a defective parent, parenting the partner's parenting contributes to the genealogy of defiance. The situation encountered most in therapy is one in which the mother feels the father is too severe. When she intervenes, she forms a coalition with the child which excludes the father and sets up a rule that the child does not have to do what father says and that father's judgment can be ignored. The implicit notion that the child need not listen to the other parent adds to the child's power. The fight about how to parent may go beyond the disciplining moment. It can also go on in the child's presence, but the child is not allowed to be a part of it. The following example illustrates how this situation is dealt with in a therapeutic interview. It also illustrates a type of ambiguous ending we consider important.

Case Example: A Deadly Disagreement

Sharon and Tony were referred by the Children's Unit of the Psychiatric Hospital following the release of Joe, their 8-year-old son. He had been hospitalized as a result of a serious suicide gesture, in which he locked himself in the bathroom with a rope after saying he was going to kill himself. Sharon, a young attorney, mentioned in the first interview that she had been involved with legal cases where men had been violent. Tony was a newly graduated male nurse. The first interview was uneventful. Both seemed immature in their thinking about marriage and parenting. She was implicitly critical of him, and he was defensive.

Sharon (at the beginning of the second interview): Tony didn't want to come today.

Tony: What do you mean, you said you didn't think we needed to do this.

Sharon; I just don't think we need to do this.

Therapist; So why don't we quit? (No one got up to leave)

Sharon; (Wanting to know what to do about her son, Joe's, defiance) What can I do? I don't want to make Joe mad. He always gets mad at me.

Therapist: Whenever you tell him what he needs to do, it sounds like you are asking Joe's permission. . . . What did your mother do when you kids misbehaved?"

Sharon related two stories in response to this question. When she was age 5, she hurled a shoe at her father in a fit of rage. It struck him in the eye, causing bleeding, but she was not disciplined. Another time when she was age 8, her mother was trying to get her and her sister to help clean the house. They were uncooperative, and her mother began crying. It wasn't clear what was behind the stories.

Sharon: I refuse to do anything physical with him. What else can I do?

The therapist told a story of a woman psychologist he worked with who in 15 years of practice had never had to physically restrain a child. They were seeing a family together one day. The 9-year-old boy was challenging and defiant, and the colleague told him in no uncertain terms to sit down. He did.

Therapist: It was the forcefulness of her personal presence that did the job. She didn't do anything physical, but she was very clear he should sit down. I don't think you are clear enough."

During the interview Sharon maintained steady eye contact with the therapist, who found it odd. Her eye contact was both challenging and beseeching. While being interviewed about the marriage, she became angry with the therapist and told him she had put up with Tony in ways the therapist wouldn't understand.

Therapist: (To Tony) Do you worry about how angry you get with your son?

Tony: No.

Tony then talked about how he felt endlessly misunderstood by his wife. He went on to talk about his family. They were loud, but no one ever got hurt. Sharon countered with how she has seen men arrested for some of the things he did.

Therapist: How do you understand what she is saying about you?

Tony: She thinks I am abusive, but I'm not. I am tough, I am loud, but I have never hurt Joe.

The discussion continued in the same manner. She inferred that he was dangerous and not trustworthy, but there were no stories to support her allegations. The therapist stayed with the position he took earlier.

Therapist: Your interfering with Tony's parenting is a problem. It creates a secondary problem in Joe. It sounds like he thinks you are both impossible and he chooses not to listen to anyone. But why should he? When you tell him to do something, it sounds like you are asking him. You are too tentative to be taken seriously.

Sharon glared at the therapist. The room was silent.

Therapist: Time's up. We have to quit.

The interview which was not supposed to begin was at an end. She took her son by the hand and walked out abruptly and wordlessly. The husband who didn't want to come remained in the office.

Tony: So do we make another appointment?

Therapist; If you want to come back. But you both started out by saying you did not want to be here. So, I thought we had already ended. If you want to come back, you can make another appointment.

Tony: (Glanced at his wife, who was in the hall outside the therapist's view) I guess we won't make an appointment.

Therapist: Good luck. I will be here at least five years, if you change your mind.

They did not return. The therapist never heard from them again. This illustration gives a sense of the open-ended quality therapy can have with closure occurring in the family's outside life. The therapist wishes they would have come back. The sample also examines some of the dynamics of parenting and marriage and the ways in which they effect the child. Sharon was locked into a political position as a young attorney who felt men got away with too much. She refused to do anything physical, yet was also too apprehensive to use the force of her personhood. There is a question as to whether she was using her son to defeat her husband. Tony was temperamental and explosive and made mistakes. But the therapist was addressing the problem of how to make the marriage a working peer relationship. Joe's childish omnipotence had been groomed into the role of marital power broker. He was suicidal over the slow death of an invisible patient—his parents' marriage.

The parental component of the family is naturally exposed when we talk about children. But there are two other family components that are part of the picture, the problem and the solution. Both are crucial ingredients of the parenting context, they include the marriage (or marriage variant) and the parents' family of origin.

MARRIAGE AND THE SECOND CHANCE AT GROWTH: DANCING IN THE DARK.

Children, of course, identify with each parent. But they also identify with an invisible member of the family, the marriage. The most delicate patient in the family is the marriage. While it is often an important component of the way children behave and grow, it is difficult to deal with directly. We assume the defiant child is, in part, objecting to something about the marriage, or attempting to correct something in it. We usually deal with this aspect through innuendo or inference. Defiance becomes a problem because the family rule patterns do not permit communicating about relationships, thus the marriage relationship cannot be discussed, except in the most elemental ways.

The hidden component of the parental dyad is the love relationship between the parents. Some components are in the dynamics of the present. Some are symbolic and based on unconscious fantasy life. The benefit of two parents may be that it teaches the children how to better deal with ambiguity, with multiple, and sometimes contradictory, rule systems.

There are few, if any, other institutions in the culture that are run by a dyad. A dyadic peership poses an interesting problem. A young child was attending nursery school in the basement of a church. He came home one day and told his parents he had gone upstairs to visit "God's house." Then he said, "But God wasn't home . . . and neither was Mrs. God." Prior to that, the parents had never considered the possibility of a Mr. and Mrs. God. The nuclear family is unusual in the fact that it is run by a dyad of coequals. Would the world work better if there were a Mr. and Mrs. President, or a Mr. and Mrs. Mayor? It is our impression that, in fact, institutions are run by a father and mother. The father role is likely to be more explicit, while the mother role is often implicit and not related to rank.

Case Example: A Mother's Healthy Defiance

Much of defiance in children is related to unease and lack of unity in the marriage. In the following example, an African American family with four children, had moved from a large, Eastern metropolitan area to a small city. They were referred because their second son, Ken, a 16-year-old young man, who weighed about 220 pounds and looked like Mike Tyson, was in trouble. He was a combination of quiet and bold. It was easy to have frightening fantasies about this young black man. They arranged for psychological testing and sent the results in advance. Ken was viewed as "highly egocentric" with "depressive and psychopathic features." The family entered therapy because of him and their marital distress. The family story and the dynamics which had unfolded over the preceding 5 years were painful.

The family had been referred nearly a year earlier by a psychiatrist who was treating the mother for depression following the death of her father. The psychiatrist viewed the husband as domineering and emotionally unavailable. The father called for the appointment. The therapist detected a surliness in his voice, implying he did not expect much from the therapist. The therapist responded by saying it sounded discouraging, then challenged him a bit by saying, "What makes you think I can help?" The father's tone changed, and he indicated that he felt confused about what was needed. Both he and his wife each had experienced some therapy, as had the depressed psychopathic son. The therapist said they all needed to come. Father said he needed to check with his wife. That first contact ended with the therapist saying, "Call me when you are ready. I will be here at least three years." He called the next day.

Dr. D. was a good father and a kind, motherly man. A college football player who went on to Family Medicine, he was also forceful and tough. He had worked in clinics with needy, disenfranchised families. He made an effort to be successful in the culture of medicine, but he did so with a desire to nurture and to mother. His mixed agenda did not lead to solid financial success. It would be wrong to suggest he was uncompromising. He had a strong belief that if you do it the right way, you will be successful. His wife, an articulate, self-possessed, lively, and appealing woman, told him that was not always true in business, at least for a black man in a small city.

The mother, Mrs. D., was pressuring for change in all parameters of her family. She wanted to go back to the city they came from. Father was against the move because he had just purchased a new practice and wanted to make it work. Since her father's death, she became oriented around being more personal and more creative. She respected her husband's desire to do well economically, but she did not want to wait around until that happened. On the other hand, his compass was oriented around what would make more money for the family. The therapist found her to be an honest, courageous, and clear-headed woman. There was no assurance her plan would work well for the family. Neither spouse wanted a divorce, but both acknowledged her plan could result in one. It was difficult not to admire her desire and her nonmanipulative, self-possessed assertiveness. The therapist was attuned to her desire for health, wholeness, and life in the present. She was being defiant, but in a healthy, self-possessed way.

They had been married 17 years. She had been on his side and acknowledged that she benefited from his hard work. She was upset by the fact that he was knocking himself out, coming home late, and being irritable with her and the children. There was considerable tenderness in her defiance. After therapy began, they experienced a flight into renewed intimacy. He began the new practice, and she went to work organizing the business office. As the practice was being reorganized she felt he was taking advantage of her. Although he had not lied, she felt he had been dishonest with her by not sharing some important information regarding the uncertainty in his plan. He was protecting her from pain on the one hand, but on the otherhand he was fearful she would veto his dream if he were honest. Interestingly, their son, Ken, could be diagnosed with conduct disorder or oppositional defiant disorder. That was why they brought him in. But when they discussed the crisis that upset Mrs. D., the therapist could see that Ken handled his mother's distress in the same manner as his father. Not a bad child, he was close to his mother. He showed flashes of great talent, but he had a way of failing to put things together, especially if he feared he would look like a failure. He never showed distress. He was remarkably impassive when things were difficult. He would act as though it was no big deal. He was defiant, but quietly so. This is a situation in which the mother is searching for more personhood. It's not clear where they are going, but neither parent wants a divorce.

This example is hard to condense because all of these components are important. This was a defiant family. The son was defying the parents, and the parents were defying one another but still working toward more intimacy. The son's behavior expressed the struggle in the marriage in an abstract way, and finally the marital struggle was exposed concretely in the therapy. The therapist characterized the son as being like Dennis Rodman, the notoriously naughty professional basketball player. He was difficult to live with, but he was talented and, if treated right, could contribute a great deal to the team. Mother and Father liked the analogy. Ken was a lovable character on one level, but impossible on another level. The conflicts in the family evolved with distress, but they retained a warmth and appreciation for one another as their lives progressed.

SUMMARY

Parenting is a complex process. It demands the investment of parental personhood at all levels. Parental maturity, role flexibility, and the ability to learn from our children facilitate healthy family life. Parental practices and family and contextual risk factors are associated with children's behavioral problems. It is important that the parents become patients. If they are able to change, it will help their defiant children immeasurably. When attending to the parental dyad, it as also crucial to consider the marriage. The dynamics of defiance are often part of the marital struggle about how to remain an "I" while constructing an intimate relationship.

3

The Dilemma of Childhood: Raising Healthy Parents

"Nothing exerts a stronger psychic effect upon the human environment, and especially upon the children, than the life the parents have not lived." (Jung, 1996)

"Mental illness is inherited, we get it from our children." (T-Shirt)

"We get the children we need." (Colleen Miner)

A child's birth creates an irreversible biopsychosystemic *we*—the family. Children are mysterious beings who sustain families and the child's survival requires a family. We are suggesting that children will do what they need to do in order to sustain the family and to force parents to be healthy parents. A fundamental assumption, shared with Jung, is that children are burdened by the unlived lives of the parents. Their behavior, especially defiant behavior, is motivated by their desire to help the parents grow up so they can provide a healthier atmosphere for the children. It may help to know that age has nothing to do with being grown up.

CHILDREN RAISING PARENTS

The film *Back to the Future* provides a fascinating model for thinking about the effects and motives of children. The main character is a marginal, passively defiant adolescent boy. He has an eccentric adult friend, a self-absorbed and crazy, but not sadistic man—a model for an adequate therapist. The young man lives in a family with a cranky, disappointed, alcoholic mother and a demoralized, ineffective father. He time travels to the past where he encounters his parents as high school students. He becomes a protecting spirit to them, especially his father, and improves the conditions under which they marry, so that the quality of the marriage is changed from resignation and acceptance to appreciation and adequacy. When he returns to the present, the family's life is completely transformed. The parents are livelier and, as a result, healthier. The point is that children, including adolescents, struggle to increase their parents' health so their own health can improve. They try to add to the parents' self-esteem so their own self-esteem can increase.

But children should be warned: it's hard bringing up parents these days! They have so many ways to be distracted, and the demands put on them are overwhelming. Over the past several years we have become more and more intrigued by the fantasy that children raise their parents. The idea began as an oft-repeated, paradoxical, humorous question in numerous family therapy interviews. It appeared as a way to interview children about their families. We ask, "When you worry about your mother and father, what do you worry about most?" They frequently answer, "I don't worry." Of course, we don't believe them and say so, "I have never heard of a kid who didn't worry about their parents." The fact is they usually don't worry with their heads and their mouths, but they devote their whole selves to worrying. They reshape themselves to push the parents' growth or to fit the parents' needs. The most persuasive needs are not the conscious ones, but those represented by the parents' unlived lives or fantasies of the future.

This pattern of thinking is a therapeutically useful, depolarizing way to acknowledge the motives hidden behind children's behavior as they are simultaneously fighting to be an "I" while pushing the family to be an adequate "we." The symptoms of defiance and opposition, while serving a protective function for the children, induce honesty in the parents and pressure them to acknowledge themselves and to examine their motives and assumptions regarding parenting. This forces parents to search for their "soul self." Jung's comment makes intuitive sense, but how do we incorporate it into the therapeutic process? It tells us that the unlived life of the parents pressures the children. There is a defiant quality in growth. It is simply unfair that children grow up without parents' permission. When working with families, it is difficult not to be impressed by the impact of children on family life. Too often there is an attempt to neutralize their power by excluding or isolating them from therapy interviews. This chapter considers the impossibly broad question, "What is the nature of the child?" with the purpose of engaging children as part of a family therapy project.

WHAT ARE THE EFFECTS OF CHILDREN ON A FAMILY?

Children Perpetuate the Complex Biopsychosystemic Entity We Call Our Species

They are dynamic packages of genetic and cultural information we send into a future we cannot see. Most of what they carry is unconscious. In addition to perpetuating the species, children extend the family into the future.

Children Teach Us about Loving and the Delicious Intimacy of We

The birth of a baby induces a quantum leap in the way our lives are organized. Children induce the experience of *whole-person intimacy*, that biopsycho-systemic-cognitive-intuitive experience we never get enough of and few know what to do with. We all want more intimacy than we can tolerate. This is because the intimacy is not all comforting and clear, but involves pulses of deep pain and hatred as well.

A Child is Always Defined within a Relationship Context

When we describe a child we inevitably characterize the group to which he belongs. Of course, adults are defined by their relationship context as well, but we are more often tricked by the optical illusion that implies adults are individuals. It is easier to pretend adults are separate from the context. The child is part of a context, and the context is part of the child.

Children are Generators of Ambiguity

Children induce dilemmas for parents and therapists. Does the baby's crying represent hunger or a need for help, or is the baby simply manipulating the adult world? Two choices are possible. Do what is necessary to reduce ambiguity, meet children's needs, set limits, and establish consequences, or learn to bask in the pleasure of ambiguity within a context of caring. There is a dialectic in the experience of being simultaneously amused and frustrated. Children disrupt the fantasy of the reasonable and force people into the real-life realm of the nonrational. They apply pressure that undermines the best laid plans of parents and their expert consultants. While adults stumble off balance, children have that incredible lightness of being which they bear easily. They are sheer spontaneity and lightness and their defiance seeks to stimulate those qualities in the parents. This lightness is the therapeutic by-product of multilevel frustration—the sudden pleasure of absurdity.

HOW THE CULTURE DEALS WITH CHILD-INDUCED AMBIGUITY

The issue of childhood depression and the rise in popularity of selective serotonin reuptake inhibitor (SSRI) antidepressants offers an opportunity to illustrate the difference between the cultural thinking patterns and the assumptions on which this book is based. The word on the multimedia street is that there is much undiagnosed, and therefore untreated, childhood depression. We agree, but we call it extensive demoralization rather than depression. If a child is irritable, doing poorly in school, feels unpopular, won't do the dishes, and fights with his sister, he may be depressed. Therapists are urged to find those children and treat their depressions. However, there are no studies to show antidepressant efficacy when these medications are given to children. One study, while acknowledging the lack of efficacy, goes on to say that "there is no evidence of harm." Pediatricians and child psychiatrists, in their efforts to treat the masses of children in pain and their frustrated parents, rely on the medications.

On a pragmatic level one can understand this pressure. It is rough out there on the professional front lines. There is tremendous cultural pressure on practitioners to do *something*. This demand on practitioners can contribute to the problem of children's demoralization. The demand on children to do something (e.g., get good grades; go to a better college; work harder so you can buy more computers, more VCRs, mammoth houses). However, the problem of the "I" in the context of a healthy "we" is ignored, superseded, or forgotten. Discouraged, defiant children are a by-product of this dilemma. A need to go backwards to a simpler age is not being applied here. The past is always simpler; we survived it. Life is lived in the strange conservatism of the present. Happiness is represented by the integration of the self.

If a child is annoying or unhappy, he may be suffering from a bad case of being an honest observer of a sociopathic (i.e., manipulative) or overwhelmed system. Before parents haul out the pharmacological arsenal, they need to consider how their own emotions contribute to the child's experience and what their own frustrations produce in the child. If there is anything we wish to change in the child, we should first examine it to see whether it is something that could better be changed in ourselves (Jung, 1966). How far can any parent stand to go with that idea? Do practitioners dare address the question in an ADD or ODD evaluation?

A side effect of a medication-promoting process is that doctors are pressured to *do* something. Insurance companies, who have somehow found a way to guide clinical practice, advocate the use of drugs. There are other possible interventions, of course, but the possibility of carrying them out is eclipsed by an oversimplified, nonclinical assumption. Therapeutic intoxication with medication helps the culture marginalize despair. In a relationship, the summation of pain and frustration we call "depression" leads to a deeper, fuller acknowledgment of being. We are forgetting the critical importance of being (Kundera, 1993). Children remind us of being. Their defiance ruptures our paralysis. When our paralysis remains secure, they become desperate, then defeated. The defeat is what we are too often calling undiagnosed depression. Depression is the defeat of defiance.

The objective of this book is to acknowledge and attend to cultural, family, and personal problems which are reflected in and expressed by defiance in children. Rather than decontextualizing children's behavior with a diagnosis or concretizing it with a chemical fixative, we prefer to use the strong relational context which is stimulated in families to turn things into their opposites and create new relational possibilities.

Case Example: Distress and the Pressure of Health

"I want to have sex eight times a day," says Emily, the defiant 16-year-old daughter of a 43-year-old virginal, born-again mother, and a repressed, overearnest engineer father. Mother's family background was sad, lonely, and nonintimate. Her recipe for goodness is based on a rigidity she found at church. Father learned that if he disagreed with her, she would be hurt, hostile, and unavailable. If he supported her, she would allow him to "touch her," and have sex six times a year, usually on Friday nights. Emily is infuriated by Mother's repressive simplicity. She rages with desire, overpowering everyone, and becomes terrified when anyone takes her seriously, as the therapist did. Emily is sure to match her mother's consistent, self-abnegating goodness with equally constant defiance. Mother's self-control is a mask for her rage and loneliness. Emily's defiance is an attempt to destabilize that mask.

This brief example shows how defiance becomes pressure for health. Family therapy turns things upside down, metaphorically, and looks at things in reverse: intellectual clarity leads to obfuscation, amplification of virtue induces evil, and enforced consistency leads to chaos.

Children dwell in a more natural reality that does not distinguish between *play* and *serious*. *Purposeful*, not serious, is the opposite of play. In some traditions, cracks in time occur at the point of seasonal change, which allow access between the underworld and the daylight world, the conscious world and the unconscious world, or the daylight world and the dream world. Halloween, for example, is a derivative of a pagan festival marking the change from fall to winter. At the change of season, cracks in time develop, allowing the spirits of the underworld to roam the daylight world. Therapy is a process that opens the cracks in the flow of the normal. Children move more freely in these cracks than adults.

WHO IS THIS CHILD?

In Every Child There is a Uniqueness not Explained by Family History or Genetics

Contrary to the common cultural belief that the child is a blank slate, we believe that there is a personal daemon attached to each child. A daemon is an attendant spirit, not a demon. Each child is uniquely a self, a mystery of "being recreating itself" (Hillman, 1996). Each soul is given a unique daemon before being born, and the daemon selects an image or pattern for that soul to live in the world. The companion daemon guides the soul here. Forgetting all that took place in the process of arrival, the soul believes it entered the world empty. This sounds mystical and may be difficult to understand, but there is some useful material here.

The daemon recalls the nature of its image and what belongs to its pattern, thus it carries one's destiny. This daemon idea is not entirely practical, nor does it fit with more science-based theories of personality. It comes out of the dream world, or underworld. It is a useful idea even though it is not solidly grounded. It would be as if one lives in a shadowy room with curtained windows and every once in a while catches a glint of sunlight through an opening in the curtains. Even though one cannot describe it, it is important to remember having seen it. We do not understand ourselves very well. We must therefore give up the fantasy of understanding our children or someone else's children. Within each individual there is a mystery, which is out of reach. Children are more fully souls than parents know, not just extensions of the parents. Care must be taken not to corner these souls. The greatest maturity is required of parents to acknowledge and appreciate the uniqueness of each child, especially at a time when schools and diagnosticians are overdefining them.

Children are Icons of Improvement

The power of unlived lives is unleashed by the statement, "I did not succeed, but my child can succeed with my encouragement and support." Children become icons for parents' worship of future possibility. Usually the first two children in a family are most cornered by demand. Parents' idealization of children leads to force-feeding and overprotection and neglect of the self. The child is programmed to believe, "I must live for my parents, to assuage their despair" and burdened with the obligation to get the family into heaven. A father noted that he had an epiphany upon realizing he wanted his children to lead the life he led, only with less pain. "I either punished or ignored them when they did things that departed from my image. On the one hand, I pushed them to be me, on the otherhand, I was afraid they would turn out like me."

Children are Packages of Energy-for-Repair

Naughty children arouse demoralized parents. Arousal is a form of being alive—a short-acting antidepressant. Anger temporarily interferes with depression. Children may frustrate parents as a way to keep them angry, because they cannot be rageful and depressed at the same time. Thus a child's depression often arises out of his inability to solve a problem of parental depression.

Case Example: A Father's Fear of Emotional Pain. Arthur was the most perplexing, defiant child the first grade had ever seen. He was difficult at home as well, but with much less voltage. Because his rages were so tear-filled, the school guidance counselor believed he might be depressed. When the school's interventions failed, they assumed there was a more serious chemical imbalance behind his behavior. When Arthur, Pam (the mother), Edward (the father), and Kristin (the sister) came for treatment, the therapist learned that

Pam had been treated for the past year for depression with antidepressants and individual therapy. She said she felt much less burdened. As the story unfolded, the therapist learned her history of relationships was unfulfilling. She came from a family of distant, sarcastic people. She was angry with them and expected nothing from them. Edward was a successful small-businessman who believed in positive thinking. He was a kind man who was loving toward his children. His father took his own life when Edward was age 15. He acknowledged no feelings about his father's death. He said he "understood why it happened."

As the therapy went on, it became evident that Pam was frustrated by Edward's niceness and pervasive inability to acknowledge emotional pain. His niceness was a mechanism he used to keep her at a distance. The therapist saw the family 14 times. Arthur became increasingly belligerent and destructive in the office and the therapist ended up restraining him on two occasions. Questions about the marriage were ignored, thus the marriage was discussed only superficially. The therapist's assumption was that Edward was fearful of mental illness in himself and was unavailable for the intimate, heterosexual, peer relationship that defines marriage. He kept his wife at arm's length. She tolerated it early in the marriage, believing if she loved him enough he would become more loving. He became more loving with the children but not her, which left her feeling more lonely. She was depressed by this loneliness and by her failure to relieve her husband's personal depression.

Arthur's outrageous behavior was his attempt to keep her alive and to provide her the intimacy she needed. It worked, but at considerable cost to himself. His depression was the result of his trying to relieve his mother's depression, which was the result of her failed attempt to relieve her father's depression. When the therapist undermined Arthur's superficiality, the mutual marital dissatisfaction poured forth, like pus from an abscess. Pam, who was still unhappy, now knew that her unhappiness was not a personal defect. Arthur got the most out of therapy. He had some remarkable rages in the middle of interviews. He shed the skin of oppositionality and weepy hunger, and the profound sadness which led to the diagnosis of chemical imbalance faded away. One can see how Arthur's "chemical imbalance" was linked to complex, multigenerational dynamics in the family. Fear of intimacy is often linked to unarticulated fear of mental illness, craziness, or depression.

PARENTAL FALLACY: BLAME VERSUS INVOLVEMENT

Our culture emits complex messages about the impact of parenting on children. Prominent sources, such as Hillman (1996), suggest parents are not to blame for the way their children turn out. That's an interesting idea. Therapists are not inclined to blame parents. Parents do a fairly good job of blaming themselves. Family therapy asserts that parents *do* make a difference. Problems arise out of the parents' naiveté about relationships or out of their personal emotional hunger.

The problem is that the culture tends to be overly simplistic and too concrete in the way it connects parental behavior to the resultant personality and behavior of children during growth and adulthood. Therapists must guard against cornering people with the etiology of their problems being connected with their parents. We argue against concreteness, not against parental influence.

Parental influence embedded in family patterns is important and its impact on children during family therapy is inevitable. A confounding issue is that the most powerful influences are unconscious. In the example above, the parents want their child to be polite and well-behaved, but their naive assumptions about life push mother into a crazy, embittered, self-defeating defiance. This becomes more of an issue with family-oriented individual therapy in which the individual constructs a reality made up of fantasies about the family, which remain unchallenged by other family members.

PARENT-CHILD PROCESSES THAT SHAPE CHILDREN'S BEING AND BEHAVIOR

In this section, we shift our perspective a bit. We have been using children's concern about their parents' growth as a way to understand intergenerational conflict. However, and in obvious contradiction, we are also implying that the *being* of children is largely a mystery. Acknowledging contradiction is vital. We are organizing our thinking about children around the idea of what is useful therapeutically—complicates understanding by explaining defiance relationally.

There are three important relational processes which shape a child's identity. They include identification, reaction, and projective identification. Each of these processes is embedded in family patterns. The parent is a role model for the child. At the same time, the child reacts to a parent's behavior. To cite a simple example, in the case of a punitive, abusive parent, a child may grow up to be submissive and depressed (*reaction* to the abusive parent) while another child in the family may grow up to be abusive and punitive themselves (*identification* with the abusive parent).

In projective identification, the child is shaped by the parental fantasies about the child, including hopes (who the parent wants him to be) and fears (who the parent is afraid he may be). This is a powerful, yet mysterious process. It is a fundamental part of loving. The process is essential and omnipresent in parent-child relationships, just not very accessible. Identifying the projective identification that exists in a defiant family, even in part, offers the possibility of more freedom for all members. The simplest example of projective identification involves the single mother of the 3-year-old boy with an abusive father. After the father leaves, the little boy becomes belligerent, and the mother is afraid of the child because she sees her abusive, degrading husband in him.

METHODS FOR EXPLORING THE CHILD'S IDENTITY

It is important to experience the family unconscious as a way to give some meaning and context to defiant behavior and to develop the content for the processes noted above—identification, reaction, and projective identification. The processes may be explained by current dynamics, but they are difficult to understand and often related to the symbolic understructure of the family. However, modern psychiatry, with support from pharmaceutical and insurance industries, often refers to the realm of the symbolic, mysterious, and difficult-to-understand as a "chemical imbalance." The therapists learn about the symbolic understructure from taking a history. When these stories elicit affect in the interpersonal world of the family interview, change is possible. The collections of words we call stories take us into the metaphorical understructure of the family. They help the family own its troubles. We attempt to gain access to a family's metaphorical world, not so that we can manipulate it, but so that the family can embrace and more fully experience life.

QUESTIONS THAT MAKE SYMBOLIC EXPERIENCE ACCESSIBLE

The following paragraphs present questions that create access to the symbolic world of the family. This information lives outside logic in the world of intuitive reality. It can be dangerous if treated too concretely.

Who Is the Child Modeled After?

When you think about the family trees from both sides, who does the child remind you of? She is named for my grandmother who was so shy, but used to be in plays in the community theater. His eyes are just like Tony's, my mother's brother who committed suicide. One fantasy for how a child's identity is formed goes as follows: the first is modeled after mother's mother, the second is modeled after father's mother and the third is father's buddy or girlfriend, or both. The fourth begins to have some freedom from preset family demands (Whitaker, 1989). The basis for this fantasy, which is only true in 70% of cases, is that the relationship with the mother is the model for intimacy in the next generation.

What Were the Prebirth Fantasies about the Child?

A simple example relates to a family with two children of the same gender. The second is likely to have a slightly ambiguous identity, based on the prebirth fantasy that the child would be the opposite gender. The child may have a unisex name. Barbara, called Bobbie, is the tomboy who wins the punt, pass, and kick contest. The boy, Kim, is sensitive, tender, and artistic. Prebirth fantasies of the child are blended with what was happening in the family at conception, during pregnancy, and at birth. The "vulnerable child syndrome" (Green and Solnit, 1964) provides a model for understanding the symbolic implications of history. Basically, an event with powerful emotional repercussions occurring during the pregnancy, perinatal, or early postnatal period, affects how the child is seen because he is the product of that pregnancy. Such a child may have exaggerated importance in the family.

QUESTIONS ABOUT THE NATURE OF CHILDREN

Who Are They? What Does the Therapist See?

The child is an I. By that we mean the I is itself, a labyrinth in the land of the unknown. The I is, in part, the mystery of who the child is. We cannot know it, but we must respect it. When we attend to the I, we attend to the world of the unknown. Acknowledging it with open eyes enables us to deepen our relationship with this world. The child's uniqueness is a blending of the personal daemon with an amplification of some parts of the parents. The therapist uses intuition to embellish the sense of who the child is.

Who Do They Want to Be?

Who they are trying to be is murky territory which becomes more accessible as children get older. It is also helpful in dealing with parents, who are themselves hypertrophied children. The therapist finds out about who the parents' models are and who they want to be by asking who they model themselves after. Who are the children's role models?

Case Example: A Role Model Solves a Dilemma. Anna, age 15, began treatment after a serious suicide attempt by drug overdose. Her parents were locked in a deadly divorce which resulted in both living in the same house. The psychiatrist who made the referral said Anna was the most depressed child he had ever seen. When it came time to plan for Anna's return to school, her parents became concrete and demanding, treating the therapist as though he should be able to read the future and implying he was stupid because he couldn't. They wanted a plan, yet no suggestion was sufficient. Two angry interviews ensued. "What if Anna gets depressed in school?" they asked. Midway through the second interview, Anna interrupted and said, "I know what I will do if I get depressed in school. I will just ask myself, 'What would Winona Ryder do?'"

The school year began, and she become a very defiant girl. This previously shy, self-deprecating, depressed girl insulted some overweaning teachers. Winona Ryder would have been proud of her. The issue of role models also applies to parents. Who do they model themselves after?

Who Do the Parents Want, or Need, Them to Be? Who Are They Afraid They will Become?

What is an oppositional, defiant adolescent up to? He is refusing to do what he is told. He may be belligerent in his demand to be left alone, or he may be withdrawn and suicidal or anorexic, exhibiting the more passive, well-mannered patterns of defiance. He may be passively, but annoyingly, absent-minded. Our premise in working with children like these is that they feel cornered by parental pressure to conform to the parents' or community's living standards. The adolescent is protecting his integrity, but unconsciously or systemically, he is insisting that the parents become more honest and discover their own integrity. The rebellious behavior regarded as pathology occurs in the name of health.

Case Example: Pressure to Conform. Father was on the football team in high school but rarely played. Thirty years later his son goes out for the high school team. Father coaches him and pressures him to be what the father failed to be but wishes he could have been. Father becomes angry when his son makes mistakes or does not show enough enthusiasm. In this case, the father's investment overrides his son's fun. The son may get angry and insult his mother to get even with father. He might quit the team or drink as a way to get the coach to kick him off the team. Nevertheless, the most important problem is father's insistence that the son be what he could not be. Father's coaching is based on strategies and fantasies derived from listening to television sports commentators and his own understanding of why he failed. When such a family enters therapy, the child's attitude or behavior is often defined as pathological because father's behavior is an example of culturally invisible pathology. This process also applies in a slightly different way to the parents. What do they want? Where are they trying to go for themselves? By becoming more invested in themselves, parents give more freedom to their children.

INCLUDING CHILDREN IN FAMILY THERAPY

Children are commonly included in family therapy as a means of evaluating the child or of revealing hidden pathology in the family (Keith 1992). We include children for their therapeutic value. Evaluating children is different from doing therapy with them. Yet, any evaluation of a child represents a therapeutic experience, and no matter how objective the evaluation pretends to be, it inevitably deals with the abstract reality of personhood and the family we. We want to provide a way to understand children so that their relevance to any family therapy project is clear. Over the years, a question asked at family therapy professional meetings has been, "Who works with children?" We have always worked with children because of our belief, which is supported by experience, that the family is not the family without all the children. Contextual change requires the power of the whole family. Children add dynamics to the therapy. Because children also interfere with structure and control, a therapist who works with families must learn to acknowledge and value his impotence to push families around. Children are not like furniture. They are dynamic in that they attract energy from parents and add energy of their own to the family. The energy of children is not so neatly packaged in social language and good manners. They are less bound by logic and consistency. They invite and stimulate spontaneity, which has a profound effect on the interview. Thus, children's presence interferes with therapy patterns that are overpurposeful. It is possible to find many reasons for not including children.

Tips on Working with Children in Family Therapy

1. **Have a cotherapist,** especially when you are new at working with families. It is difficult for one person to work simultaneously with two generations. Freedom and flexibility increases dramatically when there are two therapists.
2. **Use simple language,** and keep your comments brief. Adopt the language of the children early in therapy. Use your imagination. Feel free to be silly, cute, or preposterous.

   For example, the mother of four brought snacks for the children to a late appointment. She gave everyone, including the therapist, an orange. Later she gave the 6-year-old a chocolate lollipop. The therapist beckoned the 6-year-old over and tried to trade his orange for her lollipop.
3. **Avoid questions.** Children experience questions as depersonalizing, as a demand for compliance, and as a demand to surrender this I which they need to cherish. It is useful to mirror comments or wonder out loud in an open-ended way. For example, a therapist commented to an angry adolescent female who is silent at the first family interview, "If I were in your shoes, I wouldn't talk either. I would probably be afraid they would jump down my throat."
4. **Attend to the child.** Children become disruptive when tension is high in a family or when they sense the therapist is apprehensive about them. Rather than dismissing them, it is more helpful for the therapist to switch his focus from the parents to the children, getting down on the floor, if necessary. Interviewing from that position can be surprisingly effective. At such a time, it is more important to interrupt the history, which won't change anyway, to connect with the children.

   For example, the therapeutic process focused on the distress behind a 11-year-old, obsessive-compulsive boy's behavior, the parents began to argue vehemently in the interviews. Inevitably, the son would come over and begin talking to mother in the middle of the argument, or sit down and cuddle up to her. The therapist wanted to disrupt the interaction. He would say, "Cut it out. They don't need your help." or, "Hey! Quiet, will ya! I'm the therapist here." The first few times it happened, all were amused including the boy. When it happened in the ninth interview, he became enraged and hid behind a chair. When it happened in the tenth interview, the boy became enraged, walked out, and slammed the door. The therapist sent his 8-year-old sister out to bring him back. She succeeded.

5. **Choose indifference over cajolery.** It is better not be seductive, but to tell the truth, in order to form a relationship with children. Children and adolescents tend to be apprehensive of people who need them. Bemused indifference lays down a better track for getting to children.
6. **Manage children in the office.** This can be a surprisingly controversial issue, but it is the therapist's office and he knows his rules. In the first interview, it serves some purpose for the therapist to observe how the parents handle their children. For example, the children may initially gravitate to the doll house and the small collection of toys. Often a parent will say to the child, "Now you sit down here and listen. Get away from those toys." The therapist responds, "Actually that's not one of the rules here. I have discovered that children hear a lot more if they can play while we talk. It's okay if they play with the toys. They aren't as dumb as adults who can only think of one thing at a time. If you find you are too jealous, you can get down on the floor and play with them."
7. **Interact with children directly.** Parents think they are being helpful when they encourage the child to talk to the therapist, or reinterpret the therapist's questions. The parent should be asked to discontinue this behavior because their help isn't needed. In fact, parental intruction is likely to reactivate defiance, which interferes with the therapist-child conversation.

   For example, the therapist asked an angry, silent 15-year-old girl to describe what her family was like. Mother cut in and said, "He wants to know what you think of our family" The therapist responded, "Excuse me, Mom, but you already had your chance. She understood me. When you interrupt like that, you make her feel dumb." When the adolescent paused, and father said, "Go ahead, you can tell him whatever you think." The therapist said, "Dad, I don't need your help. I think she is trying to decide if she should answer honestly, or be cautiously diplomatic like you."
8. **Establish a rule that adolescents have to attend but they don't have to talk.** Paradoxically, you can use this condition as a tool to encourage the adolescent's verbal participation. When she begins to speak you can say "Are you sure you want to let me trick you into breaking your promise to yourself?" If she chooses to speak, this forces her own participation. When the interview goes right, and the *family* becomes the subject of concern, the adolescent often finds freedom to speak.
9. **Insult adolescents, but indirectly.** Paradoxically, the insult makes them feel more secure. They are terrified by seduction. Anything that peaks their interest is grist for the therapy mill later on.

   For example, 20 minutes into a consultation with a family with five children, the therapist asked if Louie knew about something. It turned out

"Louie" was Tony. When the therapist came to him again in the interview, he again called him Louie. It was insulting, but not alienating. There is a playful way of insulting adolescents (and men) that helps the therapeutic alliance. In subsequent interviews, Tony playfully referred to the side of him that behaved and got good grades as Louie. Louie became a symbol of his alter ego.

10. **Know that you can only underestimate the pain of the scapegoat.** It is important to acknowledge his pain even though he will not thank you for doing so. He is struggling both to belong and to be separate in order to maintain his integrity. Though well-intentioned, the school and the police can enlist the parents in ways that alienate the child. There are many agencies that can provide punishment, but there is a kind of caring and tenderness that can only be provided by the family, more specifically, by the parents. However, there is an important distinction between personal caring and unconsciously encouraging defiance by implying that the school is stupid or that the police are overstepping their bounds.

    In the case of school referrals, therapists working with children have to decide whose side they are on. The school behaves a bit like missionaries whose righteousness and presumption of access do not acknowledge the dignity of those they serve. The therapist may work toward a functional relationship with the school, but his more specific role is to serve the integrity of the family.

11. **Remember that when parents are worried about the children, the children are worried the same amount about the parents plus 10%.** The parents' concern is usually about the children's social adjustment, what kind of friends they have, or what their grades are like. And while children worry about their parents' social adjustment, they are also concerned about the parents having a nervous breakdown or dying. The fear of a parent dying unexpectedly begins when the parents are around age 40.

12. **Be playful with the parents while the children are listening.** The parents can describe a dream or expand one of their fantasies with a push from the therapist. Playing with the parents is vastly reassuring to the whole family.

    For example, in the 10th session, a mother was urgently counseling her daughter (the one who wanted to have sex eight times a day) about what she needed to do (what mother wanted her to do). It occurred to the therapist that she might be talking about herself. He asked "What do you dream about?" The mother, caught off guard, looked at the therapist and said, "My dream is to just leave." She was attempting to stimulate remorse in the family. "Where would you go?" asked the therapist. "I don't know. I really don't know," answered mother. "That's weird, isn't it?" said the therapist, "You know what your daughter should do and where she should go, but how about you? How come you don't know where you should go? How come you don't know how to bring yourself to life?" "I suppose I could go back to school," she said. The way she said it sounded gruesome to the therapist. She was teaching her children to have no dreams. If she got serious about herself, her children might begin to think they were worth something.

13. **Feel free to digress with no specific purpose even in very tense situations.**

Case Example: Play and the Emergence of Meaning. T. J. comes from a hardworking rural family of blue-collar, middle-class parents. Father is a maintenance worker for the city and deals in used cars on the side. Mother is a school bus driver who works part-time in a fabric store. The parents are youthful, attractive people, naturally so, with little adornment. They have an appealing dignity about them. Father is an alcoholic in recovery for 15 years. An older son died at age 18 in an auto accident 8 years ago. In the past year mother had a torrid affair with a 19-year-old. The parents have talked about it both with and without their children present. She is not remorseful. The affair was deeply gratifying for her, but she ended it because it was damaging her and her family's reputation. T. J. age 15, is a tough, slender adolescent who regularly gets in fights at school. He is a good fighter, a little too good for his own good. The fights are precipitated when someone insults his family or teases him about his mother, whose affair was public knowledge in their small community. They have been arguing about T. J.'s unwillingness to go to school.

T. J.: (*scornful of everything adults do, brings interview to a halt*) This is a waste of time.

Father: Well, talk. (*To therapist*) We've been doin' pretty good. He's been goin' to the state fair every day.

T. J.: (*scornfully*) I've only been there twice, and it's been on for five days! I don't want to be here.

Therapist: What happens if he doesn't go to school?

Mother: Well I think we might have go to court for some kind of neglect.

T. J.: They can't do anything to you.

Therapist: They could too. Although, I suppose you could use T.J. as your lawyer. Nobody tells him what to do.

T. J.: I don't worry about nothin'. What is, is.

Therapist: You sound like a existential philosopher, or a teen-age Buddhist monk.

T. J.: (*The parents are smiling.*) That don't mean nothin' to me. I ain't goin'. There's nothing to worry about.

The parents talk about the future and say T. J. will learn not to be so defiant.

T. J.: I ain't gonna change. I don't need to worry about nothin'.

Therapist: The reason you don't worry about nothin' is your parents are worried about you. They worry about your future, so you don't have to. If you screw up they pay for it. The nice part is that you can be mad at them for your mistakes.

T. J.: Yeah? Well I don't care. And I'm always gonna be this way.

Therapist: Anybody who talks like that is saying they will be a kid forever. There are three ways you can stay a kid. One you end up in prison.

T. J.: I ain't afraid of prison. I got friends in Martinsburg been in Atwater (a well-known high-security federal prison). Both got the Atwater slash to prove it. (*He points to his neck*) One kid just had a baby and everything is cool for him. He got it straightened out.

Therapist: Did he get pregnant at Atwater? (*Parents are smiling. T.J. looks exasperated, but smiles*)

T. J.: He wasn't pregnant. How could a man get pregnant?

Therapist: I don't know. I was just hoping there still might be a chance for me.

T. J.: (*We have wandered into this territory before*) God! You're gay.

Therapist: Don't knock it, sweetie. Don't forget this, we queers have most of the sexy fun. (*Parents continue to be amused, T.J. is disgusted and sits back, throwing his hands up.*)

Father: What are the other two (*ways to stay a kid forever*)?

Therapist: You can be in the state hospital or you can marry a woman who will take care of all your worries.

T. J.: I ain't gettin' married. Besides, women don't take care of men. Men take care of women.

Therapist: (*Chanting sing-song*) Dream on, little dreamer, dream on, (*decrescendo*) dream on, dream on, dream on. All men are little boys, hungry for a momma.

T. J.: Well there's no woman that will take care of me.

Therapist: You mean besides your mother and your sister? Have you ever had a girlfriend?

T. J.: Yeah? Lots of them. I started dating when I was in first grade. I was seven.

Father: You must have been 6.

T. J.: No, Rob took me. Remember, he drove me and Kari to the movie. I asked her.

Father: Rob died when you were seven.

The conversation turned to what was happening in the family when Rob was killed.

Mother: I feel real bad about those times. I think that's when some of this trouble started. After Rob died I was just paralyzed, and T.J. used to go down to some boys' house. They were older than him. They had a skateboard ramp, and they taught him how to skateboard. I was worried about it but I was too depressed, I think.

T. J.: (*After a silence. For the fourth time that day.*) How come you are all lookin' at me? What is this, stare-at-T.J. day?

Therapist: I was just thinking about what you looked like when you were a baby.

Mother: He was cute. Really cute. We all had so much fun with him. Sarah (sister) was 5, and she thought I brought him home for her.

They talked about how chaotic things were at the time of his birth. Mother and father both appear dreamy-eyed and thoughtful at this point in the interview. T.J. was quiet, slumped down, legs extended straight out in front of him.

Mother: Yeah. I feel real bad about that time.

Therapist: Don't kick yourself too hard about those times. You would have had a hard time keeping him close then anyway. Last time you told me about how he used to come and sleep with you up until he was 13.

This issue had been discussed previously, and it wasn't clear that he came to sleep with them because he was afraid of anything. The therapist guessed that he was worried about them and came there to care about them. It was instinctive. He could not or would not explain it.

Therapist: Let me tell you my fantasy about him. I think he has a good core. He is going to go through some rough years. I believe he knows the difference between right and wrong. He feels like a kid who has been cared about. He's just screwed up right now. Just like the rest of the family. You see, I believe there is a part of him that worries about how you are doing. And this has developed into a reactive circle. The other thing is that there are plenty of people around to kick his bony ass, to make sure he gets a chance to know he is a jerk. You can give him the most loving. You're the core of his life. The center. And if you whack at him, it could make him desperate. There is no one around to love him like you do.

As they prepared to leave the interview, the parents' eyes were shiny with tears. T.J. was ignoring his parents' emotion, complaining about coming back. This wasn't helping anyway, he said.

We hope the reader can see what the therapist is doing here. There are some playful, outrageous, politically incorrect, abrasive moments that appear to have no relevance to anything. Then, all of a sudden, the therapist is reflecting on Rob's death and its effect on T.J. We are talking about the *is-ness* of this family. This is how you use the idea of the We in therapy. The idea is in the back of the therapist's mind. There is no abrupt change as a result of it, but the family now leaves with a little less puzzlement. They don't know exactly where they are going, but they face this future with a little less tension. They will return in 2 weeks.

Keep in mind that adolescents are out of their heads. They are whole persons who react with their entirety. Thus, they are not good observers of their own behavior. Another way to think about it is that they reside part-time in a parallel universe, which is not explainable in our language.

Case Example: Parallel Universes. A professor's family was having trouble with their fourth child, Charles, who was going through a siege of defiance during his junior year in high school. The older brothers and sister who lived in other cities came in for a consultation interview on Good Friday. They were a chaotic family, but appealing and honestly upset with themselves. The third child, Tom, was now living in a large city about 1,000 miles from home. The following exchange occurred about 20 minutes into the interview.

Father: Tom, what I keep wanting to ask you about, and I never get it out, is about the bad time you had 6 years ago, when you were a junior in high school. I think it would help me understand Charles a little better if you could explain why you were so pissed off back then.

Tom: Was I pissed off? I don't remember it that way.

Mother and father exhaled noisily, chuckling together.

Mother: Lord, Tom, you were awful. Don't you remember how we worked on getting you to go to the other high school, and then you changed your mind the 2nd day. You weren't going to go, so I called Dad and he came home. And you two were yelling at each other in the front hall?

Tom: God, that's random. I don't remember. I mean, I remember switching schools, but I don't remember what you're talking about. I don't remember being angry then. I mean I can remember feeling kind of discouraged and fed up. One day the counselor called me in and I started crying because I hated the school so much, and she thought it was because of you guys. Then they said I had a chemical imbalance and made me go see a counselor right away.

The moral of this story is that Tom had been in a kind of psychotic out-of-the-head state. At times like this, a therapist can seldom get children to metacommunicate about what is up, except in fairly conventional ways.

What we have outlined are interactional summaries. These kinds of processes must develop out of the therapy experience. They can be reflected on from outside in retrospect, but seldom in the middle of the experience. Adolescents are not good at explaining themselves. Nevertheless, they are fighting to be selves. They become defiant as a result of too much help, too much liberty, and not enough of love. Each is intensely a self, thus not a good observer of self. This is especially true of the defiant adolescent.

SUMMARY

In this chapter we have described our impressions of the nature of children. As we indicated, children are always defined by the context in which they live. So, we are talking about children in ways that are intended to be therapeutically useful. We think of children as making an effort to repair their families so the families can provide a context of health to support the children's growth. The greatest therapeutic errors are single-mindedness and concreteness. There are deeply unconscious processes operating within each family that shape the identity of the children. Many are disguised as cultural values which are harmful to children and families. Including children in therapy is a rewarding experience for everyone involved.

4

Therapists and the Therapeutic Process:

The Poetics of Experience

"It is not the rebellion itself which is noble, but the demands it makes upon us." (Camus)
"Technique is something we use while waiting for the therapist to arrive." (Whitaker)

This chapter is an impressionistic introduction to a particular pattern of psychotherapy with families. Our wanderings may seem disconnected and the reader may feel lost at times. The use of one's imagination can be helpful. This chapter includes a brief subjective history of family therapy, followed by a discussion of the role of psychotherapy as a process for increasing access to the self. This differs from psychotherapy as a social adaptation process, such as psychoeducation or counseling. The chapter continued by reflecting on the personhood of the therapist as it relates to the use of self in clinical work with defiance. Clinical examples illustrate some of the assumptions on which this pattern of family therapy is based.

Psychotherapy is made up of two processes. The most essential effort is to gain access to more of the self and more of one's health. Secondly, it is a process that acts as a personalized guide to social adaptation. This process works in the light, in the realm of the reasonable, where the therapist works to reduce pain and ambiguity. This pattern of psychotherapy is easier to teach because it is an academic discipline. We view the process of hunting for the elusive abstract self as a more difficult one. This search for the self may be better understood as a process of consciousness evolving. Our methods appear to be in support of the family taking greater control. This process of family therapy works in a region where the lighting is poor and the terrain uneven. Symbolic experiential therapy uses anxiety, pain, and ambiguity to promote growth. Its language is more abstract and less specific, more poetic. In the therapeutic process, the *poetics of experience* refers to a cluster of highly charged arcane metaphors created by the family and therapist. This clinical discipline is learned through practice, self-discipline, and experience.

When the patient is a family, the task of searching for and integrating the self becomes more complex as the family "we" and the self of each member must be engaged. However, the process of consciousness evolving works best in a relationship context with significant others. The problems that fall into the realm of defiance may appear too turbulent to fit this model. With the problem of defiance it seems more appropriate to restore order through the use of structure and reason, as if to say, "Hey! Knock that shit off!" However, we think this process, which carries many names (e.g., growth, gaining access to more of the self, increasing maturity, evolution of consciousness), is crucial and fundamental to the work we call family therapy.

Hunting for the self of the patient demands a parallel hunting for the self of the therapist. The search for the therapist's self requires ruthlessness, cunning, patience, sweetness, honesty, and persistence (Castaneda, 1987). The parallel we are promoting in our therapeutic work with families is that the parents must search for themselves in order to correct the problems with their children. Living for or through or projecting onto the children leads to failure to track the self.

Throughout the book are examples which point to novel behavior by the therapists, including humorous, ironic, and idiosyncratic remarks. Some examples even suggest an adversarial relationship between therapist and family. When the comment sounds adversarial it usually represents a reversal in tone. Therapists always know about joining, but they often don't know how to establish distance. Therapeutic effectiveness requires the therapist to maintain the freedom to be more unpredictable in the therapeutic relationship. Thus, what appears adversarial is a demonstration of moving out of an established relationship with the responsibility of rejoining in a different manner.

Humans seek consistency and a feeling of predictability, but when family routines become oppressive, they stifle growth. Defiance is stimulated by this growth-stifling process. Of course, aberrant behavior upsets the family which inevitably attempts to restore familiar patterns of living. Our view is that a family's desire to return to the routine and the familiar, supported by social agencies, often makes the situation worse. The resulting defiant behavior can become more desperate and destructive.

Novel behavior that breaks from expected routines has an unusual effect on our total being, our sense of values, and our perceptions. Novel behavior by a therapist alters how the family structures reality. Family patterns are so stable, that only rarely does a single novel event produce an avalanche of change. It is more likely for the effect of a therapeutic action to be cumulative and reciprocal. Unusual, unexpected behavior changes our relationship to the world. Living patterns can become routine and powerfully stable. Defiant children are often reacting to the deadening power of the routine. A polarization they develops between a deviant child and the "normal" adults (e.g., family, parents, teacher) as the adults attempt to preserve the stability that masks all compromise and pain. Punishment or consequences are used to neutralize deviance and to bring a family member back into the structure of what the parents define as normal.

Idiosyncratic, novel behaviors collapse polarization and routine in unexpected ways. Novel behavior softens concrete thinking and changes the way reality and values are organized. When defiance becomes more desperate, families are required to change how they look at behavior and life. Therapists work on ways to disrupt routine patterns of thinking and behaving. In the case of defiance, there is a level of danger, risk, and outrageousness that interferes with what is needed most—spontaneity.

One of the major tasks of this book is to describe a clinical method for using defiant behavior to help families regain control of life. For some, this kind of language leads to the impression that "anything goes," which is not so. Of course, novel behavior by a therapist can be sadistic or capricious in the name of therapy. Such danger is reduced in therapeutic work when the behavior occurs within a context of caring and it abides the community standard of morality. It also requires an underlying sense of beauty and an awareness of the aesthetics of experience. The caring and the sense of beauty are what differentiate this work from psychoeducation. The therapist's behavior, including language, is aimed at integrating a child's defiant behavior into the living context of the family. Integration is an important component of the sense of beauty. In psychotherapeutic work with families, we encounter patterns in experience that have an aesthetic quality, or a sense of beauty. Experiencing these patterns can produce an epiphany—a moment of seeing a kind of wholeness among the disparate parts of life experience. These therapeutic moments affect a person's relation to their reality. These epiphanies are often activated by novel behaviors and comments, including irony, humor, and free associative nonsequiturs. It is important to note that novel experiences are cumulative (Castaneda, 1987).

Case Example: The Use of Humor

A Brazilian family of five was 6 months from the end of their 3-year stay in the United States. Both parents were high ranking government officials who were completing Ph.D.s in public policy at a nearby university. Mother's chronic illness had exacerbated a year earlier. Camille, their 18-year-old daughter, a lovely, talented, but introverted young woman, started coming off the tracks 5 months before their return to Brazil. A family history of schizophrenia magnified her anxiety and her parents' apprehension. They were afraid she was on the threshold of becoming the next schizophrenic. She was angry about a number of things in the family, but most particularly, the parents' insistence that she see a therapist. One day she asked, "What's my diagnosis anyway, Mr. Shrink?" The therapist sensed the parents' anxiety as all awaited her answer. "I think you are a Brazilian screwball, just like the rest of the family," she responded. That diagnostic formulation gave a playful quality to the relationship. Camille became less fearful of being cornered by the therapist. Her involvement with her was flavored with increasing interest in herself. Her anxiety and defensiveness about her symptoms were reduced and she looked and behaved less like a schizophrenic-to-be. Likewise, the family's anxiety was reduced. Both the young woman and her family began to use the therapist's diagnostic formulation to refer to themselves. At the last session before the move back to San Paulo, father said, "We're just a bunch of Brazilian screwballs." This shift in identity significantly depolarized the process in the family that was pushing her into a diagnostic corner. It may seem abrupt and risky, but much time and attention had gone into the work with this family. Camille and her family experienced this seemingly offensive, almost inappropriate remark as profoundly loving and accepting. After that point, Camille became very attached to the therapist whom she had previously disdained.

Throughout our careers we have depended on family therapy when others have chosen individual therapy or pharmacotherapy, or a blend of the two. We believe in families, this means that when there is a crisis, we choose to increase the number of people on either side of the therapeutic relationship. We don't trust medication as much as we do the therapeutic process. We believe in the healing power of human relationships, especially those biopsychosystemic relationships called families. We view families as organisms with implicit methods for self-healing and self-correction. We are not against medication, rather we are opposed to its use without skepticism. Medication has the effect of reducing anxiety and pain in all relationship axes—therapist-family, parent-child, and husband-wife. It can interfere with the anxiety necessary for growth. Oddly, the most important indication for medication may be when the practitioner's anxiety level is too high.

Reconfiguring defiance as a disease or chemical imbalance interferes with the symbolic experiential work described here. We regard all psychopathology as being related to interpersonal experience, until proven otherwise. It is our belief that mental disorders are the by-product of multipersonal patterns of many family generations. The symptoms, therefore, belong to the family system. While this is a simple statement, it is a very complex idea.

FAMILY PSYCHOTHERAPY AND THE SENSE OF BEAUTY

The way a therapist conducts therapy is based on morality and a sense of beauty within the context of a caring relationship. The sense of beauty in therapy needs some discussion, but we assume the morality component is understood. An idea of this kind implies that we are talking about psychotherapy as an art. In fact, we think of psychotherapy as a craft, an applied art. A therapist is rebellious, not in a militant way, but in a creative way. Technical skill is needed, but quality is dependent upon artistry, cunning, and caring.

Psychotherapy isn't an art that produces a palpable end product. It is a performance art, like music. We see a strong parallel between psychotherapy and music. If the world of family therapy were the world of music, we would be folk or blues musicians—marginal, but deeply invested in the nuances of what we do. Individual musicians are obviously important to music, each performing in a distinctive style based on the totality of their experiences. What is not so obvious, except to musicians, is that music is bigger and more important than any performer. The musician is the music's way into the world. This is also true for psychotherapy. The therapeutic process is bigger and more important than the therapist. The therapist is the conduit for the therapeutic process. There are many ways to practice psychotherapy. With a few years of training and experience, it is possible to do good work, but for professional therapists and musicians alike, their careers are spent refining their craft. Becoming therapeutic requires practice, patience, disciplined experience, and investment of time and energy. This method of therapy is based on clinical experience and learning.

Symbolic experiential therapy is not in the mainstream of contemporary family therapy. Sometimes old-fashioned language and assumptions seem out-of-step with current trends. In the way that folk music or blues clings to the edge of the world of music, our family therapy pattern is traditional. This type of therapy is not widely taught in graduate schools. Good performance does not depend upon replicating the notes someone else wrote. Rather, learning this type of therapy depends upon a combination of motivation, talent, skill, and creative spirit. The pattern of practice is consistent and replicable, but the innovative possibilities are endless. Learning is based on experience, not on theory. Theoretical insight *follows* clinical experience. The beginner can do much of what the experienced professional does but the experienced professional is much better at handling the inevitable impasses and at remaining nonanxious when family anxiety rises. This may sound strange, but the experienced professional is more accomplished in the art of doing nothing.

Family therapy refers to a wide range of therapeutic and conceptual frameworks. However a practitioner decides to do therapy is based on her own experience of life, her multigeneration family experience, what has been therapeutic to her, combined with more formal personal and mentoring experiences. However, once she defines how she is going to work, based on what she believes will be effective, she also establishes limitations for herself. Those limitations are frustrating, but in psychotherapy, as in living, frustration is the basis for creativity on both sides of the therapeutic relationship. Knowing the limitations of the therapist is and what she does is part of the definition of integrity. The therapist attempts to understand human experience in terms of family interaction and family history in the matrix of symbolic experience.

In today's culture, healthcare providers, whether physicians, family therapists, or social workers, are inevitably invited to fix a problem located in an individual. This focus on the individual is fundamental to the way our culture thinks about health. The dominant thinking patterns in our culture are good at ignoring context. Our pattern of working is based on a different view, one that is not new. In fact, it is fundamental to how family therapy started. We expand the context of the problem so that it has to do with the whole family. We go so far as to say we don't believe in individuals, except as fragments of families. The culture acknowledges the usefulness of this perspective, but when it is put into action and produces confusion, inconvenience, guilt, or loss of innocence; support and enthusiasm quickly fade. The whole family is needed for treatment, not as a therapeutic stunt or power play, but as a simple way to enrich living and decrease the likelihood of failure. The family as a group has the power to change its living patterns. It is not likely that one person, or even a dyad, can change a family pattern. The whole family is needed to produce change. There are powerful entropic forces in family relations which easily neutralize the energy to change. The antichange agents have more power when they are not included in the therapy interviews.

For example, our model of family therapy puts us in juxtaposition with modern psychiatry and its use of the term chemical imbalance, a persuasive metaphor to support the use of psychotropic medications. It puts us in opposition with the medicalization of human experience. Even defiance can be medicalized by converting defiant behavior into a disease and calling it masked depression, bipolar disorder, or an attention deficit/hyperactivity disorder. The medical system is conservative and wary of novel behaviors.

When we make a choice based on experience, we must be prepared to meet some limitations of our choice. The limitations are embodied in therapeutic impasses, where despite the best intention of the therapist, the process is blocked. At this point the therapist has to regain consciousness of her own center, then consider how to be innovative or creative in the way they deal with the problem, so that they can get the job done, not get killed, and have fun. That is, the therapist must remain as honest as possible about what is and is not possible. Our pattern of family therapy is a form of rebellion, not because we choose to work with families as opposed to individuals, but it is a rebellion against the extremes of togetherness or isolation, and the extremes of death or eternal joy. It is a rebellion that supports integrity, as opposed to perpetual adaptation.

Family therapy is a process enshrouded in wonder and mystery. It deals with something important but elusive. We can refer to that something as the unknown, the spiritual world, abstract reality, or systemic awareness. However, despite the absence of a clear name, the process is what is most important.

Paradox and contradiction are the mysteries of the soul. The weird and the uncanny are sources of knowledge. In order to know the self we constantly seek but cannot define, it is necessary to open the heart wide and search every part. It is a requirement that we face the weird, the perverse, the sick, the strange, even the sadistic. Without embracing complexity, the soul cannot be understood. Sometimes deviation from the usual is a special revelation of truth. When normality explodes or breaks out in craziness or defiance, we might look closely before running for cover or attempting to restore familiar order. For some reason, when we encounter apparent meaninglessness, meaning is revived. If we are going to be curious about the soul, we need to explore its deviations and perverse tendency to contradict expectations (Hooks, 1995). Later in the chapter we talk more about the importance of curiosity about the soul.

Psychotherapy is countercultural, but not in a way which desires to take anything apart. It is a rebellion based on integrity that refuses to put the culture's demands ahead of spirit. It is a rebellion in the name of health and in the name of increasing one's freedom and energy. That does not sound properly altruistic, but we believe that increasing our own freedom and our own energy, increases the freedom and energy of our intimate others.

We are talking about family therapy as a clinical discipline, a craft, and a useful art that is learned by experience. The next section juxtaposes this view with the evolution of family therapy in this era. This comparison explains why it is difficult to work with families in the ways we describe; ways which can be difficult in the current cultural context, but ways which are nevertheless fruitful.

A SUBJECTIVE HISTORY OF FAMILY THERAPY

Family therapy appeared in the 1960s. In psychiatry it was based on a newly emerging scientific paradigm, known as a theory of general systems (GST). A new paradigm involves a disruption, therefore a challenge to conventional thinking patterns. The subjective part of our history begins with our perception that psychiatry initially embraced GST with excitement, but GST challenged and displaced conventional psychiatric assumptions. First, it placed pathology in a relational context. Additionally, the practitioner, who in the medical model was a source of superior knowledge, became the most experienced participant in the systems paradigm. In fact, in the systems pattern, knowledge may be entropic, whereas experience tends to be negentropic. Our view is that the rise of family therapy was a partial stimulus for a very conservative political movement in psychiatry. Remedicalization, as this movement was called, was an attempt to restore the psychiatric physician to a position as a source of superior knowledge.

Remedicalization limited psychiatry's broadening focus, and directed its specific attention to the use of medication. Family therapy was pushed to the sidelines. In the logic of remedicalization, because medication (a chemical) reduced symptoms, it was assumed that chemical imbalance caused the difficulties we think of as psychopathologies. Chemical imbalance is a metaphor that explains why medications work with some disorders. However, because of society's fascination with technology, chemical imbalance is a very persuasive metaphor. The evolution of the DSM series was another component of the remedicalization of psychiatry. In our view, the DSM series represents a regressive pattern of scientific description similar to 19th century patterns of classification. It incorporated none of the new ideas from the new systemic paradigm, emerging as a catalog of overextended metaphors for describing and pathologizing human experience. These scientific catalogs were developed by committees of psychiatrists whose clinical experience came from tertiary care centers. Interestingly, as the catalog of pharmaceutical agents expanded, the catalog of diagnoses changed. Why was that so? Why is it that we see so much more clearly what we can treat? As remedicalization gained momentum, it became less defensive and referred to itself as biological psychiatry. The concept of biological psychiatry restored the status of psychiatrists as sources of specific, superior knowledge. It is possible to be expert about neurotransmitters and medication, but dealing with people and their experiences continues to be humbling and filled with ambiguity.

We are suggesting that family therapy had a paradoxical effect on the world of mental health treatment. While initially it expanded the universe of psychiatry, secondarily it stimulated a conservatism which has become the dominant mode of understanding the realm of psychopathology. Oddly, in order to establish a place for itself in the culture of healthcare, family therapy has in recent years been medicalized. The cost of being countercultural was too high. The chemical imbalance and genetic factors of biological psychiatry are being readily absorbed into much of the therapy culture. The basis of our argument is that the ascendancy of biological psychiatry maginalizes the therapeutic process in the name of social adaptation.

While systems thinking is exciting and illuminating, it transcends the familiar reasonableness of linear thinking and results in confusion. Our culture is cautious of confusion. It thinks of confusion as simply unnecessary. Taking a pill isn't confusing. That's why it is loved. Systems theory does not get rid of ambiguity, it makes ambiguity more tolerable. As one becomes more familiar with this kind of thinking, the tolerance for ambiguity turns into thirst for ambiguity. Ambiguity becomes one version of the higher good. It almost always provides the possibility of patterns which embrace contradiction. It moves from diagnostic thinking (knowing by dividing) to observation of the whole of experience in context. This dynamic view of experience creates uneasiness in its complexity.

Family therapy began as a movement counter to the culture of more conventional psychiatric patterns. Where it had been a clinical discipline, it became an academic discipline. While family therapy has contributed to massive changes in the culture and how it thinks about psychotherapy and human experience, the switch from a clinical pattern to a more academic pattern brought an undue demand for being reasonable, with its resulting by-product—caution. Mainstream family therapy has been reunited with many of the cultural components it once questioned. Thus family therapy has been medicalized.

Symbolic experiential family therapy is a psychotherapeutic methodology that is organized around contextual and relational issues in the realm of those things we consider psychopathologies. Two fundamental assumptions that are important to keep in mind are: (a) all psychopathology is related to interpersonal experience until proven otherwise, and (b) where there is caring, all pathology is sharing or repairing.

In the following pages we suggest that many serious psychiatric problems which psychiatric thinking relegates to the realm of chemical imbalance are problems of the self. The self is not accessible by reason. It is more accessible when routines are disrupted, even briefly, by novel experiences. It is more accessible through systems awareness, experiences with intimates, play, and dreaming. Our culture prefers a psychotherapeutic pattern which is a softened version of the medical model. This model seeks to reduce tension, enhance communication, and advocate for compromise in the interest of comfortable solutions. Compromise, however, does not work with defiant families because it obscures the I, the very entity fighting for recognition through defiance. The defiant behavior is an objection to the culture's ascendancy over beingness, the self, and the family.

HOW DOES PSYCHOTHERAPY FIT INTO THE CULTURE?

Exposing the endless ambiguity of the world is the experiential therapist's starting point, but this is a difficult process. It means learning a way to engage an upset family without a theory or a pharmacy and being able to stand without hope of something better. When the family says, "What are you going to do?," the therapists answers "Nothing." Or, in a more hopeful mood, "Teach you how to suffer." In the struggle to be more human, therapists must hunt for ourselves and learn to accept arrogance, humility, naiveté, and irony. In essence, the therapist says, "The only you I know is me," and "I can't see it in you if I have not seen it in myself."

A DEVELOPMENTAL SCHEMA FOR DISTINGUISHING AMONG PSYCHOTHERAPIES

We use a homemade developmental schema to distinguish between a psychotherapy that acknowledges, nurtures, and attends to I or the self (or perhaps it might be called the soul), and a psychotherapy that operates as an agent of the culture in support of social adaptation by modifying the social selves (Keith, 1996). We draw this distinction for the sake of illumination (in reality the distinction does not exist) so that defiance may be seen as a fortress for the I, rather than as a case of bad manners in need of correction. An idea evolving out of conversations with Carl Whitaker (1991) identifies a distinction between a self (the "who I am," emphasizing integrity and being) and a set of social selves (the selves that *do*). We refer to the matrix that unites them as personhood.

Adults play the duplicitous social games of adulthood. Social life is made up of white lies and pretenses of all kinds. We used to believe that duplicity was what we saw in politicians and used-car salesmen, but we can all be dishonest. Good manners can be duplicitous or adaptive. This is not a moral issue or problem of good and evil. While a game metaphor may seem trivializing, being a good game player is crucial to survival and to healthy satisfying living. For example, family therapists are actually persons carefully trained to play the game of family therapy, which is one of their favorite games. Some games are played with passion, energy, and dedication. Some are played with awkwardness and pain. Others, because of shyness or ineptitude are avoided completely. Parents teach their children to play these games of social adaptation. It is important to remember that while the roles can be modified, the I remains an elusive constant.

Looking at ourselves from a social perspective, we conclude, "We are the sum of our relationships." However, on another level, we are more than the sum of our relationships. More than duplicitous social game players, we are a printout of earlier programming by our families. The software at our core, installed in the dream period of infancy, develops in family living during the preverbal years when we are the victims of the world of our families and the world of adults. These programs can be minimally altered. While they are powerful, they are not accessible through reason or self-reflection. We have virtually no memory of this time or these experiences. When we arrive in the adult world, we have no memory or veto power. We lack the ability to think about what is happening to us. Our self-esteem is established in this period out of the process of being loved. During this period we are irreparably and inevitably wounded by what our parents are unable to do for us out of their anxiety, fear, despair, or sense of inadequacy. Their fears participate in shaping us.

We all have a chronic undifferentiated, but relatively healthy, schizophrenic part of us that is unconscious, nonrational, and right-brained. Likewise, problems called chemical imbalances or character defects are related to these programs. They are virtually inaccessible to reason-based language. They are available, however, during play (especially parallel play), during dreaming, and in response to novel behaviors.

When we reach the age of 2, we become something of a problem. We begin to individuate and learn the rudiments of defiance. We learn to say *no*. It is not clear if our demands are based on the need for food or on the need to dominate our world and our adult tyrants. By age 2 ½ or 3 we begin to be programmed for adulthood. We start to learn duplicitous games, including different ways to say no and how to protect our innocence through self-justification. Particles of memory begin to appear. By the time we are 3-years-old, the training is in full swing. We learn not to bite just because we are upset. We learn to be polite. We learn duplicity (white lies) in the name of adaptation. But we also learn what is necessary to protect the self. At times, adaptation appears harmful to the self. But too often, the family assails our "I," and we invent ways to protect it. Defiance is a necessary part of development. Defiance becomes distorted or pathologic when those responsible for nurturing the emerging self can't cope with it by reason of their own immaturity or respond to a crisis which destabilizes their relationship to the outside world by becoming too punitive or repressive.

Today most psychotherapy is done in the realm of social adaptation, teaching us how to adapt in the world. Our model of psychotherapy attends to the software, or the program, that makes up the self. While we do not think of this software as changeable, therapy aims at gaining more access to it and making more of the self accessible. Experience does this as well. At first glance, it may appear that the fantasies behind this pattern are vaguely utopian. However, our pattern is more accurately based on an enjoyment of ambiguity, amusement at the absurdity of this life, and a freedom to enjoying intimacy with other I's.

It is our view that the use of a more linear, medical model with more serious pathology, and the relegation of these pathologies to the metaphorical realm of chemical imbalance, can have iatrogenic components. This is true especially when it fails to acknowledge the context of the problem or the subjective, symbolic, or existential experience connected to the pain. Sometimes it appears helpful, in a paradoxical way, for the child-as-patient to remain a linchpin of the family's well being. This induces adaptation to (what is assumed to be) an intrinsic defect in the child. The parents become understanding treatment aides. Their investment in a diagnostic category or medication reduces ambiguity in the family system which, in turn, reduces the pressure they put on the child. "It's only his disease," they contend.

The side of psychotherapy involving symbolic experience, is less easy to summarize. It has to do with moving into the world of *primary process*, in which there is no clear difference between unconsciousness and consciousness. For example, father's workaholism as an escape from life and intimacy takes on amplified importance and overmothering by either gender is taken on as an issue. Defiance is shaped by the effort to preserve integrity, and many therapies inevitably compromises integrity. Our therapeutic method promotes integrity and, as a result, brings difference into awareness early on, without requiring agreement in order for a relationship to be established. The parents' effort to protect children is experienced by the child as a threat to his identity. An essential component of our approach is a belief that defiance is a symptom of the effort to preserve the I and personal integrity, and concomitantly, to stimulate and enhance the parents' integrity and reinvestment in their own I.

Currently, psychotherapeutic practitioners are under heavy pressure to support cultural values. Practitioners are persuaded that committees in distant institutions (managed care companies or national professional organizations) know how to help a defiant family better than they do practitioners. Therapists should keep in mind that policies are made by committees in meeting rooms. Those who make the policies have worked themselves into bureaucratic positions in which they do not have to look into the eyes of people in pain. Remaining countercultural isn't illegal as long as you know how to take responsibility for what you do. From a clinical perspective, family therapy contains an inherent clumsiness that is a by-product of an honest reflection of human struggle.

THE THERAPIST

The role of therapist is unique in our culture. Because it is an ambiguous role, it can be anxiety provoking. A therapist is an experienced patient whose competence is in traveling (as a guide) in the world of deeply subjective experience. The role matches that of a parent who has authority, responsibility, and maturity. It is rooted in personhood, which unites our social selves with the self. The struggle for therapists is to avoid being pushed out of the therapist role and into roles which are more specifically useful to the community, such as abuse investigator, teacher, political activist, moral arbiter, and protector of someone's bottom line.

The dynamics of therapy are in the personhood of the therapist in interaction with a family's emotional currents. This is a psychotherapeutic koan, a focus for reflection, which has the capacity to stimulate our growth, professionally and personally. We are influenced in our thinking and behavior by ideas that we do not fully understand and playing with them is worthwhile. Acknowledging these paradoxical mysteries of the unknown is crucial. Personhood refers to a matrix which connects the I of ourselves, the *who I am* of virtually unchanging core of each of us to the cast of our social rules.

Our koan about the dynamics of therapy and the personhood of the therapist is particularly relevant to working with defiance. Defiance, as we construct it, occurs with the collapse of fealty. When fealty collapses, defiance occurs as a way to protect the "I" of the defiant one. Those who encounter the defiant one must be in contact with their own "I" in order that faith in relationships be restored. This change from management of the other's behavior to reflection on the labyrinth of "I" represents a shift in the coordinate system by which we understand where we are and where we are headed.

This shift in coordinates is a goal of therapy. It usually requires a series of shifts, the effect of which we have noted is cumulative. A shift represents a therapeutic moment, a therapeutic epiphany, a moment of revelation. What is revealed is not truth in a final transcending sense, but beauty. It is an aesthetic moment in which the beauty of integrity is glimpsed (Eco, 1982). What is often revealed in the beauty of the therapeutic moment is a contradiction, but an integrated contradiction. It may insult logic, but it *feels* right. The therapeutic moment is not a *transcendence* or rising above, but a *descent* and entrance into the flow of life. Swimming is not transcending the water, it is giving in to the water. In an epiphany something is revealed, usually a contradiction, and there is pleasure in the revelation. Our hearts are joined, not by the truths we share, but by the contradictions we acknowledge (Camus, 1955). This experience moves us from a group of purposeful roles to a group of selves amused by the endless absurdity of our humanness.

SOME FEATURES OF THE SELF OR PERSONHOOD

If we consider the self to be the core, personhood is the matrix for the multiple social roles by which a person is known. We are known by our social selves which are connected to the core self by personhood. The self is

- Against the culture, not socially adapted and not for sale.
- Creative and crazy, spontaneous and unpredictable, and unavailable for seduction.
- Often ridiculous, awkward, or silly.
- Largely unconscious and right-brained.
- Potentially dangerous to the social self as well as to the Other.
- Not convinced death really means anything.
- Inconsistent.
- Not anesthetized by born-again enthusiasm, or overwhelmed with despair and the temptation of suicide, but struggling with the pain of growing until death comes (Keith, 1986).

THE THERAPIST'S SELF AS IT APPEARS IN THERAPY

What comes into focus when we think about the self in therapy, is that the therapist's self appears in relation to the patient's self. It appears in an effort to evoke the patient's self. The following is a list of some of the ways the self is glimpsed in therapy (Keith, 1986).

- *Power*, whose etymology means "to be able." Thus, power is related to freedom. The therapist's power (freedom) to make demands as to how to formulate a problem and who should attend sessions is greatest at the beginning of therapy, but decreases as caring increases.
- *Integrity* refers to the therapist's capacity to live with the knowledge that she does not fully understand what others think. Her integrity does not allow others to pretend to know what she thinks. Her integrity helps her acknowledge the limitations of her view. It helps her stay clear that just because there are questions does not mean there must be answers.
- *Awareness of absurdity*. Sometimes the world seems meaningless and we don't understand our place in it. This experience can be frightening or amusing.
- The use of *play* and *humor* invites primary process to emerge from within families. Play and humor are departure points into purposelessness. They are portals of entry in the return from alienation or extrusion.
- *Anger and creative hatred*. As the therapeutic relationship evolves and becomes more meaningful, freedom for anger and creative hatred expands. There is always something beneath the anger which must be embraced and integrated.
- *Metaphorical (symbolic) reality* is the primary therapeutic medium. Therapy occurs in an experiential atmosphere separate from the outside real world. Attention to metaphorical reality translates the residue of outside experiences into the therapeutic present.

- *Remaining balanced*, thus retaining the freedom to advance or retreat from any position while remaining engaged.
- The self is present in the *development of peer relationships*. The therapist cannot be a peer with her patients until the end of therapy, however he can model this crucial relationship pattern with a cotherapist.
- The *ability to be freely loving* requires energy and self-centeredness.

Being a family therapist in the world of opposition and defiance requires a contradictory position—hubris in what she does and thinks and in the questions she asks. That is, there is a healthy defiant quality to the therapist's posture and an unwillingness to be manipulated into a pseudo *we-ness* with someone. The therapist presents fragments of her model for how the world works, not as an effort to make the family think like her, but rather to give them a model for making a model. When a family disagrees, a therapist can say, "There are a lot of opinions in this world. You just need to know that I take mine more seriously than yours." Simultaneously, the therapist must demonstrate humility about the answers she gets from the family and the initiative she see in them, constantly acknowledging in this way that they are in charge of their own world outside of therapy.

THE THERAPY

The reality of the therapy room should not be confused with the lived reality of the family's world outside. The social rules of the day-to-day world do not guide therapeutic practice. The world of the therapy room is a world apart. It is like the world of dreams, which is separated from the daylight world by a semipermeable membrane.

The fundamental goals for each family therapy project are as follows:

To restore the group spirit of the family. Health is rooted in the group spirit of the family. When group morale is improved, the family's administrative competence vis-à-vis the community is increased, so that members have the ability to deal with problems as they arise. The family we is greater than and has more power than the sum of its parts.

To translate family history into symbolic history. The symbolic history comes wrapped in stories, which takes the therapeutic process beneath the surface of the family's lived experience into the realm of myth, not the overdeveloped myths of the culture, but those that shape and guide the experience of the family. Defiance produces a heat that challenges the myths of the culture and can reshape the family myths.

To help each family member develop the affect to deepen their relationship to more of their own self. A simple restatement of this goal is to help each family member fall more deeply in love with himself.

To help family members deepen their affective investment in one another. The family is able to provide respect for the private style and idiosyncrasy of each member. In this way, the security of each self is assured. The ground for intrafamily fealty is thereby restored.

To develop a therapeutic relationship with the family as a group and with each member.

The first two goals are linked in that they attend to belonging. In this pattern, it is crucial that the family we be involved and examined. Is it intact? Is the family aware of it? The we is manifested in the morale of the family group. If the family were a basketball team, would they be a winning team or a losing team? How does the team handle dissension? The dissension may involve the whole team, or a specific dyad, like the point guard and the center. A team with dissension oftentimes has a poor win/loss record. The adequacy of team spirit is measured, first, in the family's ability to get to an interview, and second, in the family's ability to talk openly about its struggles. The third and fourth goals are linked in that they focus attention on individuation and the person.

GUIDELINES FOR THE THERAPEUTIC PROCESS

These guidelines for conducting therapy are based on our experiences as practitioners, not family therapy scholars. We do not have indepth knowledge of other patterns of therapy. We have the impression, however, that there has been a gradual erosion of clinical experience with whole families. The suggestions in this section offer support for working with the whole family.

The therapist accepts the role as responsible authority on family therapy. The families are authorities on their own lives and are responsible for their lives, but they are not experts in regard to how to do therapy. The concept of collaboration is important in working with other professionals, but does not occur with families until later stages of therapy. Collaboration carries with it the implication that the members of a relationship are peers, but therapists cannot be peers with patients. At the beginning of therapy, being a peer with patients is usually a fantasy of the therapist who is anxious about his professional adequacy. The desire to be a collaborator is likely to occur in a therapist who is fearful of taking responsibility for treatment. If the therapist attempts to set up the therapeutic relationship or the doctor/patient relationship as one between peers, the family will often move to set up a hierarchy, by going one down, "You're the doctor," or by going one up, "It's okay, we know you are new at this."

There has been appropriate concern about hierarchy in social institutions, especially in regard to gender, race, and social class issues in our culture. There are some situations in which hierarchy is either inappropriate, or coercive, but it is part of the reality of families. The family hierarchy is not merely a social construct. In the language of biological psychiatry, we can say the need for hierarchy is genetic, wired in, and crucial to our survival. The health of children depends upon parents being responsible. Our model for the therapeutic relationship is the parent-child relationship. The therapist is not responsible for the family's life, but she is responsible for the therapy and how it works.

The therapist must develop the kind of power necessary to invade the family and do battle with its members. This is not possible until the therapist has developed the courage to be herself, and to share her own free associations. It is important for the therapist to seek her own self honestly and patiently. She must expand her own person, thus modeling a pattern for growth for the family.

One of the unfortunate by-products of a desire to collaborate is that such patterns of therapy are likely to exclude children. When children are included it is impossible to deny the fact of hierarchy. Children are not peers with their parents. When it does not occur between peers, collaboration usually represents a temporary suspension of hierarchy. Collaboration represents a demand for social adjustment, and it tends to repress personhood. It emphasizes the social selves. It says, "Let's all work together on this." But if we aren't together, then collaboration becomes a lie or stimulates more defiance. Peers can collaborate, but in nonpeer relationships collaboration is a dishonest, and sometimes unethical, social manipulation. There is a place for collaboration in family therapy, but not at the beginning of the therapeutic project.

The desire to establish a peer relationship with the family is an attempt to override the therapist's obvious impotence to make a family do anything. We think of impotence as one of the therapist's most valuable tools, one she should protect and learn to value. One of the problems with defiant families is that they are likely to reach an impasse early in the therapy process. In fact, the impasse may be in place when they arrive, making them less available for therapy. This posture may stimulate a therapist into action which results in increased passivity from the family. Experience teaches the therapist that passivity in the therapist stimulates action in the family and an odd contentment with impotence arises.

Once the therapist understands his impotence, he has less need to be a political force in the family. He can express his opinions. For example:

Therapist: One thing I notice about the family is how lonely you seem, Dad.

Father; No, I'm not. I'm not lonely.

Therapist; Just so you know, I still think you are, but oddly, you don't know it.

When families enter therapy, they expose their impotence, but their impotence to change does not define weakness or inadequacy. It does not require tenderness, unconditional positive regard, and endless passive listening. Feelings are a by-product of describing one's impotence. At the beginning, what appears as a need for nurturing or extra carefulness is a two-sided transference phenomenon—cotransference.

Along the same line, empathy is a bidirectional process. Like the nervous system, it has an afferent and an efferent component. Instead of falling back into concerned passive acceptance, a therapist comes to trust her empathy, the strength of her caring, and the strength of the family to make direct interchange useful and valuable. Taking in the family's feelings may, in some cases, lead to a confrontation.

In the therapy room, the therapist is an authority on psychotherapy. However, there is an art to having authority. Art is dependent upon professional secrets. The art of utilizing authority demands a capacity for self-mocking, self-deprecation, and humility about the limits of knowledge. Self-deprecation by a therapist melts the impersonal professional image. And self-deprecation allows a therapist to challenge or to mock without being overpowering. It also depends upon the therapist's personal maturity and her ability to know and own her own sadistic side. Unacknowledged sadism may be camouflaged with graciousness and intelligence. Sadism is part of the mechanism by which we individuate from the other. The sadistic way of individuating is by denigrating the other (e.g., political correctness). Here we increase our value by cutting the other off and by assuming they are cruel or uncaring. On the other hand we may individuate by becoming more certain of ourselves, no matter what the other does, and even acknowledge our hidden cruelty or gratification from the pain of the other.

Case Example: The Therapist: Self-Deprecating but In Charge

The G's were a family of five: mother, father, an older brother, and two sisters. Bob, age 17, talked about being a witch. He dressed in a dark, Gothic manner and painted his fingernails black. His parents were stiff and tight, and assumed everyone thought of their son as an idiot. With the help of the school and their pastor, they came to view Bob's role playing as a mental illness. Halfway into a very tense first interview in which the parents could only talk about Bob and elaborate on what they feared and disliked in him, the therapist said, "You know, I think Bob is a creative kid, but what worries me, is that he has turned into such an isolate." And turning to Bob, "Had you thought of trying to cultivate some of your pals into a coven, so that you have some disciples? You know you can't be a messiah without disciples." Mother, a very humorless 6th grade teacher, lips pursed in permanent disgust, went after the 60-year-old therapist as though he were 11 years-old, "That's ridiculous. We didn't come here for more silliness." She paused, then challenging the therapist, "Why are we here anyway?" Smiling, and without pause, the therapist answered, "I'll tell you something. I have been ridiculous for a long time, and I'm good at it. I suppose you're here to learn a different way to be ridiculous." The content of this absurd message had abrasive and rude elements, but simultaneously and nonverbally, it was nondefensive, playful, and inviting. But most importantly, it was oddly self-deprecating—a social non sequitur. Continuing, the therapist asked mother how she arranged to upset her parents when she was in high school. Within the next 10 minutes, jaw loosened and smiling broadly, mother laughed at some of her own exploits as a high school senior, while her husband and son looked amazed. She had stepped aside from her dominant mother/teacher role. In her amused, nonanxious remembering, the family and therapist had access to her personhood.

The rejection of the linear involves a rejection of the narrative (Brown, 1966). The key is not to be dominated or hypnotized by any story. Play, likewise in its freely creative distortion, rejects the narrative. It does not transcend the narrative, but it interrupts and changes the narrative. The narrative is important as a place from which to begin. The therapist's questions have the quality of, "How can we help? How does the family operate? How did you learn to organize yourself this way?" From this outline comes a rough draft of a story, one that is not polished. Through the process of gathering this information, the therapist gains empathy for the family and its members and gets a feel for them and how they handle relationships. Then the therapist makes a move away from the narrative with irony, joking, or a personal association.

In the preceding example, the family avoided talking about the family and emphasized Bob and his troubles. The therapist abruptly jumped out of his narrative and promoted a novel idea which brought mother into a confrontation, which, in turn, led to more of her self being present in the interview.

We believe a therapist should allow anxiety and ambiguity to increase. Anxiety and ambiguity activate the family's administrative competence. The self is activated and nourished by ambiguity and by intimacy. Reason and treatment planning imprison and anesthetize the self. One of the side effects of raising anxiety is that the family transfers it to the therapist. This is a time to introduce a cotherapist. In the case of Bob, the therapist raised the family's anxiety by helping Bob become a better witch. This forced mother into a confrontation, which was handled directly, but playfully.

An interesting problem comes up when a therapist lives by the non sequitur. He inevitably gets them back. Non sequiturs stop the flow of interaction and stimulate reflection. If the child or other family member learns to use them, the therapist should admire them ("Touché'!" or "Ouch!") and find a way to associate around them, thereby integrating them into the conversation. Associative communication is a variation of coconstruction in the world of multigenerational systems.

Case Example: Handling the Defiant Child's Non Sequitur: Associative Communication

The therapist had interviewed the father about the family, then the earnest, do-it-right older sister. Next came the angry, combative, defiant son, Scott.

Therapist: What's your family like?

Scott: (*Scornfully, with curled lip and in no mood to contribute to the narrative*) This family is like a pile of shit.

Therapist: (*Deadpan and without changing tone*) Is it well-formed or creamy shit?

Scott: (*A grin flickered under his dark scowl, then the scowl was restored.*) It's mixed.

Therapist: Is it dried out, or does it still stink?

Moving to the metaphorical level is a rejection of the linear, but it also has the effect of integrating the non sequitur. At this point, all are smiling and quietly laughing.

Scott: I don't see where talkin' is doin' any good.

Therapist: This isn't supposed to do good. We're just giving each other a bad time. You are pretty good at it, for a kid.

The therapist's model for living and relationships evolves with continuing experience. Much of the beginning of this book represents our metaphorical way of thinking about the world of human experience. This complicated model guides our intuition and our clinical actions. It is a model for building a model. We assume each therapist, like each family, has an implicit model for how life works. In the therapeutic interaction the models are parallel to one another. The therapist's model is more explicit, but not necessarily more persuasive. Those who can create a model can play with the model and therefore play with living. The ability to play with living is part of health (Jaffee & Whitaker, 1992).

Family therapy is like psychotherapy with a psychotic. Long-circuited thought processes activate the "it's phony" switch, which is as sensitive in the family as it is in the psychotic. Breaching the programmed family mind is induced by the therapist's deprogramming herself and advancing her own growing edge. Primary process ideas come in fragments, not in paragraphs.

The power-powerless ploy, which defines the bad people as powerful, and the patient as powerless, is a programmed response used by many New Age therapists when ambiguous circumstances exist. Part of the ploy is to view particular persons as wounded victims. This is an easy way to activate a therapeutic relationship, but it rapidly forms a symbiotic relationship between the therapist and one family member. It is a trick when a therapist quickly converts someone into being a patient by seduction, rather than by helping her become a patient by honest self-questioning, and self-ownership. Overdefining the powerlessness or pain of one person puts the possibility of continuing as a family at risk.

Experiential family therapy depends upon the inclusion of three generations. Increasingly, modern family therapists talk as if it is possible to do family therapy with one person. This is, to begin with, a semantic problem. A family is not a family unless everyone is there. When any person describes her family, she is describing her fantasy of her family and her transference to her family. The description inevitably changes when a person interviewed alone is added to a larger family group. A family is accurately described by getting the whole family together to talk about the family. This provides an experiential holographic model for the family. We believe it is possible to do a kind of family therapy with one person but, because it is intellectual rather than experiental, the quality is much different. Family therapy with one member is often done for the wrong reasons. For example, it may be chosen because it represents a compromise or a pathway of least resistance, not because anyone thinks it is best. Thus, it often is not helpful with the situations we describe here. Further, doing family therapy with one member requires a very experienced therapist with the maturity and intellectual power of a Murray Bowen. There are not many therapists of that caliber available.

A common complication of the beginning stage occurs when the entire family agrees by phone to come, but they arrive without the father. It may be viewed as impolite to send them away, but it is not therapeutic to go ahead. Here it is necessary to point out the problem of meeting without him.

Therapist: Why isn't he here?

Mother: He had to work.

Therapist: He doesn't think he is important to this project?

He may have another plan for what ought to be done. If so, they should follow his plan first, and if it doesn't work, then come back. He may not be desperate enough. "Maybe you should wait until it gets worse," the therapist suggests. Men are good at simplifying situations with reason and common sense. The therapist must remember that father's common sense or, for that matter, the common sense of the insurance world, is not the same as the common sense of therapeutic work. Common sense is usually a way of saying you ought to be dominated by my experience a way of narrowing experience through the application of a secondary process. Father's failure to arrive is his way of avoiding facing what he does not know. He avoids a trip into the labyrinth of the self. The power of the whole family is needed for change to occur. If all do not participate, those who vote against change by remaining on the outside end up having the most power for neutralizing change.

The therapist's desire to communicate privately with the scapegoat is a symptom that signals the collapse of fealty and hints that the parent coalition is not taking care of the personhood of family members. It means the parents have convinced the therapist that they have limited tolerance for ambiguity. The reason for meeting alone is that it is not safe to deal with certain issues with the whole group. And that is the problem which needs to be addressed. The therapeutic strategy, therefore, is to increase safety by adding people to the therapeutic project on either side of the therapeutic relationship.

SUMMARY

Readers who find themselves confused after reading this chapter should not be overly worried. It is impossible to be clear about some of what has been discussed. The most important understanding comes out of reflecting on what is written. Defiance is another term for rebelliousness. In psychotherapeutic work with defiant families, the therapist is a rebel and therapy is a rebellion. As Camus indicated, it is not the rebellion which is noble, but the demands it imposes on the therapist.

The problem the family seeks help with is defiance, but we have suggested that part of the treatment is for the therapist to be defiant in the sense of maintaining her integrity and insisting on the validity of her own view. This provides something the family can push against that forces an organizing response from the family.

The systemic view is a healing paradigm. We attempt to operationalize a view of defiance as arising out of a hunger for healing. But this is a paradigm that gently disrupts present institutions and patterns of thinking, and is therefore easily dismissed. We began by saying that psychotherapy is a craft and a useful art. Art does not replicate reality, rather it attempts to produce the conditions that lead to the experience of epiphany. This results in a breaking through to a deeper involvement in the richness of family life. The second part of this book addresses how the ideas presented in the first four chapters are implemented in the clinic setting.

5

Beginning the Therapeutic Project

Dr. K. received an urgent call from Mrs. F., a local probation officer, who was referred by her pediatrician due to her daughter's defiance. The following interaction was over the phone:

Mrs. F. was used to dealing with difficult families and children. She was controlled, but anxious, as she talked about her 17-year-old daughter and a boyfriend. Her daughter had had an abortion a year earlier and was emotionally inaccessible. Dr. K. suspected Mrs. F. was a single mother. She needed to "talk to someone today!" She asked to come in alone and for her daughter to come the next time.

Dr. K. responded, "I don't have any time today. Who else do you have to talk to?" "Well, my husband," she replied. He was surprised to hear about her husband. The initial impression of mother being a single parent may mean she and daughter are symbiotic. The problem may be the emotional intensity between them, or she may view her husband as unhelpful.

Common sense and urgency suggest that if mother came alone it might be useful. This would be an error because it is important to start with the whole group. They are a close family of four. The younger daughter, Amy, age 14, sounds like the one with the most wisdom. Father was a director of the Youth Detention Center.

Therapist: "It sounds like you are driving her crazy with your desperation. She may be defiant, but she will always be your daughter. You aren't losing your daughter, you're losing your little girl."

Mother: "I know, but what should I do? I feel so stupid"

Therapist: "I don't think you should do anything. I think you have lost the power struggle. Parents are supposed to be stupid. Why don't you try to find some fun in being stupid. It goes with the job. Don't underestimate how much fun it can be for teen-agers to make parents feel feeble."

Mother: (*Mrs. F. moaned, signaling amusement.*)

Therapist: "I can see you the day after tomorrow at 2 o'clock, but everyone ought to come.

By the way, keep in mind it is easy to underestimate how much pain she is in."

Mother: "What do you mean?"

Therapist: "I can't explain now. Just keep it in mind."

Mother: "Okay, we will see you Monday at two. What if Katy won't come?"

Therapist: "I will be disappointed. Tell her you have decided to give up trying to understand her, and you want to do something about your own pain. The therapist you talked to said she ought to come. Bring as much of the family as possible."

THE FIRST PHONE CALL

Therapy begins with the first phone call. That was not an unusual call. It seems a good, even benign, solution to start alone with the most anxious member of the family. The problem is that how the therapist begins defines the problem. If the family is not there, it is not family therapy. If all four members show up we would be pleased because it tells us something about the covert cohesiveness of the family. Then it's the therapist's job to make it possible to work as a group. If they show up without Katy, the defiant daughter, we would be disappointed. But we suppose that part of this upheaval is getting the family ready to be a family of three after she leaves and we only have her spirit to talk to. If mother and father show up we become aware that there is some manipulative defiance in the family on the part of the parents and that they want to define the treatment plan. We would be disappointed, not with children, but with the parents. In the phone call Mrs. F.'s desperation was hysterical. It is possible to make inferences from the beginning of the phone call. Mother probably runs the family with her franticness. If mother shows up alone, we would cancel the appointment. We do not want to begin this way. We might say to her, "You are calling me because of my expertise. If this is going to go anywhere, it will take everyone, not just you and me. This may sound impolite, but please, don't ask me what to do then not do it."

There are clinical reasons for this stance. At the beginning of therapy the therapist has the power to make demands. This power diminishes as empathy for the family develops. The family has invited the therapist to be a healer. A healer operates within a structure. If a family objects to a therapist's structure, the therapist should suggest they find someone else to work with. By deciding not to see mother, the therapist is defining his professional self and professional structure.

Another therapist may not trust this pattern of working, or may be lead by his discipline to work in another way. This is one way to work with the craziness we call defiance. Forming a therapeutic alliance with the mother may have some benefit to her and may generate health elsewhere in the family. It may stabilize things or lead to discovery of marriage problems, which could lead to marriage therapy or a separation. The medical maxim of "do no harm" applied here would suggest not treating the symptom until a thorough exam has been completed or the family situation may become worse.

This chapter describes the critical initial stage of therapy with defiant families. Like any journey, the way it begins influences the outcome. During this stage the therapist is active and responsible for establishing the tone of the therapy. He is a professional in charge of beginning the diagnostic stage of the therapeutic encounter. The relationship with the family is professional, not personal. Competence is the professional precursor of personal integrity. We believe the therapist should present himself as a nonanxious, attentive, competent professional who is interested in getting to know the family, and can be helpful. A simple suggestion is that the therapist think of himself as a generation older than the oldest member of the family. While the family is the expert on their living, the therapist is the expert on family therapy.

The problem in defiant families is often long-standing. Recent events often precipitate a crisis. The initial phone call is a variation of, "We need help. Jim's been suspended from school. He is on probation and out of control. We've tried everything, and we are at our wit's end. If we don't get help for him, we're not sure what will happen next." The family is overwhelmed by the presenting problem. The parents are frustrated by the escalating behavior of their child and at failed attempts to solve the predicament. A call to a therapist is a last ditch effort to regain normalcy. The family is usually less than optimistic about the possibility of change. They feel mystified and defeated by circumstances outside their control. Frequently parents are asking themselves what went wrong, what could they have done differently, and how did things get so out of hand. They want to find a simple answer to a complex dilemma. Mainly they want to regain authority over their child. They want their household to calm down and their excessive worry to stop. Our assumption is that they would like to get something out of life, instead of endlessly fending off catastrophe.

ESTABLISHING THE GROUND RULES

Therapy works best when done with the family system. Requesting attendance of the whole family, we explain to the caller our belief that there is a correlation between the number of family members involved and the effectiveness of the therapeutic effort. If extended family members live in the household, we suggest they attend as well. The resistance to bringing the entire family can be high. There may be conflicting work schedules and activities for the children. At other times a family member is unavailable or unwilling to attend. Parents don't want to expose nonproblem children to the situation, as if that's possible! The fact is that most children are relieved to come to a setting which will provide help for the situation. Occasionally the identified patient wants to be seen alone in order to sustain his campaign to save the family through self-sacrifice. A parent who requests to have an adolescent seen alone may be concerned for the child's well-being, while protecting an upsetting relationship. Due to the habituated conflict between parent and child, a parent may feel the child can open up better if they are alone. Additionally, the child may not want to expose himself to further family disapproval. It is common for the family to define the problem as residing within a single family member. After all, he is creating the disturbance and drawing the scrutiny under which the family finds itself. At times relationships are so volatile that no one wants to sit together as a group. It is best to accept the caller's description of the problem but insist on scheduling with the family. We might say, "I understand your reluctance to get everyone together. I think we have the best chance to be successful if everyone comes in."

The therapist assumes responsibility for defining the contract for therapy and who the key players are. Family members may push against the structure established by the therapist. The project will fail if all are not included. It is essential to present a succinct explanation for how the therapist operates and the expectations for beginning therapy. We believe it is easier to involve the whole family from the beginning before individual alliances have a chance to develop.

It is important to remember that therapists are in a position to put pressure on the family to take action on behalf of themselves. This is a difficult process. Because the therapy is for them, if they have a better way to go about dealing with their problems, they should be encouraged to go ahead and do that first! In the meantime, there are other patients requiring therapy. Therapists who see everybody who shows up under any conditions are salesmen. Professional integrity involves giving families the opportunity to not come.

Therapists need to develop an awareness that guides interaction around the issues of defiance and helps families negotiate societal power struggles. Too often therapists who need to understand defiant families do not. They are thrown off balance by the social outrageousness of the defiance without perceiving its interpersonal roots, or they may be dissuaded by the family's fear of exposure and vulnerability. Defiant families are pathologized in the community's attempt to begin intervening. They end up feeling hopeless and overwhelmed and attempt to turn responsibility for their daily living over to professionals.

The process of joining is particularly significant. Defiant families are often reluctant participants during the initial stage of therapy. They arrive at the therapist's office feeling vigilant and defeated. They have been under scrutiny from the community, and consequently they are embarrassed. They assume a defensive posture when asking for help. There is pressure from outside forces, such as the school or legal system, demanding family members change or the child and family will face sanction. Joining can be complicated by the negativity families demonstrate toward therapy. Negativity may appear as hostility or indifference toward the therapist. This is not a personal attack, but rather a reaction to being a reluctant patient. The therapist needs to remind himself that the family is driven by psychological self-protection. They have tried to tough it out on their own. They may have a difficult time forming meaningful connections with others, particularly authority figures. In some cases, they may be overly hopeful at a new beginning. The therapist should not be seduced by their distrust or by their enthusiasm and should strive to remain professional.

Issues of attachment and intimacy abound in these families. A defensive posture has not often served them best. When defiant families enter therapy they are locked into a negative assessment of the identified patient, yet are resentful of all negative evaluation directed at other family members. It is difficult for them to see defiance as serving any positive function. Exposing how the family operates beneath the obvious outbursts is not easy for them. They don't think that way. They are locked into the negative fallout from the defiance. Most defiant families are not used to looking at or talking about relationships, except in superficial ways. This is uncomfortable, usually prohibited territory for them. What assurances do they have that the therapist is invested in their best interests?

THE FAMILY ARRIVES

The therapist is a clinician/healer engaged in a professional discipline. Healing is an art and as Paracelsus said, "Where there is no love, there is no art." The family pays for the therapist's ear but must capture his heart. When a family enters a therapist's office, the professional practitioner conducts the first interview by taking the history. This practitioner role is more active than the role of therapist. The beginning stage depends upon a nonanxious therapist presence. It is essential to pay close attention to all levels of information, verbal and nonverbal. In the first interview, family members are usually on their best behavior and are most compliant.

As an analogy, recall how effective elementary school teachers operate. They are tough for the first 3 weeks. After that they can enjoy the children but, having established a firm persona, they can go back to it when necessary. By the end of the first interview, the therapist will have learned about the family's pain and their failed efforts at solving their problem. At this point the therapist becomes invested in the process.

The presenting problem is the family's ticket of admission to therapy. It is easier to focus on a problematic child than to face fears of being an incompetent parent or therapist. Parents know intuitively that the child isn't the only problem, but they can't or won't articulate what else is wrong. The child has become successful at diverting attention away from other family problems. His behavior has become the central organizing feature of the family. The therapist looks for opportunities to broaden the focus as therapy begins. In the initial stage there is a dynamic tension between the therapist and the family. The family wants to get at and solve a specific presenting problem, while the therapist wants to get the family to develop a sense of who they are collectively and individually, as well as to assess their interaction. The therapist must keep in mind that they do not need another failure, as they have certainly experienced other failures. It is critical to establish ground rules for therapy, otherwise it is useless to do it at all!

The pattern for therapy in the initial stage should be a mixture of businesslike and friendly interaction. We begin by asking everyone's names and maintaining a cordial attitude. We prefer to refer to the parents as Mother and Father and to the children by their given names. We really do not want them to feel at home. We make it clear that we make the rules regarding therapy, and that we maintain the freedom to break the rules we make. We don't think we demonstrate caring basically because it is impossible to care for people prior to developing a significant relationship. Pseudo caring is synonymous with politeness. The family requires our highest level of competence, which is demonstrated in how we conduct the interview and the connection we are able to make with the family. Our vision is clearest in the first interview but becomes clouded as caring increases. Honesty is more important in our view. We establish a style of sharing our opinions and perceptions that can either be accepted or disregarded by family members. Commenting on the positives and reassurance are kept to a minimum.

In response to, "Can you help us?" "I don't know, it sounds like a mess to me!" stimulates rejuvenation and honesty. It brings back more families than sugar-coated reassurance and empty caring. Reassurance, in situations like this, is poisonous. Defiant families have no trouble finding people to reassure them. They have problems finding people who are honest while remaining engaged. We believe in every family's ability to self-correct and move in the direction of growth. The fact that they don't believe in themselves creates anxiety that fuels defiance.

It is not uncommon for parents to say, in answer to our question, "How can we help?" "I'm not sure you *can* help. We've tried everything and nothing has worked. The principal said we needed to get help for Billy, but I can tell you we've tried. He's just too out of control. I get a call from his teacher every day. It's getting to the point that I dread hearing her voice. What do they think we should do?"

"Stop answering the phone," says the therapist. Pause. "You know, I was just reading an article about Cuba. You know they don't answer the phone every time it rings. They see it as an intrusion into the rhythm of life." The therapist offers alternate solutions from the first contact, with the hope of disrupting the tunnel vision of the family.

The contradiction about the initial interview is that it focuses on the family, not the identified patient, which changes the tone of the conversation. When school officials find out the family has seen a therapist, their desperation goes down, and they are likely to stop calling. Likewise, when the defiant child has a chance to feel less defensive, he will be less defiant and desperate. This is a psychotherapeutic placebo effect. We tell them "enjoy it, it won't last," as a method of defeating the hysterical optimism which may make children more defiant. The initial convening of a family makes a difference, even when other clinicians have been involved. If the family was evaluated for attention deficit/hyperactivity disorder, chances are that an interactive conjoint family history was not taken. If they were seen in the family court system, the family probably wasn't contacted for a family history. Simply convening the family can be very therapeutic.

When the family arrives for the first session, the therapist should be attentive and skillful in order to be a good diagnostician. He should be alert to the overall family mood and the demeanor of individual members. The standard way of conducting the first interview is to begin by asking the father to describe how the family works. The person of highest rank and the most emotional distance, usually the father, is interviewed first. The mother is the expert on emotion and relationships in the family. There are several reasons to save her for last. Family members are less influenced by her views if they are kept until the end. Secondly, she is likely to be the most upset. Early emotional arousal may often be a camouflage technique, like the mother duck who swims away from the nest faking a broken wing in order to protect the nest. Triangulation with any outside agent (e.g., school, police, divorced parent, former therapist) is another dynamic to watch for. Although such an agent may be part of the problem, they are not the explanation for the problem. The therapist needs to matter-of-fact maintain a demeanor. When one attends to the entire context, almost nothing a family does will seem outrageous.

Initially, the therapist gains a feeling for who the family is experientially, making use of his intuition to guide the interaction. It is important to pay attention to the system until there is a sense of the gestalt and to be aware that counter transference to families is powerful, omnipresent, and unconscious. Knowing one's vulnerabilities is essential in working with defiant families who are good at pushing the right buttons to elicit strong negative emotions. All therapists have points of vulnerability based on their own pathologized fragments, such as families with alcoholism or physical or sexual abuse. If things get out of control, stuck, or overwhelming, the therapist can seek consultation from a colleague. We recommend routinely conducting a three-generation consultation in the early stage with every family. A model of such a consultation appears in the chapter on the extended family consultation.

The therapist must resist becoming bogged down by specific issues. Likewise, it is important not to corner anyone early in the therapy. The therapist challenges the meaning family members give to events by revising or modifying their statements. For example, an acting-out school-age child's behavior might be reframed as an attempt to keep mother from being too depressed or to disrupt habitual marital conflict. These modifications are introduced as wonderings or optional ways to think about problems. It is similar to casting seeds to see what might grow later. For example, "Did you ever consider that Billy's behavior is an attempt to keep Mom from being so sad and discouraged about her life?" rather than, "Billy is just trying to keep Mom from being depressed." Options presented in an open-ended manner come from the therapist's perception of the situation and are meant only for the family to consider. They are the therapists postulations, not definitions that demand acceptance by the victims. They can be consciously discarded because the therapist really doesn't know them yet. Families that remain dogmatic in their perception of the problem have more difficulty making progress than those who are open to new viewpoints. It is helpful for the therapist to make one interpretation the family can agree with in the first session. If this isn't possible, a quick consult is recommended because a rough ride is sure to follow.

It is common in the initial stages of therapy for the family to be curt and begrudging, as if to test the therapist's competence. The therapist should keep in mind that the problem belongs to the family and simply ignore defiance and be polite. If the family is persistently begrudging he might say, "Why don't we quit? I'm too feeble to work with a bunch of people who are angry about being here," and follow through. Another tactic is to be amused by their posturing by saying, "This would make a nice picture for the family Christmas card." The therapist should not be afraid to state the obvious, such as "I hope it's not me you're so mad at," or "Looks like I'm in for a rough day."

The themes of a family's conversation can be guarded and devoid of emotion in the initial stage. This caution is intended to keep the conversation from moving close to who they are. Children who are upset by family discord are irritable and want to be left alone. They often use the same tactics with the therapist that have been successful at negating their parents. For example, during a session the therapist talked to family members about how they each saw themselves and the family. When the conversation was finally directed toward the identified patient, he began crying. He had anticipated being scolded for his behavior and was prepared to do battle. The therapist had not challenged him, which allowed different aspects of his behavior to emerge. His mother was surprised as she "hadn't seen him cry for a long time."

It doesn't do any good to beat up impossible children who are acting out. This is what they have come to expect and they invite it. They lose their fear of punishment and are often gratified by scolding. In fact, they may welcome it as a way to settle the family down and restore a familiar equilibrium. This makes the parents look like they have it right and proves the children's love for their parents. It is more important for the therapist to build rapport, demonstrate empathy for the plight of the family, and develop a relationship. This is challenging because the defiant stance says, "I dare you to talk to me." Defiant families recapitulate behavior that has created problems in their lives. The content may vary, but the process remains the same. The events in therapy are a microcosm of their life as a family. It is important to pause and think about the whole family and the context they find themselves in before jumping to an individual diagnosis or treatment plan. The family needs to take stock of themselves by exposing their interpersonal processes. A good question to ask is, "What do you worry about when you are not worrying about Bob?"

Another scenario for entering therapy is the family who arrives ready to turn all responsibility for decision making over to the therapist. The family is giving up due to frustration and a sense of impotence about their situation. Parents with defiant adolescents often fall into this category. They are tired of being ignored, harassed, and threatened. They hope the therapist will be able to connect with their child and develop a relationship that will positively influence the child's behavior. Keep in mind that it is most important for the parents to connect with the child. They are the ones who are responsible for him on a daily basis.

Connecting prematurely with the defiant child can be a pitfall. Bonding with the scapegoat is tempting, but hazardous. In the first interview, it is important to restore parenting to the correct generation—the parents. Their job is to *be* parents, not to *do* parenting. It is highly unlikely that any therapist will initially provide a conspicuous idea that will make much difference. Advice breeds resistance and brings out the defiance of the parents. Resistance is defiance with a glaze of good manners. Even as the parents resist, however, they may present today's crisis as urgent and needing the therapist's immediate attention. They stimulate anxiety in others as a way of dissipating their own. If the therapist reacts in ways to suggest that he is fearful or uncomfortable, the family assumes that they are somehow not quite right or that the therapist is not up to the task of dealing with them. They gladly turn over their problems to the anxious therapist and wait expectantly for him to screw up. The more recalcitrant families keep their fingers crossed during the interviews. We suggest the therapist act as if every interview is the last. It is not necessarily a failure if they do not return. If the family's initiative is not sufficient, community pressure forces them back.

It can be a difficult balance for the therapist to maintain a nonanxious presence in the face of the presenting problem. The therapist's responsibility is to demonstrate a willingness to get to know the family but not demonstrate so much initiative that the family feels overcontrolled. Like hesitant deer who run if someone trying to feed them moves too close, defiant families run away if the therapist is too helpful or interested initially.

If the family decides not to enter therapy or to find another therapist, it is simply a no-fault failure to relate. We feel strongly about the therapist's role in establishing the structure for therapy. This kind of nonanxious, amoral integrity has an impact in a culture of experts being pressured to treat everyone fast and friendly, like a McDonald's worker. The family makes decisions based largely on how to control anxiety. Reducing anxiety does not lead to health, any more than a surgery patient deciding when and how to make the incision so it will hurt the least. Patients are experts on their own lives, but they are not experts on how to do therapy. It is the professional's responsibility to arrange for the therapy to work.

Therapy is a process of being with families and initially living through situations with them. It is not a magic bullet or a permanent solution. A major goal is to help the family become more expressive and accountable—to become full emotional partners. They need to expand their ability to express themselves in other ways than they are used to doing. In the early stages, defiant families feel persecuted by sources outside their control. They need to express their power-based sense of injustice and unfairness. It is essential for parents to maintain their authority to define right and wrong, rather than to be observers. The therapist should avoid assuming or being placed in the position of rule maker. The therapist's role is as coach, not player. The coach does not go to the field but remains on the sidelines. The family's patterns of interaction, attitudes, and behaviors aren't defined as essentially wrong, but are examined in light of whether or not they enhance family relationships. It is important not to amplify the presenting problem until the therapist learns more about the family. The goal is to keep the family's esteem intact during the initial encounter, if at all possible. Therapy often fails if the family starts to hate themselves too early in the process.

The best advice we can give professionals is to understand the complexity of defiant families. There is always more happening under the surface, if we aren't distracted by the overt problems. These families are sensitive to being put down or negatively evaluated. Parents usually feel guilty and may actually arrange for the therapist to blame them early on, so that they can then feel temporarily innocent or vindicated. Meeting with the entire family is critical to understanding the complexity of the family structure and interaction.

Beginning the therapeutic project entails establishing a structure for the therapy process from the first phone call. The therapist is in charge of who attends the sessions. Maintaining a nonanxious presence in the face of the family's urgency to solve the presenting problem is key to the early stage of therapy.

KEY FACTORS IN TREATMENT

Developing Trust

Initially there is a multifaceted problem of trust. Defiant families test everybody with their suspiciousness. The overt component is the family's distrust of the therapist. The covert component is the therapist's distrust of the family. It often feels as though they are leaving something out of their story. The therapist can make this issue explicit by saying early on, "It feels like you are holding important stuff back." Defiant families spend an inordinate amount of energy maintaining a defensive perimeter. They do this by reshaping their history. But not talking about what is painful won't create change. Chaos is another component of the defense found in defiance. The need for a defensive perimeter is stimulated by the burden of blame placed on the parents by the community, family, friends, and themselves. There is a sense of shame that as parents they have caused the problems with their children. Furthermore, they have been led to believe that the resources necessary for problem resolution lie outside the family. These notions further alienate and fragment the family.

It is important to remember a simple truth: You can only do the first interview once! When therapy begins with part of the family, it is more difficult to expand the system at a later date. Loyalty and trust issues only increase. If the identified patient is seen alone in the initial stage of therapy, the family receives a covert message that the problem does, in fact, reside within the acting-out child. Resistance to including other family members at a later date is probable. When they do participate, they do so as paranoid outsiders or voyeuristic commentators. It is essential to pay attention to developing a relationship with the family. The therapist needs to know how the family views itself, the quality of various relationships, and how members resolve conflict and solve problems. If the family is not present, there is difficulty forming a sense of who they are contextually. There is only the fantasy of how someone else views the family. The temptation can be to form a relationship with the problematic family member or with a member who is more emotionally available, but this is a common mistake that quickly leads to an impasse. It's better to fail to begin, than to begin and fail. Too much compromise wears therapists out. Errors based on compromise tend to be irreversible. The therapist should not insist on the whole family participating as a therapeutic trick. If the family is not there, there is no power for change. When the adolescent is diffident, ignorinng him and talking to other family members, especially the father, can be helpful. If the interview goes well, the teenager will try to be included. The relationship is defined in the initial encounters. Errors based on integrity tend to be reversible and therapeutic.

Challenging Defeat

Challenging the parents' sense of defeat is a major task of the initial therapy. In order to do this, pathology must be redefined as an effort to grow within the family. Problems are reframed to include the family group by focusing on the benevolent effects of the identified patient's acting out.

Case Example: Tough and Tender. Jim, age 16, has been extremely defiant and, when frustrated, suicidal. Susan, age 22, is his older sister. Dr. Owen explores positive alternatives for understanding the identified patient's behavior.

Therapist: Do you think Jim takes the blame for fighting? Like, somehow he assumes that he's supposed to make it better?

Susan: I think maybe Jim blames himself for a lot of the things that go on in our household that really aren't his fault.

Therapist: Yeah. I get that feeling from a lot of what your Mom was talking about, when she said he was always a good baby and a good kid.

Susan: Yeah. He was always supersensitive. He's very supersensitive, and he tries to overcompensate for that because it's not really acceptable today for a guy to be as sensitive and as caring as he is. I think he tries to beef himself up by running with a tough crowd. He's got—I don't want to characterize his friends, but—he's got good friends who aren't going to get him into trouble, and he hangs out with them a lot. They're good kids. And then he's got some friends—and good kids do bad things. I mean, I'm sure he's been drinking with a bunch of his friends, whether they're what I call the good kids or the bad kids. But there are some people that he hangs out with that don't give a damn about anybody. I think that's what he's trying to be like because he hurts himself by being so sensitive. I think he shoulders a lot of the responsibility for the family. There's just no communication whatsoever. We don't talk.

Therapist: You're close but sort of shoulder-to-shoulder, or almost back-to-back. It's not like you embrace each other. You're not close that way. Is that what it's like for you?

Dr. Owen accepts negative descriptions, but adds a point of view otherwise overlooked. Behavior is broadened to include other aspects of experience that are neglected, and the contradiction is altered by thinking of Jim as difficult, yet tender-hearted.

When working with adolescents, sometimes sparing the rod saves the child. Most often the referral for therapy is in the form of a request to "fix" a family member, usually a child who has become intolerable at home, at school, or in the community. The request for help comes out of desperation over the situation. The family has an explanation for why they are here, but the reason is a compromise. They have already agreed upon what to worry about. For example, when the therapist asks about the marriage, the wife confesses that her husband is angry because she worries all of the time. They agree on that, but the therapist embellishes the issue by questioning, "You mean if he is angry with you, you start talking about junior?" Parents have difficulty comprehending what contributes to the defiance in their child. They only see parts of the picture.

Establishing the Family's Identity

A key factor to assess early in treatment of defiant families is their sense of identity and spirit. These families are often a fragmented collection of individuals who are overwhelmed by the circumstances of their lives. Their intimacy is based on defying community representatives. There is a low level of intimacy despite how well put together or successful they appear in their occupational lives. Frequently these families have a powerful family secret, such as alcohol or drug abuse, an affair, or parental pathology. For example, one of the most common covert forms of defiance is the unwillingness to confess sadness or pain about the lack of pleasure in the marital relationship. Defiant families can feel overwhelming even to the seasoned therapist due to the chronic nature of problems, the high level of acting out, and the pornographic nature of the material presented. It is easy for a therapist to be seduced into a problem-solving mode, or worse yet, to become timid so that the family establishes the tone of therapy by insisting it proceed according to their plans. The appearance of not being rattled by the family is essential when things become heated up.

Keeping Your Therapeutic Cool

Creating a therapeutic alliance can be a challenge. Slowing the family down is a useful maneuver, especially since they demonstrate a sense of urgency and acceleration due to crisis. They have a tendency to test the therapist by dumping volumes of information and emotion. If the therapist becomes anxious and fearful, the family will sense this and therapy will not start. Insulating oneself from family anxiety allows the family to step back and regain balance. Life is rarely shocking, but it is upsetting to them because of their investment in each other.

In listening to the family's story, the therapist should attend to small moments, as when the child showed evidence of being soothed or there was an affiliative moment in the middle of the war. The child's upsetting behavior is often a caricature of one of the parents and the therapist may feel bemused as he observes the nonverbal process. Looking for the dialectics of the behavior, he may pathologize the virtuous and depathologize evil-doers. Families test the therapist's ability to deal with conflict and gruesome information. If they feel the therapist is not up to the task, therapy will bog down and become a laborious process. In these cases, the therapist may become symptomatic. As the family's caution fades and they feel confident in the therapist's ability to cope with them, they become more reflective and more spontaneous. They become more spontaneous when they become aware the therapist does not need them. We have had some odd experiences with defiant families, particularly when we say something that makes our caring for them overt. They don't come back. We might conjecture that it represents their satisfaction that someone finds them lovable, but we don't think so. We think they experience loving as a frightening burden. They are fearful of obligation, and the unknown hazards of a world which embodies tenderness.

Adopting the family's language is an unconscious method of joining. It shows the family the therapist is collaborating on a deeper level of caring. Using similar words, phrases, and gestures decreases their sense of alienation and demonstrates active listening. This is not a contrived situation, but a genuine interest on the part of the therapist to connect with the family. Symptoms of identification develop, for instance, when father and therapist remove glasses to rub eyes simultaneously. Mother and therapist may rub the side of their faces simultaneously. It isn't clear who started the mirroring behavior. This unconscious mirroring lowers defensiveness in the family and is symptomatic of the two-sided cotransference of developing mutual empathy. For example, families may have peculiar words for describing things. The therapist is alert to the use of language, vocabulary, and level of understanding. In one family, the wife was describing the ways the marital relationship caused her stress, especially the husband constantly putting her down. She meant to say the relationship was *infuriating* but primary processing took over and instead she said *inferiorating*, which described their interaction in more graphic terms. The therapist used the word inferiorating when he sensed the husband was putting the wife down.

Talking over a family's head may be embarrassing to them, leading to frustration and misunderstanding. This is a common problem in medical practice.

The therapist can't assume that the message sent is the message received. Families often do not understand psychological jargon. Summarizing your understanding of the picture they are painting can aid in this area. During the initial stage, asking what the therapist means can feel demeaning to the families. It is better for the therapist to state that at times his language may be idiosyncratic to the profession and that he takes responsibility for any misunderstanding.

A therapeutic alliance establishes an opportunity to share thoughts about personal experiences. It establishes the possibility of increasing intimacy without invading the family's world. It may be difficult to establish a connection with a particular family or family member. It can be surprising when simple topics promote a level of connectedness. For example, the G. family scheduled an appointment due to 8-year-old Randy's defiance at home, his bullying kids on the way to and from school, and his explosive temper and moodiness. Throughout the session Randy listened but chose not to join in. He successfully dodged any interaction aimed at him. At the end of the session, the therapist asked him if he had any pets. Randy acknowledged he had a dog. "What kind?" asked the therapist. "A rottweiler," answered Randy. 'No way," said the therapist, "I had a rottweiler a few years ago. Her name was Britta. She was a big baby." Randy looked cautiously at the therapist, "No way! My dog is named Britta. She's a real wimp." The therapist made a connection.

Defiance as Acting-Out to Relieve Anxiety

With defiant families we expect high levels of acting out in three generations. This is their standard method of derailing change. The question to keep in mind is, what is behind the presenting problem that is helpful to the family? How does this behavior restore unity or add to the health of the household? If the identified patient has difficulty controlling impulses or wants to leave the family, we wonder with them who else has similar, but covert, and partially unconscious, feelings or experiences. Who does the child take after? Which parent is most like the child? How did they behave as children? What problems did they have? How would their parents handle similar situations? The therapist should always be looking for common intergenerational themes and threads that hold the family story together. Questions should include: What influences from the previous generation are exerting themselves on the family? What family legacy has the family inherited? What do they have to live up to or overcome? This process lowers defenses and creates a positive group spirit. It's not easy for defiant families to talk about the previous generation because the history may contain painful memories. However, it opens up the possibility for storytelling.

Case Example: Blueprinting the Therapy Process. The following case illustrates a process often played out in the initial session. The therapist wants to develop a broad sense of the family while the parents want to jump into the presenting problem. The therapist blueprints the process for the session, but still the father has his own agenda.

Therapist: Today I'd like to get to understand how this family works from each of your viewpoints. Then we can talk about the problems that got you all here. Let's start with you Dad.

Father: What exactly do you want to know about us?

Therapist: I would like to know about your relationships with one another. Who gets along, who fights, who keeps the peace, things like that.

Father: It's hard for me not to jump right in and talk about Jim. He's the real reason we're here.

Therapist: I know, we'll get to that later. Right now it is most helpful for me to get to know your family, the bigger picture.

The therapist maintains control of the session through acknowledging the father's dilemma while asserting his goal to understand the family as a group. Defiant families feel pressured to do something about the problem despite its chronic nature. Getting into the problem area too quickly leaves the therapist with the distinct disadvantage of not knowing much about the players. In the initial session, the therapist must provide the direction of the interview.

It is important to note the relationships described and the viewpoints of each family member. A holographic picture of the family emerges naturally if the therapist avoids detailing problems within the acting-out family member too early. Asking families to talk about relationships is complicated. They can describe each other's role in the group, but delineating dyads and triads requires a thinking process foreign to most families. Families that are able to describe themselves in terms of relationships possess a higher level of systems thinking, which we think is correlated with maturity and health. Most families describe individual idiosyncrasies within the groups, usually focusing on negative characteristics. In the first interview, the therapist directs the flow of the encounter by seeking out each person's perspective of what it is like to be in the family. For example, in the S. family, Mr. S. described a cohesive, well-connected group. He felt that they talked easily, shared, were involved, and understood one another. As the session progressed, the oldest daughter who was so compliant as to be disappointing, described a very different family. Her description made it sound like her father was delusional. She believed they all cared for one another, but at a distance. They only talked superficially, and nothing substantive was ever discussed. Her younger sister (the driven child) agreed with this perception. She thought her father described the family as he hoped it would be, not as they really were.

In the first interview the therapist makes an attempt to assess the family *espirit de corps*, or the family we. All members are implicated in the problem. The defiant family is often characterized by its avoidance of being a family. The major symptom is a failure to acknowledge the whole; they prefer to keep things fragmented. The family feels nonintimate while describing vivid predicaments. Because the members have difficulty describing how the family operates, the therapist is often left with the feeling that each person is describing a different family. It is like the well-worn story of the four blind men describing an elephant or the impeachment trial in which the United States Senate described the president's actions in salacious detail but without emotion. Their observations are delimited by political implications. Each describes a unique perspective of the group with little description about how they see themselves.

During this part of therapy, the therapist searches for cohesiveness within the family as well as a sense of family ethics. The therapist asks questions like, "Can you tell me about times when you enjoyed being together? Tell me a story about what it was like when you were growing up. Try describing your family like a basketball team."

Case Example: Looking for the Family We. The following excerpt is taken from a session in which a 17-year-old son was referred to therapy by his family physician. The adolescent had become increasingly confrontational at home and school, had a history of drug and alcohol abuse, and had recently threatened suicide. The family convened to discuss how they were managing in light of recent events. The therapist's goal was to get a sense of how family members saw the family functioning and to assess the level of support in dealing with the son.

Therapist: So, the thing that's helpful to talk about is what the family is like. Can you start off talking about what the family is like as a group?

Father: Okay, I'll start and then they (*the family*) can join in.

Therapist: Why don't you start and then we'll go around the room, and I'll ask them to talk. What I'm interested in is how you each see it.

Father: Okay (*He is hesitating.*).

Therapist: You can think about the family like it was a basketball team; I want to know how the *team* functions—how it operates.

Father: Well, we have one family member who likes to take the ball and run. Everybody else seems to like to work within the rules. I mean, I know I've dealt with teenagers for quite a few years. You can't always get them to do everything you ask them to do, because of the teenage-hood—I understand that. However, my son seems to take the ball and run by himself. He doesn't seem to want to work within the rules. I'll set rules for the girls and they always seem to work within the rules but always on the outskirts. They never really bust out of the parameters that I've set. Jim consistently busts through the parameters. He's done it since he was 2-years-old.

Therapist: He likes to take the ball and shoot.

Father: Exactly, at least from a basketball standpoint he's our shooter—sometimes wild, sometimes from half-court.

Therapist: Like a rookie.

Father: Like a rookie, yeah, like a rookie—always crazy. And, I don't know, Mom and I are the coaches. We set rules for the kids. If I were to compare us to our peers, we're probably stricter than average, although we're not fundamental bible-thumpers who don't have cable or a stereo. We have those things, but we try to monitor everything. I'm probably stricter than the average dad.

Next the therapist explores the oldest daughter's perception of how the family operates. She is chosen to go next because of her position in the family. She is the eldest, and most likely to defend the marriage.

Therapist: Susan, what's your view of your family? How does it look to you?

Susan: Well, I'll agree with my dad that when it gets right down to it, we're probably the closest family we know, but we don't like each other.

Therapist: Really. Actually, that's a fascinating, contradictory idea. How does it work?

Susan: We don't get along. We don't talk to each other. We're just kind of there. But it's sad—with lots of tragedy, like when we were looking for my brother. That really shows you that we are tight. You know, when it comes right down to it we'll do anything, you know, but with everyday things we just don't get along.

Therapist: Hmm. Do you have any idea what you're fighting about?

Susan: Stupid stuff. Our personalities are so different, or maybe they're just so much the same that we don't get along. I hear that a lot. When I was Jim's age, my dad and I never spoke a single word. We did not get along. We fought almost all of the time. Me and my sister used to pull each other's hair, punch, bite, all the time. There were times when we'd just get into arguments and I'd go out and fight, or Sara and Jim would go out and fight. I've screamed at my mom, or we've screamed at each other. I mean, I don't know.

Therapist: No idea what's behind it, though, about what makes it hard to be close together? Like maybe he (*father*) wasn't supposed to get married because he was going to be a priest or something?

The message is that the parents have histories and come out of a living pattern that colors the present. Father is like a priest—calm, cool, and partially disengaged. In fact, he started out to be a priest and studied at a seminary. After getting the oldest daughter's view, the therapist turns to the youngest daughter to ask her to describe things from her vantage point.

Therapist: (*To Sara*) Do you want to say how the family looks to you, Sara, from the bottom of the totem pole?

Sara: Umm.

Therapist: How much younger are you than Jim?

Sara: Like a year and 1 month. Umm, no communication whatsoever. We don't talk, and we fight about stupid things, and then . . . (*Jim shifts back and is looking toward the ceiling*). I'll fight with someone, and then I'll just push them away. I'll just say, "Shut up, I don't want to talk with you." They just frustrate me even more.

Therapist: Do you ever think that some of the kids are closer to Mom and some are closer to Dad? If the folks are having a struggle do the kids divide up?

Sara: I think Jim would probably talk to my dad and, probably, all the girls would talk with Mom.

Therapist: Oh, a men against the women kind of a deal, you think?

Sara: Probably.

Therapist: (*Smiling*) Between your parents who's the most fun to fight with?

Sara: I don't really fight with Mom that much, but I fight with my dad all the time.

Jim: (*Leans forward, smiles, looks at Sara, and laughs. Good nonverbal signal that Jim, who has been silent, is alive, that he belongs and is in on the interview.*)

Therapist: Do you ever get him to back down?

Sara: Not really (*Mother giggles, commenting on father's view of the family. This contradiction of his perception makes us wonder if he came in with the wrong family*). It's like both of us just have to have the last word. It's like, just leave. I don't want to talk to you. That's probably the most frustrating.

Sara: Me and Jim will stick up for each other a lot (*Jim nods his head in agreement*). I mean, I know we're not as close to each other as we used to be, but if I'm fighting with Dad, Jim will jump in, and if Jim's fighting with Dad, I'll jump in.

Therapist: Does anybody else get involved in your fights with your dad?

Jim: Like a tag-team?

Jim's spontaneous comment hints that the therapist is engaged with him. Once there is engagement, the initial questions become less relevant and everyone's role softens.

Therapist: Yeah.

Father: Yeah, it is if you've got to take the brunt of it.

(*Jim is smiling and looking toward Sara and his father*)

Therapist: So then together do you defeat your dad? Because that's a great strategy.

Sara: Well, sometimes.

Therapist: Most kids don't know that if they gang up on the parent they might get somewhere. If they fight one-on-one, no way. If you're really smart, you could even draft your sister.

The second generation's responsiveness to the therapist's humor is a hopeful sign with defiant families. It suggests they can think and speak metaphorically. Early in therapy, the therapist introduces playfulness into the interaction through ambiguous remarks. Note that many questions are veiled suggestions. This may seem inconsequential, but it is crucial. We often find defiant families unable to be playful with one another. Their anxiety makes them concrete. Families that pick up on the playfulness or teasing appear more hopeful and alive. For instance, one family's daughter was chastising her mother for coming home with alcohol on her breath. The therapist teased the daughter, saying, "You sound like a concerned mother." She got mad, saying, "I'm not the mother. I'm the daughter." She was incapable of playing with the notion of being the mother and remained concrete about her role. The impact of humor in this case was unconscious and was evidenced by the daughter's anger. She resisted the metaphorical playfulness. Of course, she was worried about her mother and displayed a defiant manner. This type of maneuver gives the therapist a sense of the rigidity of the role structure within the group. Can family members play at being in the generation above or below them? Can they pick up on, or enjoy the teasing and playful nature of the therapist? Families who can only be deadly serious are problematic. They have become habituated in their attempts to relate to one another and avoid any attempt to soften rigid patterns.

In the first interview parents can be discouraged by a defiant child's good behavior. They might say, "You probably don't believe we have so many problems." The therapist acknowledges the parent's frustration by saying, "It's good to know they can behave. Don't worry, I believe what you're saying. It's not uncommon for children to behave so well initially. If he falls in love with me, he'll get worse." A strange component of the problem of defiance is that the child proves his love for his parents by being naughty. The therapist accepts the parents' description of the problem without increasing their defensiveness. Otherwise, they can end up feeling marginalized. There is value in the parents seeing the child behave well in this context and recognizing that he's not entirely "screwed up." There is more to him than a naughty boy.

Usually by the second or third session, the therapist sees a different picture of the family as issues are played out. An adolescent might come in and demand, "I want to go back to school, but the principal won't let me until you talk to him." The therapist answers, "I'll be glad to talk to the principal, but it is his decision whether or not you return to school. Maybe *you* should work something out with him." At this point in therapy the therapist has a better sense about how the family operates.

The Pornography of Defiance

During the initial stages of therapy, defiant families are notorious for titillating the therapist with salacious details about their lives. Graphic distortions may entice the therapist into gathering more information or engaging in active problem solving. Following either direction becomes an inadequate attempt to solve the metaproblems or alleviate metasymptoms, taking the therapist toward a dead end. The focus needs to remain on relational and process issues. Dealing with specific details initially doesn't really help. It is more important for the therapist to trust his intuition that the family will do what needs to be done. Families repeatedly attempt to corner the therapist with the graphics of their situations. For example, the S. family was going into great detail about all the awful things their adolescent son had done, including drunk driving, stealing, and punching a classmate. While it was tempting to gather more details about the rule breaking dealing individually with each infraction would only help the family overlook how misunderstood and alienated their son felt. The therapist chose instead to explore the parent's apprehension and worry for their son, rather than their anger. If the therapist is seduced by salacious details into focusing too narrowly on detail before getting a picture of the process, he ends up either cornering the acting-out child or cornering himself into a state of impotency.

The initial narrative of the family provides the therapist with the opportunity to experience what the family is like. The therapist wants the family to describe a wide array of issues, thereby presenting a wide-angle view of themselves. A broad perspective is necessary to develop a picture of intergenerational family dynamics. If significant specific disclosures occur during the initial session, the therapist makes a mental note of them but continues charting the big picture without asking for clarification or going deeper. The therapist wants to know what issues the family has been working on, but the goal is not to be trapped into dealing with serious problems early in the encounter. For example, during an initial family session, the mother began ranting about finding pictures of naked women in her 12-year-olds' room. She was going on about how awful this was and what terrible things would happen to her son for looking at them. The boy was clearly embarrassed and humiliated. The therapist said to the son, "I guess you need to find a better hiding place." To mother he said, "This sounds like an important issue for you. Let's talk about it after I get a better understanding of the family as a whole." This is an example of the therapist paying attention to process. By diverting his attention to solving a problem, the therapist would lose an opportunity to understand the importance of the issue to the mother. Black and white thinking can be a trap; it reaches a dead end. The challenge is to make all parties feel heard so that therapy does not end prematurely. If a parent is dissatisfied with the encounter or feels undermined by the therapist before a therapeutic alliance has evolved, there is often a premature termination.

Premature Intervention

Defiant families frequently push early for solutions to chronic problems. They corner the therapist before the underlying family dynamics can be understood. It is tempting for the therapist to offer solutions, but families rarely consider them. It is more useful to observe the family mood to discern in what ways the identified patient mirrors other family dynamics. How do other members express defiance? Is there an undercurrent of anger in the family? Why is the identified patient willing to sacrifice himself? The next case illustrates the complexity of sorting out the dynamics in defiant families. The sheer volume of information is overwhelming.

Case Example: Premature Problem Solving. The family, consisting of Mr. and Mrs. S. and David, age 16, attended therapy because of David's increasing depression. He was missing school, smoking pot daily, flunking 10th grade, and recently put back on probation for theft. He spent most of his time alone in his room and was irritable whenever demands were placed on him. Mr. S. abruptly left the family a year ago after 20 years of marriage. Mrs. S. was devastated and didn't know why he wanted a divorce.

David feels that his father divorced him as well. He comes around only when David is in trouble and then acts as a disciplinarian. They spend no quality time together. David can't remember the last time he and his father did anything together. David is clearly begging for a closer relationship to his dad. Mr. S. says he doesn't want to reward his son's delinquent behavior by spending time with him. Mother feels impotent to change anything and she is terrified her son's behavior will escalate to the point of suicide. The parents describe problems developing since David was age 13. David says he hasn't felt right since he was 7 and diagnosed with attention deficit disorder. He is a bright kid with horrible self-esteem. Two older daughters are away at college. All members of this complicated family appear demoralized. Father wants individual therapy for himself due to chronic health problems and increasing depression. Mother attends both individual therapy and a divorce-adjustment group. David sees the school counselor, their pastor, and his probation officer. His parents have scheduled a drug and alcohol assessment the next day. What is behind the symptoms? Why is David willing to sacrifice himself? How does the defiance act as a unifying force in this family?

During the first session, David is the only one willing to say what he thinks and feels. He is the emotional barometer of the family. His acting out is the only way to involve father. Father persists in asking what he should do to help his son. The therapist offers a solution before understanding the family dynamics. He tells father that he needs to increase his involvement with his son and that his interaction should not be contingent on whether his son is behaving or not. As expected, father defends his position of withdrawal, saying that if his son wants to spend time with him, he should straighten up. Otherwise he will not back down. The son is relieved that the therapist challenges the father. However because the challenge is premature and fails to allow an understanding of the dynamics behind the presenting symptoms, the family does not return.

When the joining process is successfully negotiated, there is a qualitative shift in the therapeutic alliance. The family is more willing to share bits of their craziness and fears. If family members don't know how to play but are at least willing to remain engaged in the experience, there is hope. The therapist is viewed as an ally, despite any previous confrontation. Trust begins to develop and the family lets its guard down so that a more vivid picture of family life emerges. The therapist is able to be less active and to trust the family to bring up topics central to its struggles. Tension is still apparent, but the therapist is now viewed as someone who can be a guide in their attempts to become more fully involved in their own family process.

Case Example: Evolution of a Therapeutic Alliance. The R. family came to therapy due to the suicidal threats, drug and alcohol abuse, truancy, and school suspensions of their 16-year-old son. The son was extremely belligerent as therapy began, openly expressing indifference to his life. His mood controlled the family and intimidated his parents. He sat sullen, hat down over his face, ignoring anything going on in the session, and refusing to talk. Other family members were more willing to get involved, sharing their worries about him and each other. No force was exerted to make him open up or talk. At the end of each session the therapist shook each person's hand as they left. The son always walked out, making sure to ignore the therapist. During the second session, he threatened the therapist about getting too close, saying if he came too close again he would hurt him.

In the third session, there was a shift in the son's demeanor. He was still defiant but his approach softened during the hour. It was nothing earth shaking, but he just seemed less angry. Mr. R. said that following the last session he and his son had a talk on the way home about his concern over his son's indifference about whether he lived or died. They had talked more openly than ever before. As the session ended, the therapist went through his usual ritual. When he extended his hand to the adolescent, he returned the hand shake and even looked him in the eye. This shift in behavior was significant. The therapist didn't make a big deal of it but noted that in the next session, the adolescent was more talkative. This qualitative shift relaxed other family members and therapy moved into the working stages. Giving the adolescent his personal space and pacing of involvement in the therapy allowed him to maintain his integrity and join when he was ready. Chasing would have been a duplication of the interaction with his parents. The therapist did not need to have the adolescent comply, therefore he could comply.

SUMMARY

The initial stage of therapy is critical. The relationship begins with the first phone call. The therapist establishes himself as a competent professional, setting the ground rules for the therapy process. If the therapist compromises his standards at the beginning of therapy, it is hard to recover. Maintaining a nonanxious presence in the light of the family's urgency is essential to the therapeutic endeavor. Defiant families challenge even the seasoned therapist because they are complex, chaotic, resistant, and at times pornographic with the details of their lives. They maintain a defensive perimeter until they have tested the therapist's competence. Forging a therapeutic alliance is key to the initial stage of treatment. A holographic image of the family emerges if the therapist avoids premature detailing of the presenting problem.

6

Therapeutic Jambalaya: The Middle Phase of Therapy

The middle stage of therapy is crucial in working with defiant families. It is the heart of the therapy—the working phase. Capturing the essence of this stage is difficult due to the subtle nuances of the relationships and interaction among the therapy participants. The goal of this chapter is to illustrate key dynamics and techniques that are central to this stage. This is done through case examples and discussion. The reader should keep in mind that even with the most illustrative case examples, the therapeutic process will not come alive the way it does in practice. Listening to a recording, similarly, doesn't allow one to feel the music or experience that visceral reaction that a live performance permits. The case examples highlight the dynamics and techniques essential to this stage, but only modestly capture the art of therapy with defiant families.

Issues of joining and distancing, maintaining family initiative, and understanding and disrupting the undercurrents of conflict are emphasized. The focus of treatment moves beyond symptom relief. The family system is mobilized and attention shifts within the family, so that each member can take a turn being the patient. Scapegoating is minimized and the struggles between individual rights and family responsibility become more clearly defined. An agreement is negotiated to invest time and effort into family issues. The involvement of the family is established, with the family, rather than the identified patient, the center of treatment. By this time the therapist and family have created a workable alliance, allowing the therapist to move in and out of the family. The middle phase begins when the parents become patients and start asking questions about themselves in relation to their child and in relation to one another.

Personal involvement is the hallmark of work with defiant families. Setting limits or establishing behavioral contracts is not enough for change to be internalized. In order for family therapy to be successful, personal involvement must be combined with technique. The collaborative alliance between family and therapist is paramount in working with defiant families: It allows them to feel safe to explore their darker sides, acknowledge contradictions, and see perversity in their self-righteousness. They also become more willing to take the risks required to repair family dynamics and relationships.

Our approach to therapy is specific to each family and is developed during the hands-on process of therapy. Key to the middle stage is the therapist's ability to achieve a delicate balance between distance and closeness. She must be at times bold and irreverent, almost arrogant, and at other times caring, nurturing, and humble. Defiant families have a history of frustrating, neutralizing, infuriating, or ignoring community help. Only through working with this tension between proximity and distance will the responsibility for change be placed squarely in the family's lap. When the therapist holds firm in the face of adversity, the family's willingness to take risks increases. Family members are able to be more vulnerable with their struggles, more personal and more engaged.

A therapy session is similar to a musical jam session. Each participant is responsible for her own tune. We are not sure at the outset whether the music we create will be synchronous or chaotic. The goal is for each person to participate fully in order to create the possibility for growth. It is a stimulating process when things are working. Out of sheer discord comes a melodious tune as family relationships begin to take shape and gain significance. At its best, the middle stage of therapy is unpredictable, alive, and on the edge of out of control!

JOINING AND DISTANCING

There is no correct distance for conducting good psychotherapy (Whitaker, 1971). It is critical to maintain freedom to care for the family from a certain distance, taking care not to be locked into any permanent position. Concerned indifference is the essence of the middle stage. An alliance with the family is offered in the belief that the relationship has the power the family lacks on its own to effect change. The therapist trusts her intuition, is active in participation, and self-discloses when appropriate. The use of play, humor and absurdity, deviation amplification, side taking, and challenging of roles all facilitate joining and distancing. Joining encourages finding a common ground and sharing perspectives and experiences. Any sharing by the therapist becomes pertinent to the family, not as a disclosure to aid the therapist in personal growth, but as a means of servicing the family while acknowledging one's own limitations. Distancing moves the therapist out of the system to keep from being absorbed by the family process. Through this distancing the therapist models individuation. She may become disinterested, change the topic, redirect, look out the window, talk to the cotherapist, bring in a consultant, and so forth. Distancing includes silence, especially when struggling with family initiative. If the family can accommodate each other's and the therapist's quirks with caring, affection and respect can develop.

Equally important is the therapist's ability to establish and suspend alliances with individual family members or subgroups with the notion of working toward growth within the family. Therapy is foremost a relationship between the therapist and the family system and within that relationship exists the possibility of person-to-person relationships that can be deeply intimate. The therapist functions in service to the group, not the individual. The therapist must already have a framework for understanding family dynamics. Sometimes these fantasies about a family's dynamics are almost correct. Having a hypothesis is important. It is better to assume to know what is going on and be explicit about it than to be confused. Pushing a point of view makes family members think about it and compare it to their own point of view. We listen attentively when families tell us what they think.

An energetic alliance is formed as the therapist and family coalesce. This alliance is imperative to growth within the family. When change is facilitated within the therapeutic system, family myths are often shattered. The identified patient's defiance is redefined as helping mother avoid depression or as increasing marital unity by providing a common enemy. The presenting problem is reworked into an intergenerational context of defiance. The focus is often a struggle between family members, with the pathology of the defiant member as an amplified model. Maintaining an interpersonal context is crucial to this stage. There is temptation to form alliances or meet despite absent members. Family therapy keeps defiance within the context of the family system. Family work provides guidelines for growth and healthy development. It makes satisfying connections with others possible. Blaming is reduced as the context is clarified.

Therapy takes on a qualitative difference. Behavior usually reserved for home is played out in the sessions. Family members are more open in demonstrating key issues that perturb the system. Interactions are richer and more intense and stimulate dialogue among family members. The therapist is free to back out. Family members expand their roles and expose their personhood. Therapy moves beyond the reality of daily events of living into the family's symbolic understructure. Experiencing the family's private life in this way is crucial to the success of therapy. At times the therapist is a participant observer who takes care not to interrupt the action. At others she is central to the interaction, pushing the family to new awareness. Family members begin to examine their contributions to problems and become involved in expressing themselves rather than blaming others.

During this stage, a family describes its life in more detailed terms—the passive language and vagueness has usually ended. The worlds of fact and fantasy are explored. The bilateral process is expanded, creating a supersystem with the therapist as the new ambiguous, destabilizing member. The therapist is no longer excluded from the system but is strategic to the ongoing productivity with the group. She listens for themes of how the family functions and how it handles problematic events. She listens for their emotional tone, attending to the overall mood of the group. Defiant families often lack a language for emotions. They have difficulty with the perspective that empathy allows. Parental maturity increases as they focus on what the symptoms say about their parenting as well as the fact that their child is hurting. It is the therapist's job to remain involved and to highlight family dynamics and options.

Both family and therapist question the status quo. The therapist actively pushes the family beyond its comfort zone, but the therapeutic relationship is powerful and intimate enough to tolerate this activity. If the therapist has passed the family's testing and hung in through tough situations, the family becomes progressively willing to enter into a deeper collaborative relationship. The therapist's caring moves the relationship into fresh territory. Tolerating anxiety and intense emotion becomes an issue for everyone involved in therapy. When crises erupt, the therapist must tolerate personal anxiety while the family tolerates anxiety about their uncertain future. The therapist balances active participation with detachment while encouraging the family in its efforts to solve dilemmas. The limits of interpersonal influence are recognized, as well as the painful binds families and parents unavoidably experience.

The therapist must be aware of her personal expectations and values, such as "lying is bad" or "all parents must be more mature than their children." Imposing her expectations can corner the family or create a crisis. Righteous indignation may work for Judge Judy, but it rarely facilitates risk taking and openness. In defiant families the lessons to be learned through experience are costly. Behaviors can be shocking and embarrassing, but they need to be acknowledged so that family members can learn from them. Strange, perverse behaviors are related to the steady dialectic between belonging and individuation. Crises that erupt during therapy may include an adolescent challenging parental or therapist authority, a family choosing inadequate solutions, or therapy reaching an impasse or being abandoned altogether.

Case Example: The Humanness of the Therapist

T.J. age 15 (who we met in Chapter 3), was kicked out of school. Therapy focused on T.J.; his noncompliance, and his freedom to say anything he pleased. His parents responded punitively to his insults or glared at him with anger.

T.J.: Well, I'm going downtown tonight. I don't care what you say, besides, what can you do?

Father: If you go downtown, I will call the police. They don't want you down there.

T.J.: Yeah, well, what are they going to do, give me a ride home? What are they going to tell you, take me to a f——— counselor?

Mother: T.J., you are in more trouble than you know. If you go down there, they are going to put you on probation.

T.J.: Shut up b——! (*Mother is silent*) Yeah, I blame others for my troubles. But why did I punch Mike in the face? For Christ's sake, it was because he said my f——— mother was f——— Bill, and goddamn it, you were. Don't tell me to think about my family when you forgot to think about Dad and me and our family. You were off f——— the biggest asshole in town, and a 19-year-old asshole! Damn it Mom, he is only 4 years older that me! How do you think that made me feel? (*T.J. was sitting in a chair in the corner, with a parent on each side, staring at him. He avoided their stares.*)

During heated interchanges, the therapist reacted to the negative language. What does the therapist do at a time like this? Does she say, "Don't talk like that. That's inappropriate," or, " We don't talk like that here!" Does she sit quietly and do nothing? Or does she shake her head and say, "What a minute T.J., you sure are good at burning your mother's butt!" In this case the therapist was thinking, "he is being simultaneously outrageous and honest. He is giving me a look at his pain. He feels double-crossed by his mother. He is worried about what is going to happen next. He says he will move out on his 16th birthday. He knows he's in a bad space. He needs and wants his education, but he can't say that yet. To the extent he can be helpful to his family, he is more therapeutic by being out of control." T.J. gets up and walks toward the door.

Therapist: I'll tell you what I think about this. Nobody should talk to anyone like that outside of the movies. But I believe that is how the family talks. You have an explosiveness to you. I would be real tempted to knock his head off for talking like that to me or my wife, even if I was mad at her. But in his case, he wins the battle when you explode. I think what you do is say 'Ouch, that hurts me!' I don't know if I am right or not, but I do know what I believe. I believe that he is scared and I believe he is in pain, but like most of us, he is too frightened and feels too insecure to say it straight. Like I say, I don't know if I am right, but I think you will get further with him if you think like that.

The affect that emerges out of this stage fuels the therapy process. The therapist contributes to the openness of the session when she is able to share personal thoughts and feelings that relate to the therapy process. The therapist can't fake genuineness—either she has regard for the family or not. The therapist brings not only expertise but humanness to each encounter. T.J.'s abusive language toward his mother needed discussion, so the therapist shared her experience. Experience plus humanness equals maturity. A mutual respect develops from this equation. The family begins to see the therapist as a guide or coach, not a savior.

It is critical not to micromanage the family despite temptations to the contrary. The parents attempts to co-opt the therapist into assuming responsibility for decision making, particularly in setting limits for children. They might ask, "Should we ground Sam for smoking pot? Is it okay to schedule a parent-teacher conference for our 17-year-old son to see if he's failing anything?" Issues are open for discussion, but the parents must weigh the pros and cons of action. Micromanaging implies parents aren't capable of making appropriate decisions for their family. Empowering the parents to take action, rather than encourage a passive stance of "therapist knows best," is crucial. The therapist should support family initiative to take risks and explore options. The more they assume responsibility for decisions, the more permanent the changes will be. The healthy parent and therapist knows that freedom and responsibility increase together.

ACCESSING THE FAMILY'S SYMBOLIC WORLD

One of the key ingredients in the middle stage of therapy is the therapist's ability to listen *through* what is being said rather than *to* what is being said. The therapist moves beyond the reality of daily events into the family's understructure, paying close attention to picture images or metaphorical words that are generated. The goal is to access their metaphorical language and create a context that invites the family to share their symbolic world. Therapy is a process of shifting between metaphor and reality. The therapist attends to the process and listens for meaning embedded in the family's descriptions of their daily life. By operating primarily on a symbolic level, the therapeutic relationship becomes an interactional metaphor (Connell, Mitten, & Whitaker, 1993). Through sharing a more personal investment, the therapist experiences the underbelly of the family.

Therapy in this stage moves into the nonrational. The therapist and family share mutual stories. Storytelling is initiated from real or clinical material that is triggered by the family. The family can pick up on or ignore these anecdotes because they come out of the therapist's creativity and may or may not spark something for them. Communication is therefore less censored. The therapist listens to the metaphorical language that the family uses to describe its life and conflicts, connecting with family members as they expose their fears and weaknesses. Engaging the family at a symbolic, rather than literal, level has a powerful impact. Defenses are minimized and anything is possible.

Case Example: Storytelling Softens Defenses

The therapist shared a personal anecdote with a mother who worried that she might hurt her defiant first grader. She remembered being angry at her younger son, chasing him through the house, when her older son screamed, "You better run and hide because I think Mom is crazy!" This was a time when she became alarmed that her anger was out of proportion to the situation and a when her children were therapeutic to her. The remark gave a glimpse of the frustrated mother behind the professional role. This story facilitated discussion about the client's abusive upbringing and fear of repeating what was done to her. Despite this fear, she had never hurt her child. In fact, she was quite creative in her discipline.

Every intimate relationship has a private language. Likewise, a private language evolves during this stage of therapy. Through communication, a shared, symbolic language develops within the therapeutic system that enhances the level of connectedness of the therapy participants. It makes the process of therapy more vital. Families have stories about their lives that can be retold and reworked during therapy. The content is usually familiar, but the retelling enhances the possibility of its significance.

The therapist is part of the family system in much the same manner as a favored aunt or uncle. She is integral to the reshaping of family relationships. Family members feel free to comment on the therapist's interpretations. They may say, "Wow, that's way off base," or "You're getting to know us so well that it's scary." They feel free to challenge the therapist as "boring" or call her on her observations. Because the family's guard is down, their inner workings can be revealed. Family symbols become apparent.

Recognizing the symbolic importance of events or possessions can clarify unspoken issues. For example, a patient was distraught because her refrigerator broke and she had to buy ice every day to prevent her food from spoiling. She had just gone shopping for food and had no money to replace anything that spoiled. Her spirit was low and she was overburdened. The emotion associated with the event seemed out of proportion. The therapist learned that what made her cry wasn't the many tasks she had to perform, but the fact that the refrigerator belonged to her mother, who hanged herself a year earlier. The daughter didn't want to give up on the refrigerator, even if it was old and broken.

THE DIFFICULTY WITH INTIMACY

At times it is difficult to be intimate with the family. The therapist finds her personal reactions to be unsettling. Father may be more abusive than initially suspected, putting the therapist in an uncomfortable position as the abusive behavior is sorted out. In one family the father berated the adolescent son, frequently humiliating him in public places. The negative countertransference to the father was strong as the therapist worked with the family to understand their dynamics. The therapist must guard against usurping parental authority, especially when the parents are weak and ineffective. It does the family no good to have the therapist in charge. At other times, the therapist experiences complete impotence in the face of destructive behavior. Admitting defeat in such cases is the only option. It disrupts the family's fantasy that you have unusual powers.

Case Example: The Understructure of the Family

Mrs. O. is a 32-year-old mother of two who has recently returned to college. Her 8-year-old daughter, Melissa, has become increasingly problematic at home and at school. She talks back, stomps around, refuses to do her chores or homework, fights with her 3-year-old sister, and constantly defies any limits set in the household. Mr. O. works third shift, consequently he is unavailable emotionally and physically. He is unsupportive of his wife's attempts to go to college.

Mother: I've had it. This week I got three calls from Melissa's teacher about her behavior. She has been impossible at home—a real drama queen. I've tried everything I know.

Melissa: Well, how would you like to be me? It's Melissa get me this, Melissa you're such a brat, Melissa watch your sister, do this, no, do that. What do you expect?

Mother: Melissa, you're exaggerating as usual.

Melissa: (*Sarcastically*) Why don't we trade places for one day and I'll boss you around and see how you like it!

Mother: See this is what I'm talking about. The attitude is awful. I know I am a witch lately. Sometimes I think, my god, I sound just like my mother and believe me that is scary. Bill is no help either. He is just like having another kid around.

Therapist: Are you suspicious Bill and your mother are coaching Melissa on how to be a pain in the neck?

Mother: (*Smiling*) It sure seems that way.

Therapist: It's overwhelming to manage the household and go to school. I remember when I returned to college with two young kids, it was hard to manage all the responsibilities. My oldest son was not happy with the changes. One day when he was mad he said, "You used to be a nice mommy before you went to school." What a blow.

Mother: My only hope is a better life for my family if I can just finish school. (*Mother begins crying*) No one in my family thinks I can do it. I get no encouragement from my husband or parents. I have an A average and no one says 'good job.'

Therapist: What keeps you going?

Mother: Sometimes it seems like I'm feeling my way in the dark. I don't know anything about parenting besides what I see my friends doing. My friends are more help than my family.

The therapist acknowledges the difficulty of all Mrs. O. is trying to accomplish. She is burdened by not living up to her own expectations. Sharing the therapist's story fragment from her own past shifted the discussion to real problems of balancing family, personal needs, relationship, and career. Mrs. O. equates "acting like her mother" to being a failure as a parent, which was exacerbated by her daughter's defiance. Becoming a witch is terrifying and unpredictable, but it can be fun. The dance of defiance and failure are thus intimately intertwined.

Therapy focuses on the understructure of family life. Inadequate parental role modeling is a frequent theme in defiant families. Creating a parental team is crucial to dealing with the defiance. The parents often are raising their children with the goal of avoiding being like their parents. The goal translates into *what not to be versus what to be*. There is no model for parenting. Often there is a history of abuse or neglect, with children raising themselves while assuming responsibility for younger peers, or there is a lack of intimacyor feeling of being loved. Defiant families tend to be at the extremes, without a sense of balance. They are overinvolved or underinvolved. Parenting styles are enmeshed and overprotective or chaotic and distant. There is no sense of what is needed or there is a belief that what is needed is for someone else to change. They are habituated to the problem.

FAMILY INITIATIVE

There is a shift in responsibility for sessions in the middle stage of therapy. The therapist provides an opportunity for the family to come together and work on issues pertinent to daily living. The session usually begins with something akin to, "So, tell me what adventures you have been on since we last got together," or "How's life?" or perhaps, "How goes the war?" The therapist waits until someone in the family brings up a topic they wish to discuss. This may be a current crisis, an ongoing problem, a report of a change in family behavior, or pride for what they have accomplished. The family is responsible for the content of the session. The therapist is responsible for making metaobservations, disrupting the status quo, commenting on intergenerational processes, and keeping track of time.

Case Example: The Family Takes Charge

The B. family attended therapy due to the aggressive behavior of Katie, an 11-year-old. Mother had gone through a major depression in which she had been unavailable to her three children. Katie's defiant behavior escalated to the point of hollering and threatening whenever she was asked to do anything. She was aggressive to her older brother, struck out at her mother on several occasions, and was self-abusive. During therapy the family had begun to take personal responsibility, collectively and individually. They initiated new behaviors at home and the children enjoyed having a positive influence on family interaction.

Therapist: So, what adventures have you all been up to since our last meeting?

Mother: The biggest change we've had to our advantage as far as interacting as a family was a contract that my son wrote up last week (*Joey shakes his head affirmatively*) stating that he would not watch TV, him or Katie, by themselves unless it was news. They would sit for family time to watch TV. They were not allowed to play the computer or the Nintendo game or any of that stuff. So for the last week they've actually sat with me and watched TV. That's a big change.

Joey: Yeah, except when we're in school.

Therapist: You're right, that is a huge change.

Mother: At least for us. I can't tell you how much I like it. They aren't in their rooms watching their own shows. They choose to watch them with me. It's a start!

Katie: I'm never upstairs in my own room. I have to be with some of you, because I don't like my room. I'm glad Mom isn't in her room all the time like over the winter. She had us all worried.

The family is proud of their initiative. The therapist did not tell them to go home and change anything. A key point about the middle stage is that the family's initiative drives any attempt to change. Its members are in charge of whether they need to regain control, set limits, enhance relationships, or ignore the problem altogether. They are more fully involved in their own lives. Positive change is their responsibility and comes out of their initiative. The therapy process becomes more spontaneous. The therapist feels a genuine desire to connect with the family's initiative based on caring and intuition. If something is bothersome or exciting, it is acknowledged.

Mother had always come to sessions dressed in an plain manner. She seemed to disappear into the background. During a session she and her boyfriend, Mike, were discussing things they liked to do. The therapist was stunned when Sue said she liked to dance, particularly to swing music. This was a sharp contrast to the image she portrayed. At that instant the therapist had a new vision of her, one inconsistent with the past image. Suddenly new possibilities came flooding in. The therapist underscored her enthusiasm for this new knowledge.

Mother: Everything that counts we seem together on, though. I even got him into classical music. He'll even listen to swing music and dance with me.

Therapist: Huh!

Mike: Yeah, that Grand Funk . . .

Therapist: I never thought of you dancing before! I love it!

Mother: Oh, to swing music, yeah. I'm really good at it. Glenn Miller is my favorite. I have lots of his music.

Therapist: You dance to swing music, that's incredible! That gives me a whole new picture about you. What else am I missing? (*The family laughs*)

Katie: Mom loves to get us to dance with her. Joey usually runs and hides. I think it's fun. It's one of the few times Mom laughs.

The therapist's interest in the family is renewed. Perhaps her own perceptions of the family were limiting their growth. Mother had appeared so lethargic, nondescript, and lacking vitality in past sessions. She was dependent and didn't advocate for herself. Her history of depression perpetuated her isolation. The family did not have healthy relationships or a variety of solutions to solve problems. Yet, clearly there was an underside to mother that the therapist had missed. Her dysfunction had colored the picture. Healthy play had not been obvious in family interactions.

It is not unusual for therapists to jump to conclusions about the overall behavior of defiant families. Although they share common issues, health in these families is unique and appears in unlikely places, like dancing to swing music. Family inventiveness is powerful. A caution to therapists: Personal reactions to defiant families can be detrimental to progress. Growth is possible for all families if the therapist highlights what is beneficial. Health exists in the background of defiance. Healthy, playful interactions are revealed if the therapist is listening for them. Even healthy fragments should be acknowledged.

UNDERCURRENT OF CONFLICT

Once therapy has moved to the middle stage, the system often reverts to more private styles of relating. Therapy becomes a ministage for family living. Old patterns of conflict emerge in the therapy. The therapy encounter must penetrate family relationships deeply enough to disrupt underlying patterns. Factors that contribute to dissension are dealt with to sustain motivation for change. Habituated interactions must be disrupted to reinstate wholeness.

The major methodology of this therapy stage is to encourage active participation by exaggerating or expanding issues brought up in therapy. The major goal is to help family members become vulnerable and increase participation in sessions. At this time, irreverence on the part of the therapist is often helpful. Intrusive and provocative comments make the family less comfortable. The therapist's tongue-in-cheek quality aids in their toleration of anxiety. Double meaning and confusion stimulate opportunity to redefine family relationships and experiences. Techniques used during this stage are frequently utilized to stimulate self-questioning and designed to instigate person-to-person communication. The therapist focuses on identifying repetitive sequences of interaction and speculates about the driving forces behind them.

Case Example: Moving Among Levels of Meaning

This case illustrates the therapist's irreverence in dealing with family conflict. High levels of conflict were the norm for this family. Fighting was common within the sibling group and between the parents and the children. Neither generation showed respect toward the other.

Mother: I want to talk about an incident with Chris that happened last weekend. It was horrible! He was out of control. I think he wanted to hit me, but instead he started beating on his brother and wouldn't stop . . .

Chris: (*Interrupting*) Oh Mom, you're crazy. I barely touched him, besides he started it.

Therapist: Hold it Chris. Your mom said she wanted to talk, so let her finish. (*Chris slumps in the chair and looks defeated*)

Mother: For no reason at all he just attacked Doug. I had to pull him off. I even ripped his shirt, but he still wouldn't quit. I didn't know what to do. Mark (*father*) wasn't home to help.

Therapist: One thing I've discovered, when kids fight, the responsibility for the fight is usually equal on both sides. My theory is that one kid hits the other over the head with a rubber hammer while the other retaliates by sticking a switch blade between his brother's shoulders. Parents usually see only half of the fight. If you watch closely you'll see what I'm talking about. (*Both brothers smile*)

Mother: Well, Chris did say Doug poured soup on his shirt, but I didn't see it. Chris was just nuts. He didn't even seem like himself.

Therapist: It sounds like he scared you. Do you have any sense of who he was like if he wasn't himself?

Mother: Well, he acted like his dad as a teenager and especially like Mark after he came back from Vietnam.

Father: Yeah, well, I had good reason to be angry. I had a crappy childhood and Vietnam was a nightmare!

Therapist: Do you think you can help your sons understand what was beneath all your anger?

Father: It was constantly feeling incompetent. I never measured up.

Mother: Well, Chris is short too. He has the same problems as Mark.

Father: See what I mean, she cuts to the quick!

Chris: No, that's not it. I'm really sick of the empty promises. Dad never does anything he says. We can't count on him.

Therapist: Maybe you shouldn't count on him. So far it's been a waste of time.

There are strong undercurrents of anger, belligerence, competition, inadequacy, and loneliness in this family. They have not been able to learn from one another or use each other for support. Fighting is an attempt to remain connected. Despite protests, individual family members do care. The therapist encouraged exploration of who Chris was like if he wasn't himself. This opened dialogue about him being like father, especially his negative side. Mother implied that inadequacy stemmed from both father and Chris being short. Symbolically, they never measured up on many levels. Father is inviting empathy for what he has been through in childhood and Vietnam. The therapist's remark says not, "I feel for you," but rather, "it's a waste of time to count on him." This therapeutic curve ball highlights the irreverence of the therapist in dealing with family conflict. She listens through what the family is saying for inferences that effect interactions and explain the symbolic meaning of the anger.

Case Example: What Is Behind the Anger

In the next example the therapist is trying to get at what is behind the daughter's anger. Anger is a cover emotion, designed to protect. Does the family have any sense of what drives the hostility? As usual, family members get double credit from the therapist for dumb answers. It's a three-point play if the family turns anger into laughter.

Mother: When Mike first came around, Katie was an angel. A few years after we started seeing each other, he came up to me one day and said, "You're right; she's a bitch." She threw one of her tantrums. She put a hole in the wall of my dad's house by kicking it because she was mad. She slaps herself in the neck. She pulls hair out by the clump because she gets mad.

Mike: Right.

Mother: He got to see that side of her for the first time. When you see that side of her—it's a terrifying side.

Therapist: Do you know much about it? What is she so mad about?

Mike: Stupid things.

Mother: She wants to be treated like a grown up. That's what she is telling us, and then she turns around and pulls some of the most babyish acts, like stealing candy instead of just asking.

Katie: That's because when I ask you always say no.

Mother: And crying and pouting. If she gets caught red-handed doing something, you know she was doing it just by her reaction. It's like the old adage, "we think thou doest protest too much." That's exactly how she is.

Therapist: Of the kids, is she the one you get most mad at.

Joey: (*Shakes his head 'no'*)

Sue: Of the kids at home, yes (*Family laughs*).

The family describes typical defiant behavior. Katie wants to be treated like a grown-up despite her immature behavior. She experiments with how far she can push to get her own way. Mother backs down. She is scared by the behavior and her fear immobilizes her. Katie's defiance immobilizes her mother.

Case Example: Making Connections

The next segment demonstrates the therapist asking about a connection between Jim's (the son) suicidal behavior and Mom's drinking. Jim raised her drinking as a primary concern when asked about worries regarding his parents. The therapist wants to highlight the suicidal undercurrent in the family. It is a touchy subject that has not been previously explored. The therapist brings it up again, but within the context of drinking as a slow form of suicide, much like the son's overt behavior.

Therapist: (*To mother*) How about you, do you get suicidal at times?

Mother: (*Vehemently*) No, never.

Therapist: Because steady drinking is one way to do it. You can take your time at it.

Mother: What constitutes steady?

Therapist: Something that bothers the family, bothers the people around you, interrupts your relationships.

Direct confrontation at this point would not be useful. Mother is unapproachable regarding her drinking, so the therapist doesn't approach her directly. The son's suicidal behavior is linked with his mother's drinking. This inferential method keeps defenses from escalating as they are both worried about each other's self-destructive behavior. The drinking has been brought to the foreground and will be disputed as therapy progresses. The question is expanded to dynamic consideration of the son's suicidal threats, his defiance, mother's slow suicide behavior, and at her less explicit defiance. Mother's drinking is a slower form of suicide than her son's threats, but her actions are just as deadly. She is not completely closed to the subject, asking, "What constitutes steady?" as if she is going to argue amounts.

Defiant families have strong undercurrents to their overall mood. The undercurrents usually run in a destructive direction. They may relate to overt or covert anger, fear, hostility, or anomie. Exaggerating these themes, through irreverence on the part of the therapist, instigates more direct interaction. Challenging the family to go deeper than surface emotions precipitates clearer awareness of what is constraining the system.

CRISIS ACTIVATION

Crisis within the family is inevitable at this stage of therapy. It is reasonable to predict problems as the family reorganizes and parents assert authority. The crisis is precipitated by disruption of the status quo. For example, a crisis may erupt when parents change roles, establish limits, withdraw, or end therapy. The children may act out to make sure the family stays in therapy or, on the other hand, convince the parents to quit altogether. The children may rise to new levels of challenge to see if parents can maintain both their resolve and a measure of parental unity when confronting the child's pressure. Children do what is necessary to regain equilibrium.

Case Example: Interfering with Omnipotence

Dr. and Mrs. W., 15-year-old Joe, and 10-year-old Mary entered therapy due to Joe's drug and alcohol abuse and belligerent behavior. Joe became threatening and aggressive toward his parents whenever he did not get his way. The parents were terrified of his behavior and fearful of reprisal whenever they set limits. More often than not, they backed down to keep peace. Joe attempted to intimidate the therapist with his belligerent attitude. The therapists did not want to defeat him, but clearly felt if the parents were not able to assert themselves, the situation would worsen. The process of the parents being held hostage in their own house by their son's behavior had to stop. The couple discussed options for next time Joe had an uncontrollable outburst and they settled on calling 911. Joe did not think they would follow through, after all, they had never carried through with any previous threats.

During the next outburst, Mrs. W. called the authorities to arrest their son, who at the time was out on the lawn threatening his parents. Joe remained in a detention center for several days. Both parents felt horrible about seeing him locked up. He cried and pleaded for them to take him home, but they refused until treatment was arranged for his drug and alcohol abuse. Joe was shocked that his parents followed through with the plan. Treatment for this family was long and painful. The parents periodically second-guessed their well-intentioned motives. Over time they were able to function as a team and remain in charge of the family. In this case, Joe's actions were extreme and dangerous. Therapy can be effective, but it can also be feeble. When the pressure of defiance is overwhelming, it may become necessary to employ community sanctions.

Defiant, omnipotent children and adolescents need clear, firm limits. It is important for parents to remain in charge despite challenges to their authority. Younger children who lack boundaries are afraid of their own impulses and feel compelled to follow through with their threats. Their sense of danger is not well-developed, so they feel invincible when acting in a self-destructive manner. Adolescents need boundaries as well, but the issues are more ambiguous when they defy them or lose their fear of sanctions. The nature of limits changes as children grow up and spend more time out of the parents' sight.

It is critical for parents to become comfortable in an authoritative position and with the reality of not always being popular or well-liked. Children quickly learn how to push parents' buttons. "I hate you," or "You're the meanest parent in the world," are statements meant to hurt and force the parent to back down. Parents need more sophistication to pay attention to nonverbal messages and not get embroiled in content-based nonsense. Parenting is a tough job; one that requires the ability to tolerate being disliked.

Case Example: The Family Crisis

Mother discusses a crisis with her oldest son, Steven, who has been defiant since school age, both at home and at school. He has been expelled more times than any could remember for such things as swearing, fighting with peers, and hitting teachers. In this interview mother is there with her boyfriend, Mike. The therapist wanted to understand the recent events that precipitated mother throwing Steven out. Clearly, she has tolerated years of defiance.

Therapist: What finally happened? Was he as rebellious at home as he was at school?

Mother: Oh, yes. The reason I threw him out was because I told him to do something one day and he said, 'Fuck you!' I said, 'Wait a minute. I'm your mother, and you don't talk to me like that.' 'Oh, go to hell,' he said. 'I can do whatever I want and you can't stop me.' I told him, 'Why don't you just call your dad and get out now. I'm not putting up with this anymore.' That's when I was in the middle of my depression. I just couldn't take it anymore. His behavior made me more depressed. He was so hateful. Steven always got away with more than anyone else did because he was Momma's boy. Until the last episode when I sent him to live with his dad. I couldn't take anymore. He was 15-years-old and I was afraid of him.

Therapist: When did it break down, though—around 12 to 13? Usually something happens and it gradually deteriorates—then they get kicked out.

Mother: It was probably around 11 that I started having serious problems with Steven—when he started smoking.

Mike: Twelve.

Mother: I found out he was smoking, and I confronted him about it. He picked up a butcher knife and was going to cut his wrist because I had confronted him about smoking. I took the knife and proved to him that I could still tackle him to the floor if I had to. That didn't help because he thought he was so tough.

Therapist: Is that how you hurt your knee?

Mother: No. Ever since his father and I divorced, Steven wanted to be with his dad not me. My second husband was abusive, so that didn't help either.

Therapist: How old is he now?

Mother: Sixteen. He's been home for a week. I realize how glad I am that he's living with his dad. I've paid law fines. We've gone to court over him hitting a teacher. I mean, you name it, we've done it with him. I've had to pay all those fines myself. Now his dad is paying them. I'm not stuck with him anymore!

Parents of defiant children tolerate tremendous disrespect and abuse until a point at which even they can't rationalize their child's behavior. The crisis may be of grand proportions, or a seemingly trivial "straw that breaks the camel's back." In this case, mother had tolerated disrespect and embarrassment until her son became too threatening. The therapist was very matter-of-fact in her questioning even though the material was explosive. The need to understand the sequences of crises in defiant families leads to several important questions. Why is the crisis occurring now? What has triggered the motivation for action?

AMBIVALENCE ABOUT PARENTING

During the middle stage of therapy it is important to get parents to share their own upbringing and ambivalence about parenting. All adults have ambivalence about themselves as parents. Are they doing a good job? Are they teaching their children the skills necessary to survive in the world? Are they too strict, too lenient, too naive? The therapist can share bits and pieces of her own parenting ambivalence when appropriate.

Case Example: Acknowledging Ambivalence

The therapist encourages father to talk about his ambivalence about parenting. This is critical to understanding the quandary father feels.

Therapist: When you question yourself about how you're doing as a dad, how do you question yourself?

Father: Well, I guess everybody wants their kid to grow up and be the all-American kid. You know, go to college, get your degree, etc.

Therapist: I did until I found out about how some all-American kids turned out.

Father: That's right, there's no guarantee that things will turn out. I didn't go to college. I work as a shop rat. I'm just an everyday blue-collar guy. I look at my daughter (*points to Paula*), and I wish that she had finished college. You know, we borrowed money to get her through. She didn't make it and that disappoints me as a dad. Was there something more that I could have done? Should I have made her stay home? She wanted to go to college away from home, and I wanted her to go to a local campus and live at home. You don't really know what's going to happen, but you want your kids to be successful. I'm successful. I have a job, I go to work everyday, I make all my bills, I'm not in trouble with the law, I go to church. To me, that's successful. Money isn't necessarily successful. Sometimes things are out of my hands. But I consider myself to be successful.

Therapist: I was asking about the other side, though. When you worry how you're doing as a father how do you worry about yourself? You were saying that maybe you hadn't done enough for your daughter. That may be part of it, but I'm really interested in your worry about how you're doing as a parent. (*Father has avoided or misunderstood the point of the question about parenting.*)

Father; Oh, yeah, I worry about it, but I realize that she's free to do what she wants. I can't force her to go back to school now. I've told her many times, "You know, you don't want to be a hamburger flipper all of your life." The jobs like I have aren't out there anymore. There aren't any decent paying jobs out there unless you've got that degree. Nonetheless, it's still the kids' decision about what they want to do.

Therapist: (*To cotherapist*) This family reminds me of another family that had a catastrophe fantasy behind how they lived. Life was OK except they were worried about something in the background. (*To mother*) It's not unlike this thing that happened with your brother, who died tragically a generation back. It colors how you live in the present. It's as if you are afraid somebody else is going to die. (*To mother*) How did your brother's death affect you, do you think?

The therapist drops the exploration with father after approaching the topic twice and being unsuccessful in getting him to talk about his ambivalence. Father says he worries about being a father but, cannot elaborate on his fears. If parents can't be ambivalent about their role, it says a lot about their parenting relationship. Either they don't allow themselves the possibility of making a mistake, they are overly sure of their parenting, or they can't acknowledge mistakes due to their insecurity as a parent. In defiant families, this pattern of self-protection makes risk taking difficult. Questioning one's interactions with one's children is a healthy endeavor. The cotherapist asks mother about issues relating to her parenting.

Cotherapist: What makes you feel the most cornered, Mom?

Mother: Cornered?

Cotherapist: If you were making a list of the things that pressured you, what is it that corners you?

Mother: (*Wipes her eyes*) I don't know.

Cotherapist: Or maybe, what makes you feel like a failure is the fact your kids have double-crossed you and grown up?

Mother: (*Laughs*) Maybe that's it.

Cotherapist: It's not a small deal, actually.

Mother: Yeah, because I was always home with them when they were little.

Both parents wonder where they went wrong with their children. They do not have words for their ambivalence, but hopefully they will be in touch with it as therapy progresses. All parents experience it. In the next illustration there is a provocative tone in the therapeutic question to the mother. There is an assumption that parents secretly admire the independence of their children as long as it isn't turned on them. Parents and children fulfill each others' needs.

Therapist: Do you ever catch yourself kind of liking the way your daughter gets you mad?

Mother: No. I don't like getting worked up. She'll get me to the point where I'm just shaking, and I don't know what to do and I end up just locking myself in my room. One day she looked at me with these eyes that scared the hell out of me and said, 'You better sleep with your eyes open tonight.' I looked at her with those eyes and thought, 'Oh, shit, I'm locking the bedroom door tonight.' (*Laughs*)

Therapist: Do you ever wonder what you could have done differently as a parent?

Mother: I wonder about it every day!

In this case the mother is able to look at her parenting. She is not having the type of relationship with her daughter she envisioned and the defiance is more than she can handle. It is terrifying to have her daughter threaten her and worse yet to fear that she might get hurt. Mother's laughter creates ambiguity and confuses meaning for the therapist. In this case mother's laughter expresses her ambivalence. This could be related to anxiety or a desire to prevent us from taking action against her daughter. In the latter case, she is protecting her daughter even though she feels threatened by her. Attending to this underlying dynamic is important because it connects the two generations.

Mature parents recognize slivers of themselves in their children. Some of their own childhood anguish returns in their interactions with their children. It is a good prognostic sign when parents can embrace the bad boy or bad girl in themselves. It helps keep the child included, which is life saving in desperate situations. When confronted with the question, "What were you like when you were her age?" parents may respond, "Sure, I did dumb things, everybody does." That isn't good enough. It is too impersonal to be of any help. Questions such as, "We aren't talking about everybody here. We're talking about you and your life. What did you do? Is there a story? What did your parents end up thinking about it?" encourage parents to tell a story about what happened. The pathological aspect of this territory is that the parent unconsciously induces the child into doing something and then hammers the child for it.

Case Example: The Sins of the Past

Mother expresses her fear about her children.

Therapist: How about you when you were her age? What were you like when you were 12?

Mother: Oh, I was a terror. I set the dog on fire to see if his fur would burn. I was terrible.

Therapist: How much did it burn?

Mother: Oh, not much before Mom came out with the yardstick yelling, 'Get away from him!' (*Family laughs.*) Yeah, I was a show-off.

Therapist: Mom was worried about the gasoline, I suppose.

Mother: No, I was burning the garbage and had a stick that I caught on fire and I set it down next to the dog. Yeah, I was a terror. I burned the back yard, because I walked away from the burn barrel while it was burning one day. We're out there with garden hoses trying to put my dad's back yard out (*Family laughs*). Yeah, I was bad. I threw a kitchen knife at a neighbor. She was mad because we went up in one of my dad's apple trees and tore the bark completely off the tree. She yelled at us, so I whipped the knife at her. I wasn't a good kid.

Therapist: So your kids come by it naturally.

Mother: I've never told my children that I hope they have kids just like them, because I was told that and I don't want kids just like me—or, I mean, grandchildren just like me. These guys are just like me. Why do you think I worry about them so much?

Parents worry whether their parenting skills are at fault. Ambivalence about parenting is a normal reaction that requires exploration. Often they are fearful that their children will have the same difficulties they experienced growing up, or worse. Being able to talk about these issues can be healing.

Growth and development for defiant families is a spiral leading toward health. In the middle stage the therapist is watchful for what makes a particular family vulnerable. During therapy family strengths and healthy options unfold. Well-being emerges in small steps as the family deepens their involvement in the process. There is rarely a flight into health. Rather, smaller changes occur: parents might be less reactive; there is a change in the quality of the parenting, marital, or sibling relationships; or someone in the family *doesn't go* to prison or end up on probation. Moving slowly can be frustrating for a therapist who is looking for major shifts in the family group. Defiant families travel in circles in an upward spiral toward a healthy family life. As experience increases, the therapist develops the ability to notice small shifts in the family. In the earlier example, T.J., who had felt free to insult the therapist and his parents and walked out near the end of the session, came back in and said, "Thanks, Doc!" This is not a dramatic difference, but a slight change in attitude. Small changes start to accumulate when noticed.

Katie's family is affected by poverty. The children are teased and called names in school. They are assumed to be like their delinquent, acting-out older brother. Mother's inability to protect them and a history of physical abuse by her second husband further stress family integrity. The problems are overwhelming. In Chris's family, father's PTSD and subsequent violent outbursts, poverty, the large number of children, mother's parenting in the absence of the father, the older sons' delinquent behavior, and alcohol and drug abuse all contribute to the members' vulnerability around attachment in the family. Assessing which vulnerabilities to address is critical during this stage. Issues like persistent poverty are complicated and likely to continue during the course of therapy. They are important to acknowledge as stressful experiences that make it harder to trust that everything will be all right. The therapist should acknowledge the limits of the therapeutic process for specific problems and focus on issues beneath the daily grind.

MIDDLE STAGE TECHNIQUES

This section presents a few of the techniques appropriate for use in the middle stage of therapy with defiant families. The list is by no means exhaustive. Defiant families respond to maneuvers that shift the balance of power, disrupt the status quo, and exaggerate problems.

Side Taking

Side taking is a technique used to disrupt family behavior. When family conflict remains unresolved, siding with one member creates an imbalance which may increase the intensity of affect and develop momentum for resolution (Connell & Russell, 1986). Side taking often leads to an escalation of conflict and an increase in affect. We recommend gathering the following information before taking a side: (a) a description of the conflict between family members, (b) an assessment of the family's perception of the causes of the conflict, (c) an understanding of the current strategies used in conflict resolution, and (d) an understanding of the positive and negative effects of the conflict on the family system. It is essential for side taking to be an honest expression of the therapist's emotional experience.

During side taking the therapist supports or challenges a speaker's statement of information, interpretation, or opinion. For example, the therapist may agree with an 18-year-old adolescent who says his parents are too controlling by saying, "I agree. Parents who try to control older adolescents make a serious mistake. Your independence should be respected even if you make stupid choices like you do." Or to the 12-year-old daughter who is complaining about the rule regarding cleaning her room, the therapist might say, "Life is not fair. As long as you're living at home, you'll have rules you don't like. Who said you'd have an equal say in things?" or "You'll have to wait until you have your own kids before you can get even with your mother."

Side taking challenges the belief that a therapist should be neutral. The therapist appreciates the similarities and differences of family members without pretending to be accepting of all behaviors or attitudes. In the middle stage of therapy, if there is an intimate connection, the therapist's opinion carries weight. The therapist should use her influences to unsettle the status quo judiciously.

In the following example, the therapist is appalled at Chris's behavior. Rather than minimizing her response, she chooses to highlight the issue. She sides with the parents in their disgust with their son's behavior.

Therapist: What else is going on that makes you want to split?

Chris: The fact that you need a wrench to take a shower. Nothing is ever clean; my clothes are always dirty. It drives me nuts.

Father: I have to step in on that because when I walked in this morning the first thing that confronted me was Chris's clothes thrown exactly where he took them off.

Mother: His clothes and socks were thrown right in front of the TV.

Chris: Yeah but . . .

Father: Yeah but, you have to understand that it takes everybody in the family. You can't blame the shape of the house on your mom. The reason you have to use a wrench to take a shower is because you guys abuse things and they get broken. We don't have a lot of money to keep replacing the things that you guys break. It gets tough. You have to pay for part of those consequences.

Therapist: True.

Father: Look at your room—it's a perfect example.

Chris: Look at any teenager's room and it would be the same.

Father; Yeah a little mess, but . . .

Therapist: The boy needs a maid, what can we say?

Father: Yeah, but putting cigarettes out on the floor? Come on! Putting snot on the wall!

Therapist: Yuck! What was the snot—blowing snot on your hand and then wiping it on the wall? What was that?

Chris: I had a stuffy nose and I went to try to wipe my nose and clean my hand so I went like that (*flicked hand*). Rather than going around like (*wipes nose and flicks hand*) throwing it at people.

Therapist: But don't you think that's unacceptable? Blowing snot on the wall—where are the limits? You make yourself sound so innocent!

Father: I think part of that comes from watching TV (*laughing slightly*) you know?

Therapist: That's no excuse. For God's sake, he's 16-years-old. You mean to tell me you've seen his behavior on TV? Give me a break!

Father: You know the Simpsons, some of the things the Simpsons have done are gross.

Therapist: (*Humorously*) Well, I think he shouldn't watch stuff like that until he's older if that's the case.

Mother: I have fought for years because I don't allow watching the Simpsons or Beavis and Butthead, and I come home and they are on.

Therapist: Terrific, we can blame the Simpsons for him blowing snot on the wall. What do you think (*to Jenn, Chris's girlfriend*)? From what I understand, you are the one who cleaned it up.

Jenn: (*Laughing*) It didn't bother me. I am an aunt so I am used to that kind of stuff.

Therapist: Are you? How old are the other children?

Chris: I didn't know she cleaned it up.

Jenn: All I know is that I didn't see him do it. Missy came running to me and said 'Jenn! Chris just put snot on the wall!' She was like screaming about it.

Therapist: She was completely grossed out by it, as well she should be.

Jenn: I thought it was funny.

Therapist: He complains about the place being a pigpen. Well, if you don't want a pigpen, don't blow snot on the wall! I agree with your parents, you've got to assume some responsibility for the mess.

The therapist is disgusted with Chris's behavior and lets him know there are no acceptable excuses—it is just plain gross. She confronts Chris and sides with the parents' assessment of the situation. Father makes excuses for his son, and the therapist challenges him as well. She doesn't want to let Chris off the hook. Siding with the parents gives their point of view more credibility. It lets the children know that another adult finds the behavior disgusting. Chris is being gross and complaining about the mess at the house, clearly ignoring his part in the predicament. Everybody blames someone else, including the television, scapegoat in this process of scapegoat rotation!

Use of Humor and Irony

Play and humor are essential ingredients during this stage of therapy. They are means of disrupting process with spontaneity. Playfulness lowers defenses and invites primary process into the interaction. It can also be a method of maintaining a nonanxious presence. Humor is a kind of play with adults and adolescents that it can produce feelings or thoughts of absurdity while bypassing the need for reason or logic. Play keeps the therapist from being cornered by the family's horror. Winnicott said, "Psychotherapy is play. Where playing . . . is not possible, then work done by the therapist is directed toward bringing the patient from a state of not being able to play into a state of being able to play" (Winnicott, 1971, p. 38).

Introducing playfulness by teasing somebody or pretending to be their mother is consistently useful in working with defiant families. It softens the concreteness so prevalent in these families that tends to push the therapist into being concrete. Introducing small doses of playfulness early during this stage helps measure the spontaneity or inflexibility of the family. Members of defiant families often have little ability to play with each other. They find little humor in their daily lives and believe therapy is a time to talk about problems. Defiant families are metaphorolytic, especially in regard to their children, as they prefer things to be clear and to have only one meaning. This is part of the pathology. The monotony of crisis or out-of-control behavior has become the norm. The therapist's job is to avoid being stymied by family members concreteness and to teach them to be more playful. This attitude of playfulness is crucial. For example, in the next illustration, the therapist is trying to engage the 4-year-old daughter who comforts her mother throughout the session. The therapist is worried that the child is afraid of her. Teasing breaks the ice and also says to the family that serious family issues can be discussed without deadliness.

Therapist: (*To Mom*) Maybe it is because I look like such an old grouch. (*Family laughs*) Maybe she thinks I eat little girls for breakfast. (*Daughter hides her head in mother's shoulder*) I already had breakfast so you don't need to worry.

Play materials also have an important function in therapy. They can help to soothe and engage children who are bored or too young to participate. They also allow such children to be part of the process without disrupting it. Because adults gravitate toward puppets or blocks to play with their children, it is helpful to keep a play house, dolls, small cars, puppets, drawing material, books, and blocks out for easy access. When children are bored, restless, or anxious with adult conversation, the therapist can offer them something to do to remain in the session and manage their own feelings. Younger children can become disruptive when issues heat up or topics shift into toxic areas. They are keenly aware of family issues on an experiential level and thus serve as affect barometers. When intense issues come up early during the middle stage of therapy, there is often a need for a bathroom break.

Humor is a form of play. With younger children the therapist may use toys, draw pictures, or play with puppets, but with adolescents and adults play often involves play on words and humor. Ironic humor is a form of play that increases ambiguity in a way that enriches perception and interaction. If one looks at a Picasso painting of a person from his abstract period, she might say, "That's stupid—it doesn't look like a person." But if she looks at it and focuses on it, the distortion of art adds to the way she sees the actual person. Distortion enriches the way individuals see the world. Play and irony may be disorienting at first because they temporarily disrupt our view of the world but they can ultimately be pleasurable and exciting.

Play connotes a carefree oscillation and a quality of being engaged or committed. It also involves a quality of intimacy that is private and fun. Bateson's story about the monkeys at the San Diego Zoo whose ferocious combat never results in any injuries is appropriate here. The monkeys are responding to some premonitory signal that says, "this is play and not for real." Bateson thought of psychotherapy in the same way. All human emotions can be experienced in that microcosm of living—the therapy room. There is an aspect of the experience which says, "this is not for real." The feelings have the same intensity they would in a real situation, but the implications are not the same (Bateson, 1972). "What is characteristic of 'play' is that this is a name for contexts in which constituent acts have a different sort of relevance and organization from what they would have had in non-play. It may even be that the essence of play lies in a partial denial of meaning that the actions would have had in other situations" (Bateson, 1979, p. 125).

The therapist also capitalizes on silly or absurd things that happen in therapy. For instance, a family with several acting-out-adolescents is having a session. The adolescents are being uncooperative and, at times, verbally belligerent, despite attempts to involve them in the discussion. The therapist stands up to shift positions only to find her skirt is rolled up in the wheel of the chair. As she falls into her chair and wonders how she is going to get her skirt unstuck she says, "Wow, I'm sure this inspires confidence in my ability to be helpful!" The family begins laughing and one of the adolescents helps her unwind her skirt. It's important to have such an ability to laugh at oneself and to appear human to the family. Like any good stand-up comedian, the therapist used improvisation that catches on. Families need to experience the therapist as a kindred spirit in order for collaboration to be a possibility.

The therapist might play a game or play with puppets with younger children while parents either join in or watch. Younger children need to be included on the level at which they are capable of participating. They are part of the family dynamics. Frequently they have strong reactions to interactions they observe. One little boy with an explosive father said during puppet play, "I don't want to be the daddy because daddies are too scary." Both parents had minimized father's temper and its impact on their son's behavior. The topic came up spontaneously during play without cornering either parent in a confession.

It is important to comment on positive behavior children exhibit. Parents of disruptive children lose sight of the fact that their children do cooperate and behave appropriately, even if they do so rarely. The therapist can model alternate ways for parents to handle acting out that occurs in the session.

A few words of caution are necessary about the use of play. Play is a strong drug that must be used judiciously by experienced practitioners. With rigid families, it must be used carefully and in small doses, not because it is harmful to them, but because play in large doses too soon can allow them to dismiss the therapist and the therapeutic process. Play methods should not be used when the therapist is too anxious. Problems can result if the therapist gets too carried away, too high, too sadistic or too rigidly involved with the play, or if she becomes unable to straddle play and reality at the same time. Play is not used to diminish the family's anxiety. In fact, play is effective in increasing the interpersonal anxiety in the family required to give momentum to the change process (Whitaker & Keith, 1981).

Challenging Roles

Challenging roles is another technique of this middle stage. It involves punctuating or highlighting roles played by family members, then challenging members to alter their roles. Rigidly fixed roles are problematic. When the freedom to explore roles is dormant, family members are restricted from their full development. They are locked into constraining ways of interacting. When the parenting role is ineffective or absent, the family is at risk for one of the children assuming this role and, in due course, holding the family hostage.

Case Example: Mother Held Hostage

Mike was a 10-year-old referred for family therapy due to aggressive behavior at home. His parents were divorced, and he had minimal contact with his father. Mother had a series of boyfriends, all of whom Mike despised, who eventually abandoned them. During the initial session he screamed at his mother, stating his Social Security checks should be his to spend as he wanted. He berated her employment, saying if it weren't for his money they'd be in big trouble. Mother was embarrassed by her son's allegations. She placated in an attempt to quiet him down. She didn't set any limits, choosing to yield to his covert threat of "I'll hate you if you don't do as I please." To complicate matters, Mike had severe asthma. His temper outbursts frequently ended in an asthma attack, whereupon she would give in to his demands in order to restore his health. The pattern of the son ruling the household was firmly entrenched.

Following the initial session, Mike refused to come back. Mother called to say she was not able to force him to attend that day's session. The therapist could hear Mike threatening and screaming in the background. She wondered with mother who she could call to assist her in her attempt to be in charge. Perhaps she could call her father, a brother, or even the police. Whoever she chose, clearly she was going to need assistance. The mother hung up and did not make the meeting.

The next session mother brought Mike's cousin (Charlie) with them. They were the same age, played together, and attended the same school. The therapist invited Charlie into the session, and he agreed to participate. The meeting began with the therapist asking what on earth was happening in this family, commenting that the fighting overheard on the phone had to be brutal for everyone. Was Mike trying to win a contest for the loudest kid on the block or did he have to be that out-of-control to get his way? Charlie laughed and said Mike always gets his way when he acts like that. The therapist asked Charlie what happened at his house when he acted like Mike. Charlie quickly stated he would never act like that because he'd get into too much trouble. He'd probably be grounded or lose his Nintendo game. Whatever the consequence, it wouldn't be good.

The therapist asked, in reference to how arguments were settled in the household, "Who usually won?" Mike and Charlie looked at each other and the cousin pointed to Mike. Mom agreed that Mike was a fierce adversary. He was willing to carry on for hours, and she was afraid of what the neighbors would think. Mike was locked in the role of the family tyrant while mother was an ineffective parent. She worried that if she set limits, Mike would have a temper tantrum. She was afraid of his obvious defiance. As the session progressed, it became apparent that many of Mike's asthma attacks were staged for mother's benefit. He was, in fact, having few real attacks, but he became skilled at faking them. Mother was appalled. How could she tell whether the attacks were real or staged?

The therapist suggested that perhaps if Mike knew she was not going to give in to his demands, his temper tantrums and asthma attacks would decrease. She might tell the neighbors that they may hear more outbursts coming from her house as she worked on holding firm with her limits. Maybe she could get a stethoscope and listen to his breathing. She thought that might work. If she suspected Mike was faking, she thought he should lose a privilege or pay a fine. The cousin said if he were around, he could tell when Mike was faking. Mike glared at his mother during the discussion, daring her to try anything new. The therapist told the mother she would know that she was on the right track if Mike actually got worse as she asserted her parenting role. After all, she was good at setting limits in other parts of her life.

Role assignments in families are powerful. Roles may be challenged by inquiring about opposite behaviors. For example, to a mother with an aggressive adolescent the therapist might say, "Tell me about a time when your son made a mistake and did something nice for someone." To the acting-out 13-year-old female who professes to hate her sister, one might ask, "In what ways do you envy your sister?" There is a reciprocal relationship to adversarial role pairings that deserves exploration. The defiant child is locked into a particular way of being, despite behaviors that suggest otherwise. Parents overlook normal interactions because the negative ones are so hideous. Identifying the roles family members play is grist for the therapy mill. Expanding those roles facilitates development.

Challenging roles, particularly the parenting role, should be done with the notion of empowering the parents. It is important that the parents not lose face in front of children who already have the upper hand. Reestablishing the parents' authority will help rebalance the family system and return the children to the proper generational status. By predicting problems beforehand, the therapist helps the parents not feel defeated when the child's negative behavior escalates. After all, it means they are having an effect on the child's behavior. Remaining consistent in the face of adversity is the problem. Parents are encouraged to avoid power struggles with the child unless they are prepared to win.

Case Example: Playing with Role Assignments

The therapist challenges Missy about her role as parent to mother. He plays with the notion that she is a nice mother when mother comes home after drinking. Missy is angry at mother for drinking and would like to punish her. Since father has moved out, Missy is fearful about mother's ability to take care of them and no one is getting along.

Therapist: So, what's happening when you're not getting along? Is your father fighting with Mom? Are your brothers fighting?

Missy: I'm fighting with Mom.

Therapist: Oh yeah, what do you like to fight with her about?

Missy: I don't know. She gets on my nerves sometimes. She yells at me because I complain about her breath when she comes home. She smells like beer.

Therapist: Do you have to check her breath?

Missy: No, she breathes on me when she comes to kiss me goodnight, so I smell it.

Therapist: So, do you ground her for a couple of nights?

Missy: No, she grounds me just for saying something about it.

Therapist: So, you try to be her mother and she gets mad at you?

Missy: No.

Therapist: But you scold her.

Missy: No, I say please get away because I'm going to puke from it.

Therapist: So, you are trying to be a nice mother?

Missy: No, I'm not her mother.

Therapist: But if she's out being naughty, you need to check up on her.

Missy: We have some fun sometimes, too.

Therapist: So, you are a nice mother.

Missy: I'm not her mother!

Therapist: Well, I think you are. It sounds like you are part mother and Kevin is part father. It is not a bad thing to do. We parents like it sometimes when our kids take over. It is how you learn how to be a grown up.

Mother's drinking is scary to all of the children. It is a topic that needs discussion in time, but first the role of parent is played with to set up the structure of who is the mother. The therapist is also exploring the family members' ability to flip roles to nurture each other. This dialogue about the parentified child being the mother occurs often. Sometimes the child agrees she is the mother, sometimes she rejects the idea, like Missy does. What is interesting is how often this flips the parents back into the correct generation. They see themselves and their behavior in a new light. In this particular interview, the mother had been going through an adolescent period, partly out of her anger with her husband for leaving and being unhelpful. As a result of this interaction, one week later mother reported starting to set limits with her children. She explained to them that she would not always do things that made them comfortable, but that it was her life and she would take responsibility for it.

Challenging roles is an essential strategy in the middle stage. The goal is to expand the roles family members play and to assist them in being more flexible.

The use of humor and irony can facilitate this endeavor and empower the parents to assert their authority.

Deviation Amplification

Deviation amplification is a playful paradoxical maneuver used to generate anxiety in the family with the goal of disrupting the status quo. Family members are locked into static positions which thwart the search for new options. An impasse results once this entrenched position is solidified. With this technique, the therapist exaggerates the prevailing family perspective by predicting outlandish consequences for continued behavior. Another variation is for the therapist to jump to a tragic outcome they fear but do so with nonchalance. The therapist's task is clear: to push the family into new territory where current viewpoints and behaviors appear absurd. The therapist might agree with the parent of a defiant child by saying, "Would you prefer to go to the Youth Detention Center in town, or the one in Pittsburgh? Then you should start thinking about what prison you would like to go to when you reach 18. You could go to Attica because it is close to home. Then your Mom could visit. I hear there is a new maximum security prison in Wisconsin that sounds real nice. You get your own cell, but you aren't allowed to see any other prisoner, which I would like. I would hate to eat and lift weights with a bunch of creeps." This exaggerated perspective pushes the parent into a stance of "I don't think I've really tried everything. I can't send my child to jail." The paralyzing mythology of the family is then ruptured.

The intent of this technique is to disrupt the habituated family process by giving voice to the unspoken mode of operating. How the family members react to the maneuver or reorganize is up to them. The objective is to disrupt their normal style of operating. Rigid patterns take on a ridiculous quality in the face of this technique. The therapist attempts to bring about more creative problem solving within the group. For instance, in one family where the three older adolescent sons were all smoking pot and drinking, the therapist asked, "When do you guys think you'll ask your younger brother to join you in the woods for his first pot smoking lesson?" The brothers were furious at the suggestion—they didn't want him to start at all. Or to the teenage girl who was shoplifting one might say, "Why are you stealing such small stuff? It's hardly worth going to jail for that. Why don't you steal a fur or something? I heard about this family in Minnesota who worked as a team and made $300,000." These types of comments confuse the family. They are not sure if the therapist is serious. The situation is magnified, creating a distorted image. It is surely an uncomfortable narration. The key is to develop a representation that confuses the family so they can't continue the way they have been going. The more absurd the picture, the higher the confusion and the better the likelihood of disrupting the status quo. This technique serves as another way to encourage the family to take themselves more seriously.

SUMMARY

The middle stage of therapy has unique problems, such as the family sabotaging the therapist's effort to help, escalating crises, parents' inability to tolerate increased anxiety or acting out as they assert their parenting role. Other family issues, such as marital dysfunction or parental depression, may also come to the forefront. Techniques such as side taking, use of humor, deviation amplification, and challenging roles are useful in disrupting the status quo. Stimulating the family initiative during this stage is crucial to the family's growth.

7

The Heart of Therapy: A Middle Phase Interview

Dr. Carl began working with this family in bits and pieces two years earlier. He had done extensive individual and marital therapy with the parents. Dr. Owen is a consultant, who has seen the family periodically with Dr. Carl. Father, Mark (age 47), is a Vietnam veteran who was wounded in combat. He received treatment for marijuana addiction and post traumatic stress disorder (PSTD) in Veterans Administration facilities. Mother, Judy is age 43. In the past 6 months she has been a defiant parent. She is a weekly regular at a local bar, she had a one-night-stand with a professional athlete, and she had a brief affair with a man who lived with her and the children for 2 weeks. The parents were separated when Mark was away in Boston for 5 months of treatment for PSTD. There are five children: three boys, Greg (age 19), Chris (age 16), and Doug (age 15) and two girls: Missy (age 11), and Kelly (age 4). All three boys are on probation. Greg spent the last year living with mother's sister Mary and did well. Greg's girlfriend, Jenn, also attends the session. Dr. Carl is the therapist and sees the family regularly. This interview is a combination of a therapy interview and a consultation interview.

Dr. Carl: (*To Dr. Owen*) Where do we start today?

Dr. Owen: Wherever they are.

At the beginning as therapists we are light on their feet. Our minds are set at a metaphorical level, to test the meaning of what we hear as well as what we say. We don't follow details very carefully, but feel highly attentive, lightly ironic. Dr. Owen is not trying to understand them; he is focusing on himself as he listens to them. He feels centered and his awareness of the family is intense. At the beginning of the session, we are attuned to the metaphorical/process level. History, complaints, or social conversation are heard as the embodiment of metaphorical themes. We don't settle into one issue or assume responsibility for the direction of the session.

Mother: If no one has any objections, I would like to bring up the fact that yesterday while leaving the fair I picked up Doug and he definitely looked like he was on something, so I smelled his hands and he was smoking pot again last night.

Dr. Owen: So he is devoted to being a bad boy.

The family had a session yesterday, so it was meaningful that Doug would have misbehaved last night. He is a dedicated bad boy. Playful irony establishes a theme about the covert conditions inherent in the family. Why would that be so? Could it be that he is attempting to relieve mother of her sins? He is pushing her into action so that she will not need to spend time obsessing about the children being angry with her.

Mother: All of a sudden, he kept trying to hide himself from me. He kept walking way ahead of me, wouldn't let me look at him, going around in circles.

Doug: I turned around. I wasn't going around in circles.

Mother: Yes, you were when you were with that group, you took off the other way afraid I was going to get you.

Doug: That's because I thought you parked over . . .

Greg and Chris: (*in unison*) Busted.

Mother: I was parked over by the . . .

Greg: (*To mother*) I remember hiding from you when I was stoned.

Father: I don't know anything about this.

Mother: I didn't get a chance to tell you this morning. I got him home at 11 o'clock last night. Normally he would have argued with me when I said it was time to go, but he didn't. He took off ahead of me. The second clue was when I asked him to go out and bring the dog in. 'All Right,' he said, real quick.

Doug: I complained about the dog—I was in my boxers.

Dr. Owen: One clue that he had been a bad boy was that he was being so agreeable.

Mother: Yes.

Dr. Owen: He is not that good at being a bad boy.

Doug is responsive and engaged—a hopeful prognostic sign. Doug attempts to balance the dynamics because when he is too angelic his brothers become enraged with him. It appears he is not overly committed to the defiant role.

Mother: Not him, no. The other two, if they are bad, they get worse attitudes, but not Doug.

Father: All I've got to say to that, Doug, is that you know that if your probation officer has the least little bit of suspicion, you are going to get a drug test and for the next 30 days you're going to have to sweat it out.

Greg: Longer than that. I heard they have a new machine that can tell if you've smoked pot in the last 2 months. They'll bust you for sure.

Dr. Owen: (*To mother*) Then what happens?

Mother: He has deferred placement to a group home.

Greg: They told me when I was on probation if I failed my urine test I had a deferred placement too.

Doug: They told me the first time you get caught you have to pay like $50.00 charity, or something. The second time is big trouble.

Greg: You haven't failed one yet, but you have been in a lot of trouble—more trouble than me.

Mother: Greg got his community service done quickly.

Greg: (*To Doug*) You've only got two hours done and you have been on probation for almost a year.

Mother: That's right, he could be off now.

Doug: I've been on almost 2 years.

Dr. Carl: Why now do you think? What is going on now?

This is always a useful question. However, the family is not sophisticated enough to take it in, and it passes. Yet, this kind of question seeds the family unconscious and suggests, in effect, that the members consider another way of thinking.

Father: I think it's who he is hanging out with.

Mother: I think he still has a choice. This started before the fair, buddy.

Greg: I think Doug's best friend is off probation and he gets high every day. He's always afraid to come in the house. He asks, 'Do you think your mom will notice anything?' His eyes are all blood shot.

Mother: I notice.

Greg: He is stupid

Mother: Who, Doug?

Greg: She doesn't even yell at him.

Dr. Owen: (*To Chris*) Do you have any idea why this is happening to him now?

Chris: I think it's who he hangs out with, too.

Dr. Owen goes back to the question of, "Why now? Why do you think he is doing this now?" He has been the least troublesome of the boys. This is costly to him because the others resent his goodness. He feels pressured by being good and becomes the subject of sibling ridicule. Dr. Owen asks Chris because he has not participated today. Yesterday he was insightful. This question acknowledges his ability to contribute and includes him as consulting cotherapist, rather than as typical scapegoat.

Greg: He thinks it makes him cool. That's what I used to think about cigarettes. Now I don't.

Dr. Owen: (*To Greg*) My fantasy is that he feels too pressured about being good. Being the good boy gets too much ridicule.

Mother: Of the three boys he is the easiest.

(Doug looks uneasy)

Dr. Carl: I think that's true. A few weeks ago, he was feeling so much pressure he was having chest pains and went for a complete work up. Nothing was wrong with his heart—just stress. I think that is some of the reason why he is so protected by his mom and dad.

This is a fascinating mind/body connection. Doug is pressured by the context and it shows up in his chest. This is another good prognostic sign, for Doug at least. It suggests that he internalizes conflict. Psychosomatic symptoms suggest that he is still invested in the family.

Greg: Protected? What does that mean?

Mother: Protected.

Greg: Oh, you mean how you isolate him—you don't yell at him. You bust our asses and Doug can get away with anything he wants—because he is Mom and Dad's little boy.

Doug: I just take it.

Mother: He doesn't jump at us.

Greg: (*Sarcastically*) Oh, Doug, you're high. You are grounded for 2 days. God damn it Greg, get the "F" out of the house.

Mother: Like I have said that.

Greg: What do you think, Dad? (*Greg looks to Dad for support*) Look at Dad laugh.

Father: Pretty close I'd say.

Mother: I don't use that word.

Greg: Anything I do, you say, 'You're getting kicked out—pack your stuff.'

Kelly: No, you say that, Greg.

Greg: I tell Mom to pack her stuff?

Kelly: No, you say that you're going to pack up and get out of the house. You say you're getting out of this house.

Mother: He uses that as a threat on me, doesn't he Kelly?

Greg: After you say, 'I'll kick you out.' What am I supposed to say—I am moving to the guest house?

Mother: I don't use the work "kick." I say you are making your choices, Greg.

Greg: You said that before. I swear Mom that is your solution for everything—just kick me out, that will solve everything.

Mother: I don't feel it but everybody else feels it. It must be that.

Mother seems different in this interview. The angel mask she wore in earlier interviews has swung loose. In an earlier interview, she was disturbed by the children's upset with her. Here they are coming after her and she is tolerating it well. In an earlier consultation interview, Dr. Owen told her that she could not be a success as a patient until she learned the joy of being hated by her children. Has she learned the fun of being hated? Have she and father formed enough of a partnership so that she does not feel perpetually in danger of being bushwhacked by him? That would make it easier for her to tolerate anger from the children. This comment is a symptom of her emerging maturity. The therapists don't comment on it because it would interrupt what the family is doing. It would detract from an important family interaction and interfere with their initiative. It would also impede the flow of an important metadiscussion.

Greg: Jenn, when I make her mad, what's the first thing she says to me?

Jenn: I haven't been around that long.

Dr. Owen: What does he think you say?

Greg: She kicks me out . . .

Dr. Owen: Who?

Greg: My mom—that is her solution for anything I do.

Dr. Owen: If you get your mom to kick you out, can you go live at her house? (*To mother*) Do you know her mom?

Dr. Owen is presenting an option that is playful and serious. It leads to thinking in sequence. If Greg can get mother to kick him out, then he can innocently ask his girlfriend if he can stay at her house. Early in the session, it's best not to get too focused. Greg brought his 16-year-old girlfriend, Jenn, at the therapist' suggestion. It was surprising he brought her and even more surprising she agreed to come. She is a fairly straight, careful adolescent—a surprising partner for him.

Mother: We went to school together.

Dr. Owen: (*To Greg*) You ought to get a girlfriend that doesn't know your mother and then you could tell her how awful your mother is. 'The poor thing. You can come smoke dope at my house.'

Jenn: I don't think so.

Dr. Owen: So your mother wouldn't agree.

Jenn: No

Mother: She gets on Greg's case, which I think is wonderful.

Dr. Owen: So you knew her mom when you were in high school.

Mother: She was in my kindergarten class and third grade up.

Dr. Carl: (*To Dad*) How do you explain mom's relationship with the kids? They all seem to see her as a real tyrant, yet she doesn't see herself that way.

Father: The times that I have seen her go off—yeah, she's real mad.

Dr. Carl: You feel like she really does get to be a tyrant.

Dad: Well, only when the right buttons are pushed. She will start out trying to be tactful, diplomatic— then watch out!

Doug: (*To Dad*) Why do you say that? You might not even know what the word means.

Dr. Owen: That's a little disrespectful.

Chris: Doug is always picking on Dad.

Father: Yeah, sometimes I think she goes a little overboard when her anger catches up with her.

Dr. Owen: It sounds to me that when it happens, it galvanizes everybody against her. That is probably why she sounds like a tyrant, but she is not effective as one.

Father: I think especially the boys know that they can get her to a point, then all of a sudden it's all Mom's fault because she is totally out of control. She is ranting and raving and screaming. Subconsciously I think they know that, and subconsciously they feed on it.

We engaged Chris earlier for his comments on the relationship, so he feels he has permission to comment again. The children are divided. Doug is mother's partner. Greg tends to persecute mother and overlook father's sins. Our guess is that he learned it from father. Dr. Owen suggests the family is united by mother's anger and, in fact, they attempt to elicit it so that she will crumble. They corner her so that she can explode, then blame her. She sounds like a tyrant, but is ineffective in her parenting. Dr. Carl engages father as a commentator, a new role. He does well with it. Doug insults him and Chris comments on it, probably in connection to the earlier invitation to comment. Greg has the hottest temper. He is most likely to act out in anger and least likely to metacommunicate. The family is describing the process of how they work and how they handle their mother.

Mother: If they can get me to that point, they feel like they have won. They have beat me.

Dr. Owen: And you feel like you have lost.

Mother: Oh yeah, as soon as I start to lose it I end up crying.

Father: And she'll start apologizing. The kids see that as a weakness. They will feed on her apologies. See, you are going out of control. I'm talking about all of you. I've heard her apologize to you all a number of times.

Greg: She never once apologized to me. Once, when I was 12.

Father: No, a number of times.

Greg: When?

Father: A couple of weeks ago.

Greg: No. No way.

Father: Yes, I heard her. Sometimes you become selective in your hearing. You only want to hear what you want to hear, period. When you get enraged too, Greg, same things goes for you. Same thing. Half the time you don't even remember what you say. 'I said that?' Yeah, you did.

Greg: Hm, hm, hm

Mother: You're lying.

Father: Right, that will be the follow-up words. 'You're lying, aint no way I would say something like that.'

Mother: See, your dad agrees. You guys are always picking on me.

Dr. Owen: Jenn, you probably shouldn't listen to any of this. Otherwise, you're learning family secrets. (*laughter*)

Dr. Owen calls attention to Jenn's presence, suggesting she may not want to listen to this. It's a way to reduce intensity so that dialogue can continue. It interferes with the tension-building process that leads to acting out or walking out. Her presence does not seem a big deal, surprisingly. In fact, both mothers have known each other since kindergarten. Is it possible Jenn's presence gives Greg more freedom to define his position, while simultaneously keeping him more honest?

Father: I don't think they do it consciously though.

Dr. Owen: Most of what they are doing is unconscious. You feel like you're caught in this pattern, nobody can change.

Father: Nobody wants to be the first one to say, 'Okay, let's just cool this off.' Nobody wants to be the first one to do that. They all want to be this hard nose, you know, 'Hey, it's not my fault. It was you.'

Mother: There is always a fight . . .

Father: I don't take any blame for this.

Mother: Who gets the last word?

Dr. Owen: In a weird way, that's how a true family sticks together, but it's not very satisfying.

This comment redefines how pathology helps keep families involved but unfulfilled. Nothing changes. The family dialogue, however, is not disrupted.

Greg: You get the last word.

Doug: For you maybe, because you always leave.

Greg: What else am I supposed to do?

Doug: Sit there and take it.

Greg: Bust a window. (*laugh*) I have to leave.

Dr. Carl: Well, you could get down on your knees and say you're sorry.

Greg: Yeah, right. That would be bad.

Dr. Carl: You could walk up and give her a big kiss, and tell her you love her and you're sorry you are such a failure as a son.

Greg: You're an asshole.

Father: Talking about taking the wind out of somebody's sails.

Dr. Owen: That's Dr. AssHole to you.

Greg: Dr. AssHole.

Dr. Owen: That's better. (*To Dr. Carl*) You know we've got to get some respect out of this guy.

Long Pause

Greg is working at being the innocent, wounded one. He is not owning anything. Mother is trying to own her part of it and get them to own theirs. By remaining innocent, Greg is teaching mother to stay innocent—protecting her. So there is tension at this point between mother's having grown up some and attempting to promote growth, and Greg attempting to preserve the endless, unsolvable war. Dr. Carl reminds him that he could offer to apologize and show mother his affection. The metamessage is very straight, but the literal suggestion is poking fun at Greg a little. He feels the poke and lovingly tells Dr. Carl he is an asshole. Father seems to think Greg scored a hit, but Dr. Owen helps out with more irony, "Dr. Asshole to you." Parents often underestimate the pleasure therapists take in being insulted by adolescents.

Chris: You don't have to worry about being kind and sweet in front of Jenn. (*Gets up and takes garbage to trash*).

Greg: I don't know. I've said everything I had to yesterday. Plus, I am not in a bad mood today.

Father: I think if they could just get focused enough to put down their guards and walls that they have up, and start functioning a little bit better . . .

Greg: What are you talking about?

Father: Every word out of their mouth, I even noticed it this morning. Instead of just saying, would you mind stopping that. It's would you stop what the hell you are doing it's f . . . bothering me. It even happened that way this morning. I said, do you really have to talk that way to each other. Can't you just say please stop, you know nice calm words, no, it's always got to be loud. You know, that's how I dealt with things. If I got loud, all of a sudden this small person got this tall. You know then I could deal with them. 'Cause then I could just blow them over. My boys, sadly to say, picked up that technique. They'll do it to their mom while she is cowering in a corner like this. Cause they know they can do it.

Greg: I never put her in that position. I always leave. I've never made her drop and cry the way Chris does.

Mother: I disagree with that.

Greg: When? Bullshit.

Mother: I cry like crazy, every time I had to make you leave the house. I'd cry when you wanted to come . . .

Greg: Good.

Mother: I'd sit there rocking like a child. It hurts me, Greg. You act like it's a solution to make me feel better. It isn't. It's my only way of making you understand your choices . . .

Greg: All it does is piss me off.

Mother: . . . that there is a world out there that you are going to have to live in. And I have tried so hard to teach you to swim before I threw you in the pool. But, I am terrified you are going to drown.

Chris: That's how I taught Skeeter to swim. (*laughter*) I threw him in.

Dr. Owen: Who is Skeeter?

Chris One of my best friends.

Dr. Owen: Was there water in the pool?

Greg: There is no water in the pool.

Chris: Yes, there was. It's 9 foot.

Greg: I was just being an asshole.

Chris: He swam in the pool.

Greg: (*To Mom*) Don't look at me.

Mother: Why?

Greg: 'Cause I don't want you to.

Dr. Owen: Do you know why you don't? What happens to you?

Greg: It annoys me.

Dr. Owen: Why do you think?

Greg: I don't know. LOOK! (*pointing at his mother*) Quit it.

Chris tells an amusing story here and some playful bantering follows. Greg interrupts it with a command to his mother. This is an example of a microinvestigation into why Greg does not want his mother to look at him, but he deflects it to Doug. Is he saying, "I don't want to mean that much to you?" Does it disrupt part of the family belief system if they start to mean more to one another? Maybe the point is that if the We starts to be resuscitated and to show signs of life, it creates both apprehension and hope. There has been so much distress connected to attachment in this family.

Mother: I always look at the person speaking.

Greg: Look at Doug. His eyes are red. I think he was doing something this morning.

Mother: They are red Doug.

Doug: My eyes are always red.

Mother: No they're not. I've known those eyes for 15 ½ years.

"I've known those eyes for 15½ years." This line captures an important point. The mother, regardless of gender, loves her growing child profoundly. He may no longer need the love, but still desires access to it. In this sense she is an anvil, a presence who feels the hits, is not damaged by them, and seldom hits back. We are aware of the erotic tension this produces in the sons and daughters, but what about in the mothers? In mother's case, her husband regressed to prepuberty, and she ended up acting out sexually. In another version, the rising erotic tension might produce an attack of sexual indifference in the mother.

Dr. Owen: It's probably the look of love. That's probably what she sends out to Greg.

Missy: They're always red, cause you're always sleeping.

Greg: I don't know, I just don't like it when she looks at me. I've never been able to take a back seat from her. It pisses me off when she bugs me.

Mother: Every since he's been itty bitty tiny.

Greg: Yeah, she hugs me, I push her off. I can't . . .

Dr. Owen: You still have the same bad habits from yesterday. (*Missy raises her hand*)

Mother: You're not in school, pumpkin.

Missy: So.

Dr. Carl: That's just a 'Notice me!'

Dr. Owen: Go ahead, Missy. I'll tell you if you're interrupting.

Missy: Is tobacco the same as a cigarette?

Missy carefully interrupts with Doug's help. She raises her hand to interrupt with a slightly irrelevant question about tobacco and cigarettes. Doug turns the conversation to how much the children know about pot because of the parents' heavy use in the past.

Dr. Owen: Not exactly.

Missy: See. (*Looking at Doug*)

Dr. Owen: A cigarette is tobacco with paper wrapped around it.

Greg: (*Laughing*)

Doug: See.

Missy: It's not the same.

Mother: But I believe that Doug tells her that it's tobacco cause it doesn't look like a cigarette, when he is actually smoking pot. I think that's where she is coming from.

Doug: No, she knows the smell because of you and Dad.

Greg : Yeah, you and Dad used to burn the walls down. (*laughing*)

Doug: In the car going up to Boston the whole way there. We were all getting a contact buzz.

Greg: Yeah, you guys must have really thought we were stupid or something.

Doug: Missy sitting there looking at the cars going by (*nodding his head*).

Father: No, I've explained it to you before. We didn't think you were stupid. We knew you were smart. We just didn't want to flaunt it in front of you.

Greg: Flaunt it—you smoked it in the van on the way to . . .

Doug: You stacked things up so we couldn't see the bowl getting passed.

Mother: And we would spray the Lysol.

Greg: Yeah, but that's bullshit. You shouldn't be doing that in front of your kids.

Doug: All the smoke is rolling back.

Everyone was talking. The kids are a group against the parental team. What is important is that it gives a graphic description of the parental misbehavior and heavy marijuana use.

Greg: That's probably why I hate you so much. No, hey, I don't hate you.

Everyone begins talking at once.

Mother: SSHH! One person at a time, please. (*Mother restores order*)

Dr. Owen: Why do you hate her?

Greg: No, I changed that. I don't know why, but I've thought it's wrong to say "hate."

Dr. Owen: I think that would make the minister mad or the Sunday school teacher mad if they smoked pot around you. But the good thing about it is that they've taught you guys how to misbehave.

Dr. Owen is on thin ice when he says it isn't good behavior for parents, but the children should be grateful to have parents who taught them how to misbehave. Therapy is not social services, nor is it the court system—it is not the arbitrator of community morals. One important function of the therapeutic process is to disrupt dichotomizing. That is part of the process for repairing the we. The court system does not or cannot do this. This is another difference between evaluation and therapy. Evaluation measures the family process against a community or professional standard. Therapy measures the family process against its own standard. It is interesting that they take the point away from Dr. Owen and elaborate on the wrongness of it. In this way, the wrongness is belonging to them, rather than being inflicted from outside. The therapists are not in the position of accusing them, but of loving them. They establish an alliance with the family which allows it to emphasize its healthiness. Family members then take responsibility for their mistakes or bad judgment.

Greg: (*Laughs*)

Dr. Owen: But they are also trying to teach you how to get it right.

Greg: You can't do that in front of kids.

Dr. Owen: Well, you can do that in front of kids.

Chris: Dad just said he was doing that.

Doug: And get the kids high?

Mother: Greg's right. What we did was very, very wrong. And I felt guilty of what I was doing.

Mother's behavior stands in marked contrast to four months earlier when she was tentative and defensive. Then, she was more like an excluded older sister to her children. Now she is more comfortably a mother—sinful, but self-owning. This is evidence of the good individual therapy she had. She is modeling intersubjectivity, something healthy parents do. She acknowledges and accepts the children's point of view, even though she has a different point of view. She does not denigrate what they experienced. Father is also more solidly behind her.

Mother: Yeah, but the fact of the matter is, it has stopped. It stopped. At least we've recognized our failing and changed it.

Greg: That don't change nothin'.

Mother: It doesn't change what happened. No.

Dr. Carl: It's a weird thing in this family though. I think Greg was feeling uncomfortable about the feelings he was having when Mom was showing him love. Then Missy interferes, and starts talking about tobacco. She's so jealous, she wants attention.

Dr. Owen is operating from an "amoral" or a "metamoral" position. He assumes the parents care about and love the children, and whatever happens happens out of their love for them. He sounds way off when measured against appropriate social behavior. But this is therapy—it is different from social behavior. The key is that the misbehavior is of secondary importance. It is antisocial (naughty), but it is also self-restoring. The therapists would be more upset by denying or self-righteous behavior by the parents. Dr. Carl comes in at a different metalevel, but with basically the same theme: talking about loving is hard to tolerate. It is hard to tolerate because some members have not been loved or have played at being indifferent to loving.

While Dr. Owen is in the flow of the discussion, Dr. Carl has remained outside of it. Metaphorically, Dr. Owen is in the water with the swimmers and Dr. Carl is in the boat, watching carefully. Dr. Carl makes an excellent metaobservation, which attends to an overarching component of the family process as exemplified in this interview. This is a sweet example of an experienced cotherapy partnership working simultaneously at different levels.

Chris tells Greg to listen so he can get it. That's good. He takes a turn on the therapy team acting like a cotherapist. Greg has made it furthest out of the family, but the game board has tilted and he is sliding back. He both desires to be back in and is uneasy with it. He goes after mother with jabs and looping punches. They are hard shots, but she deflects the punches, never hitting him back as hard as she could. She stays right with him at the same level. She does not pull rank.

Missy is persistent, probably as a result of the egocentricity of adolescence. She is the muffler of any affect which can lead to more warmth. Is this an adolescent precursor of the female ability to deflect an erotic moment into a discussion of the check book or a question of when they will buy that sofa? Or is this rudimentary hysteria in action?

Missy: Na Ah! (*Raising her hand*)

Dr. Carl: And now you guys are back to fighting and you're on the defense about ways you've acted like a kid with your kids. And . . .

Greg: What the hell are you talking about?

Dr. Carl: And it's so much easier to fight than it is to love.

Chris: Listen to him, and you'd know.

Greg: I'm lost, I'm lost.

Missy: (*Raising her hand*) I started talking about tobacco, because he whispered to me. (*pointing to Doug*) Yeah, you don't even know the difference between tobacco and cigarettes.

Dr. Carl: Yeah, well he may be jealous of the love between the two of them too. I am not saying . . .

Greg: Missy, quit changing the subject.

Dr. Carl: But I think you are very jealous about the love that goes on with any other kid other than you.

Greg: Because she thinks the world revolves around her.

Dr. Owen: What did you say, Chris?

Chris: I wonder if we can make a profit in selling this tape as a comedy.

Dr. Owen: No, it's not that funny. It has some funny parts to it. It's got sadness to it, too.

Dr. Carl: Yes.

Greg: It's because it's a big joke.

Mother: No, it isn't. It's reality.

Greg: This family is a big joke, is what I'm saying.

Mother: The reality is that this family is a family forever.

Greg: Was a family.

Mother: And what . . .

Greg: WAS A FAMILY!!

Mother: And what broke it?

Greg: You.

Mother: Me?

Greg: Yeah.

Mother: And what did I do?

Greg: Kicked him out.

Mother: Okay . . . I can . . .

Father: You don't think it was necessary?

Mother: I can understand that.

Greg: I was used to it. That was my way of life.

Mother: Son, can you go back a little bit in time though, and remember what it was like before he left.

Greg: Yeah.

Mother: Do you remember when Doug called Aunt Mary with none of us knowing about it? He begged her to take Dad. Do you remember how we all jumped around the house happy when the police took him?

Doug: No.

Greg: That pissed me off . . .

(A lot of talking at once)

Chris: I wasn't even there.

Greg: You called the cops on Dad.

Mother: (*Talking to Greg*) We were crying, but the same time we were pleased that he was going to get some help. At that point I still wanted to keep our marriage together. It wasn't until the next day with the knife.

Doug: You still had this stuff going on—you didn't have to kick him out then. You guys still could have . . .

Greg: Well, I don't know, maybe that was necessary. (cleaning his nails)

Mother: It was to the point . . .

Greg: Cause he would've killed somebody if he'd stayed.

Mother: It was to the point, ask your dad. He was at the point where he was going to hurt one of us. Look at how he choked Greg twice. Your dad is glad that we separated because now we're all together and have a chance to heal.

Doug: We're not all together really.

Greg: Yeah, we don't even have supper time.

Doug: We don't have lunches together, we don't have anything together. . .

Greg: For Christ's sake, we live on fucking TV dinners—that's bullshit.

Doug: We don't have any family time or nothing.

Father: But we're in the process of changing that.

Missy: No one comes home for dinner in time.

Father: It's in a process.

Mother: It's hard to make a supper when everybody is in and out . .

Greg: That's why you set a time and stick to it.

Mother: We did that.

Greg: Do you know how easy it is to blow off your rules?

Doug: There is barely any reason . . .

Greg: No offense Mom, but I got to be a better parent than you.

Mother: No, I know I'm not St. Mary. It's hard for me to live up to that. I'm trying.

The interview becomes very active. They are attending to the absence of a we, and acknowledging what is necessary to begin reconstruction.

Father: But everything is in the process of being changed.

Doug: When Dad was there, nobody tried to doing anything stupid.

Chris: It was great.

Doug: Nobody tried to.

Greg: I was afraid to go home.

Mother: Because he jumped down on you. But if I tried to jump down on you guys, or even point my finger at you . . .

Doug: Because we're not afraid of you.

Mother: You start yelling abuse.

Greg: I don't start yelling abuse. Abuse!

Chris: It's just kind of funny when she does it.

Greg: Yeah, Mom, it's cause it's funny. When you yell at me it's funny.

Missy: Your eyes pop out.

Mother: My eyes pop out, so it's funny to see me angry.

Missy: No.

Greg: No, your nose starts twitching. I just can't stop laughing. I mean you're pissed off and I'm laughing.

Mother: You don't act like your laughing.

Missy: But it's not funny.

Dr. Carl: Well it seems funny to me. You're saying please don't hate me because I kicked the bum out because he was being unacceptable. And they do hate you, So I don't know, you can learn to be loved or to be hated. Because they are real clear at saying they hate you for doing what you did.

Dr. Carl makes a solid focusing comment about mother and what they think of her. Drawing it to an extreme helps Greg be a little more subdued and less absolute in his thinking about mother. They are redefining and updating their mother-son relationship. The therapists stay out of the discussion.

Greg: I don't hate her, I just don't like her.

(*Kelly goes to sit on Mom's lap.*)

Doug: Missy wasn't even scared once, when you were drunk that one night.

Mother: We're not talking about that right now. We're talking about the other issue.

Dr. Carl: Good job, Mom.

Greg: No, Mom, I don't hate you. I just . . . I don't know what it is. You just seem more like a stranger than a Mom to me. I don't feel like I know you.

Mom: Back to the issue, what Dr. Carl was saying, with me kicking Dad out. And that is why everybody hates me.

Greg: No, that's not it.

Mother: OK, your Dad and I have sat down and spoken about these things. Both of us feel that the problems were 50/50—Half him, half me. Neither one more than the other. It wasn't my fault—I think—is how I want to word this. I couldn't take anymore. It wasn't your Dad's fault that I couldn't take anymore and that he was lost and didn't know what to do. (*Kelly gives her mother a hug and kiss.*)

Greg: It's because you're psycho, and he was an asshole.

Mother: But at least now we're finding ourselves.

Greg: Psychos and assholes don't work right.

Father: You didn't think I was a little psycho?

Greg: You were more than psycho, you was crazy. You were way out of control. You were a prick.

Dr. Owen: You are asking questions and then you are acting like any answer doesn't mean anything. You laugh off every answer.

Greg: Because I think this whole thing is a waste of time.

Chris: He's actually humoring himself—he is the prick. Ha ha ha!

Mother: As far as this being a waste of time . . .

Greg: It is a big waste of time. Because nothing is going to get done.

Mother: It is the only "medication" there is for problems our family has.

Greg: It don't help. I leave here so pissed off . . .

Dr. Owen: That's okay.

Chris: That means they are doing their job

Dr. Owen: That means you are having an experience.

Dr. Owen's comment about asking questions is a useful, all-purpose observation. Mother's "medication" for this family metaphor is good. Dad supports the therapeutic process, as well. Likewise, Greg is discrediting the interviews by indicating he feels "pissed off" when he leaves. Dr. Owen says, "That's okay. . . That means you are having an experience." These moments are important. Therapy, when it is effective, can evoke strong and confused feelings. It gives the therapist a chance to define the usefulness of what is going on even when it is confusing. At times, the therapist may feel confused. It is not wise to define oneself that way. When a therapist feels confused, it is better to back up a little and attend either to the process or to the affect.

Father: This morning when I came walking in that door you were 99% happier than yesterday when I walked in. It is because you got some things off your chest yesterday that you did need to get off your chest without even realizing it, and it made you feel better. Do you recognize that? No, you would rather try to find another reason why you are happy then recognize that some of these sessions work. I'm not saying all these sessions work. I have yelled at Dr. Carl several times that his therapy don't seem to be reaching me.

Greg: It ain't fun to yell at Dr. Carl. He doesn't get pissed. You can't piss him off.

Dr. Carl: Are you raising the issue with your parents just to get them to admit that they're failures and losers and there is no hope? Then you will be happy.

Greg: I don't know.

Dr. Carl: I don't know doesn't count. You have to make something up. Do you suppose you feel like a failure so you want them to feel like failures too. My crazy thought is that you can't stand the passion that you feel for your mother so you have to fight with her instead.

Greg: What!

Dr. Carl: I'm not that technical.

Greg: She pisses me off.

Dr. Carl: Fighting is the next best thing to making love, because you really have to care or you are just not going to do it.

High-powered, direct interpretation by Dr. Carl is important in the middle phase. He points out that Greg, in his critical remarks, attempts to maintain the dissatisfying status quo. If the family begins to get healthy, he won't know what to do. It will disrupt his working epistemology about the family. This is a high-quality interview. The polarization of good and bad is collapsing. It can be difficult to see around the misbehavior in these families with their distorted pornographic material. The therapists attend to the members' adequacy amidst the chaotic experiences they have lived through. This is an example of the philosophy that where there is caring, all pathology is sharing or repairing. Drs. Carl and Owen are pushing the family to pay attention to the core of loving and caring and mutual importance in this family. The therapy team relates pathology to ambivalence about loving. Their methods are often, clumsy but better than overintellectual, and they handle it in a way that continues to be engaging.

There is a time to stay involved, even if it is just to wonder out loud. It is okay for the therapist to be wrong or awkward, as long as he pushes the family's reflection. Reflection is inherently valuable for the defiant family. Sometimes the interview is like a jam session—fooling around, keeping the herd a little restless so that something can happen. But they are also involved. In this case, you can see that everyone is tuned in and contributing. This applies even to 4-year-old Kelly who says nothing, but moves around the room, attending especially to her mother. Dr. Carl makes a bold remark about Greg's erotic feelings for his mother. He makes it safer by defining it as a "crazy thought." It is exactly correct, but difficult to bring into this family setting. It is crucial because it makes the undercover, sexual processes briefly accessible. If it has the desired effect, those feelings become less terrifying.

Doug: We got along just fine when Greg didn't live at the house. We got along just fine.

Mother: He accepted a big old hug whenever he walked in the door. I gave him a hug at school and he didn't get upset.

Greg: Except that one time. She came to my chorus concert drunk off her ass.

Mother: I was not drunk.

Greg: Bullshit! Chris, she was drunk off her ass. (*Chris nods in agreement*)

Mother: I was sitting with Mary and John and they agreed with me.

Greg: Yeah, but you should have heard what Aunt Mary said after you left.

Dr. Owen: Do you know what you are doing right now? She's talking about ways she has been close to you and what you think of is the times she wasn't and the times she got it wrong. You think of the bad stuff. You arrange it so it can't make a difference.

Doug: (*To Greg*) For once listen to the man. He's got your number.

(*Doug intrudes on Dr. Owen's comments, interpreting what he is saying.*)

Dr. Owen: Hey! Cut it out! I am the psychiatrist. He understands me just fine. (*Continuing with Greg*) I think it has to do with you being afraid of being loved. I suppose I am thinking this just because Jenn is here. You are going to do it in the next generation if you don't fix it now.

Greg: Fix what?

Dr. Owen: You are going to be the father of a family just like this unless you try to figure out a way for it not to happen.

Greg: It will never happen.

Dr. Owen: (*With a twinkle in his eye*) Famous last words.

Mother: That's what I said.

Greg: Look at the size of this family.

Mother: The same size as what I grew up in.

Greg: It can't possibly work.

Missy: There's only five children.

Greg: That's too many.

Missy: Nana was in a family of 13 children.

Dr. Owen: (*To Dr. Carl*) They must think I am not doing a very good job with Greg—everyone is trying to interrupt.

Greg: So what you are saying is that I am afraid of being loved.

Dr. Carl: Hey! You were interrupting me.

Greg: Sorry about that Dr. Carl. Where do you get that though?

Dr. Carl: I think that is how they function at home. Everybody tries to be the therapist and interferes. Chaos develops. There is no respect. Everybody just jumps in.

Mother: This is a mild version of how we live.

Greg: What are you drawing, Missy? Let me see. A yellow face.

Father: Greg, people can change if the change is allowed to happen.

Greg: I know, I know, you've changed a lot. You did a good job.

Father: I am not referring to myself. I am looking at my family. I am so thankful my mother saw some of the things she did wrong and my sister wasn't affected the way I was.

Greg: I can't judge you. It's not my position to judge you. You're my mom. In my opinion you were doing a lot better, but then you turned to drinking.

What the family is doing here is healthy. Greg is making self-owning comments. Although he makes good moves and speaks as an I, therapy doesn't transform him, as indicated by subsequent interviews when he refers to his mother as a "f_____ whore." It sounds like mother was further into the alcohol and marijuana than we suspected, although she did some useful things. She took care of herself instead of playing at being saintly and long suffering at home. Some of her mistakes were costly, but whose are not?

Mother: That's very possible. I haven't come to a definite conclusion in my mind. I have been weighing my own discontent against my behavior with drinking.

Greg: The drinking doesn't bother me, it is what you say.

Mother: Something I could do other than being mom. All right, I found going out to play darts with people is fun.

Greg: It would be easier to play catch with us, play soccer with us. Do all the things you used to do. That was fun.

Mother: That is fun Greg, you are right, however, that doesn't give me the chance to go out and be me. I am still being Mom. I was so crushed. I was told to find something for me. I may have found the wrong thing. I drink two nights a week tops. Tuesday and either Friday or Saturday—that's all. I don't have it in the house. I will never have it in the house.

Greg: It doesn't bother me that you drink. It is the things you say. I'd rather you not talk when you are drinking. 'I love you, I love you' You chased my friend around the house.

Mother: Teasing yes, I remember that.

Greg: You remember how embarrassing that was? You chased him around saying, 'I love you—I've known you for so long. Eat some chicken'.

Dr. Owen. It isn't the drinking, it's who she is when she is drinking.

Greg: She turns into this big love ball or something. I don't know.

Dr. Owen: She is probably not dangerous.

Greg: No, she isn't dangerous. Except when she brings crazy people in the house that I have to go down to the bar and threaten—someone who tells my little sister to shut up and make my little sister cry.

Mother: I know.

Doug: Making her cry for so long and you are just sitting there laughing at everything she says.

Greg: That was wrong. That pissed me off. Make my little sister cry.

Dr. Carl: Beneath the anger is a lot of shame

Doug: I had to take Kelly down to my room because she was afraid to be near you and your friend.

Mother: Yeah, I know.

Missy: She didn't want to sleep on the pillow. Your friend had her head on it.

Greg: I had to wash it for Kelly. But other than that...

Missy: Don't look at me.

(*Everyone is looking at Missy, she puts her hood up. Someone mentions she is getting red.*)

Dr. Carl: What do you guys do with the shame you feel when Mom is acting like an adolescent? Part of it is a little duplistic because you guys are smoking outside and raising hell. You want to monitor Mom but you are not doing a heck of a good job monitoring yourselves. But I do hear the shame.

Dr. Owen: I think she has this worry that she is not more than a mother. I suppose the trick for her is to figure out a different way to get out of the role. If it pisses you kids off, it is hard to quit doing it. Its like when it pisses the parents off, the kids can't quit doing it.

Here the therapists are talking about the family. This is a useful method for reorienting the therapists and for separating themselves from the family. Dr. Carl has an interesting generation-reversing perspective regarding the children all smoking dope, but scolding mother for doing it. Dr. Owen stays with the idea.

Missy: What does duplistic mean? You guys keep using words I don't know.

Dr. Carl: Well, I'm glad you asked, and your mom explained it. She's pretty smart.

Greg: No way.

Missy: Why would she use them if she's not?

Dr. Carl: Well, she may be trying to impress Dad, you never now. (*laughter*)

Missy: (*Looking at Dad*) Are you annoyed? Looking at your face I can tell you're annoyed.

Dr. Carl: What do you think he's annoyed about?

Missy: I don't know.

Dr. Carl: Why don't you ask him? Maybe he's jealous that he can't get in on any of the acting like Mom. He has to be good.

Doug: I forgot Jenn was here.

Jenn: No, I'm here.

Father: No, no, I'm listening to what everybody is saying so that later on I can use it.

Missy: I ate a bunch of candy. I'm hyper.

Mother: Why did you eat candy?

Missy: I ate all my trick or treat candy this morning.

Mother: This morning.

She is not hyper because of the candy. Missy is uneasy because something has shifted in the family and she is having a bodily response to it.

Dr. Owen: I just think you're getting nervous because something is going on that you're not used to.

Missy: I ate a bunch of Smarties that Tricia gave me.

Mother: That was silly to eat all that in the morning.

Missy: She gave me like four bags, and I ate them all.

Dr. Carl: Did you hear what he said?

Missy: What?

Dr. Carl: You missed a golden opportunity.

Dr. Owen: I said, I think you are getting nervous because something's changed. And you don't know what to do.

Missy: What changed?

Greg: I don't know.

Missy: No, I understand.

Dr. Owen: Everybody's quiet, for one thing.

Missy: Jenn is.

Dr. Owen: Everybody's thinking.

Greg: First time, everybody's quiet. It's never like this.

Dr. Owen: But Missy's nervous about it.

Missy: Nervous about what?

Dr. Owen: If it gets quiet, it makes Missy nervous.

Dr. Carl: Yes.

Kelly: Greg and Chris smoking pot in our house, in the living room.

Doug: That was outside.

Dr. Owen: I suppose they don't even give you any.

Dr. Owen's comment is aimed at neutralizing the tattling. (*A lot of talking among the family ensues.*)

Greg: You're just mad cause you can't have any.

Dr. Owen: Do they ever give any to you?

Kelly: (*Shaking her head no*)

Dr. Owen: That's a shame. How dare they. They should at least share it.

Greg: (*Laughs*)

Dr. Owen: How are you going to grow up to be a screwball, if they don't take good care of you?

An interchange begins with neutralizing Kelly's tattling. Then Dr. Owen makes fun of the ubiquitous pot smoking and accuses them all of being screwballs. This is a gentle, but therapeutic insult. Mother defends the family honor. When Kelly pouts, Dr. Owen recants. But of course, he still said it and the statement remains. There is a purpose in doing this. It is a form of novel behavior, the kind which shakes up the family's routine reality orientation. The therapists have been supporting the family and depathologizing all sorts of weird behavior. It helps to reverse the commentary, even if only briefly, by accusing them of being a bunch of screwballs. This happened earlier when Dr. Owen suggested that the parents should be admired for teaching their children to misbehave. Mother did the saintly mother thing by bringing it back to the desirable social reality.

Mother: Because you don't want to be a screwball, huh? (*Kelly is sitting on her mother's lap.*)

Dr. Owen: You'll be so lonesome.

(*Mother caressing Kelly's hair during silence*)

Dr. Owen: I'm sorry. I'm being a rat.

Missy: Two Smarties left. (*Reaching in her pocket.*)

Dr. Owen: Are you talking about Dr. Carl and me? Haven't you noticed, we aren't as smart as we look.

Dr. Carl: So you want them to leave Mom alone and start taking on the boys again, huh, Kelly? Try to protect Mom? (*Kelly shakes her head yes*) Sorry, that everybody is picking on her. It's just cause they love her and they don't know how to show it other than picking on her. It's just like guys do to their sisters—they love them but they just don't know how to show it. So they just pick on them.

(*Family begins talking at once.*)

The therapists are working on the idea that brothers fight because of tension produced by homosexual feelings. Loving produces the need to assert or protect the self, lest it be caught off guard.

Dr. Owen: Jenn, are you doing okay?

Jenn: Yes.

Dr. Owen: You don't have to stay here if it makes you too uncomfortable.

Dr. Owen acknowledges Jenn's presence by offering her a chance to leave. He is concerned that she might be injured by the experience of being treated as though invisible.

Mother: Any type of emotion reaction I have hits right here—"Its okay Mom, its okay Mom."

Dr. Owen: One of my ideas is that everything they do with you is them taking care of you. Even when they are being mean to you.

The point about taking care of mother is important. It is a crucial example of the hypothesis this book supports: Where there is caring, all pathology is sharing or repairing. If family members are invested in and care about one another, the overt pathology is an attempt to repair the family. They are attempting to whip their mother into shape.

Greg: How can we take care of her?

Dr. Owen: She is the center of the family. Its almost like you have to take care of her in order to keep the family alive.

Father: I think what some of you kids have got to realize is that your mom is your mom and your dad is your dad, but we are also human beings and we have needs and we have wants. We have dreams just like you guys do, and sometimes we make mistakes just like you guys do. Our job as parents is to guide you so you don't make those same mistakes. You have every right to point out the mistakes that we are making, but not the right to be disrespectful about it.

Greg: What if we can't figure out the mistakes we are making?

Father: The mistakes that you have made I have pointed out to you, but you refuse to recognize you are making the mistake. All of a sudden it is Mom and Dad's fault, or Mom's fault. Like I have said, I have seen a lot of progress in you and I won't deny you that progress. But there is still some refinement. You are a still a diamond in the rough, just like me. You need things chipped away, fixed.

Greg: But you will have that all through life.

Father: Exactly, if you understand that, life will become a little bit easier for you, and the family. That's for all you guys—I am not just saying Greg—everybody in this room, myself included. I am not leaving myself out of this. The only difference between you and me is that I am finally taking responsibility for my actions. You guys don't want that responsibility. You don't want to accept it. You don't want to take responsibility for your actions. I am.

Dr. Owen: For a guy that didn't have much fathering, that was a very fatherly thing to say.

Father: More than anything I love him. I will never give him up. I just want to help him. Like I take responsibility—my rage and my anger is by no means healthy.

Dr. Owen: Can you stand it when they love you?

Father: No, sometimes I have a very hard time with that.

Greg: I have always got along with my dad. He has been the biggest asshole to me through my whole life. But my mom, she has always tried to be there for me, but for some reason I push her away.

This is a very potent dialogue through here. Greg's language is beginning to reflect that he has absorbed some of the therapeutic dialogue.

Dr. Carl: It is interesting to me that you guys can freely hate and admonish your mother, but you don't go after your dad. What your dad needs is to get what he deserves, which is a little bit of sharing the load here. (*To Dr. Owen*) If they hated him a little more, maybe they could openly love their mother a little bit.

Dr. Owen: (*to Dr. Carl*) Why do kids treat their father that way? Are they afraid of his rage if they hate him?

Dr. Carl: I don't think so, in Mark's case. I think they feel like he can't stand as much hatred as Judy. I think they are careful with him out of some sense he needs their protection.

(*Long, thoughtful pause*)

Dr. Carl: (*To the parents*) Part of my theory is that you guys don't want to go belly to belly. Can't tolerate much love with each other and it's no wonder to me that the kids can't either. You see, they don't have a model for how to love as adults.

(*The cotherapist's dialogue expands to comment on the parental dyad.*)

(*Silence*)

Dr. Owen: It will be interesting to see if they can fix it.

Greg: I'm trying, I'm doing a lot better, seriously, like last year, a year ago.

The interview goes on further, but this gives enough flavor of the therapeutic dialogue. In a sense, Greg volunteered to be the patient by protesting the need for therapy. Reintegrating him was part of repairing the fragmented we. There are a few simple themes that are worked on throughout the interview. Greg is simultaneously reentering the family and differentiating from mother. He is protecting father, perhaps because father is also out, or perhaps because he needs to identify with father at this point in his development. It is possible that as oldest child he more fully embodies the marital we than any of the other kids, and thus feels more distress over the marital disruption. He is punishing his mother for her sexual infidelity without saying so explicitly. The last segment of the interview is omitted, where Chris and his anger become the center of concern, and the whole family becomes the therapist. Missy, who has been an irritant during the first part of the interview, makes some very touching observations about Chris. Then in the last 10 minutes, we deal with a specific issue about how the parents should handle Chris' underachievement at school.

Some of the important dynamics in this interview are as follows:

1. Greg is induced into the patient role. He has been absent for much of the family work while living with his maternal aunt, Mary.
2. This is late-stage therapy for Judy. She is practicing existential interacting and going through an existential confirmation.
3. Therapy focuses on the mother-son relationship, most specifically, Greg and his mother.
4. Father is taking some practice moves at being a healthy father.

5. Father is learning to be a patient, much of it vicariously, by his identification with his sons. He has had a lot of recovery-oriented therapy.
6. Missy is breaking out of the weird role she plays—that of being involved but as a disruptive force. This role could lead to a lifetime of inadequate, disappointing relationships. In the early part of the interview, she demonstrates her capacity for avoiding family intimacy. However, later in the interview, she makes a deeply insightful comment about why Chris would like to have a baby.
7. The foundation for we-ness is being established. Fealty is being restored. Judy and Mark have a parental We that supports both of them and gives something for the children to challenge. They can even challenge Judy's recent acting out.
8. This is individual therapy for Greg, without making him out to be a sinner. His patienthood is initiated with concern for him and his feeling of being isolated and double-crossed.
9. The most central theme seems related to how to handle intimacy, and how intimacy stimulates anxiety. This anxiety about intimacy is a pivotal issue in dealing with defiance. It is a covert problem in many families. Intimacy leads to confusion. Our culture finds little pleasure in confusion, so we avoid experiences which lead to it.

Though the interview touches on many important issues, some directly and others obliquely, much of the same dialogue persists. This family is at its healthiest in the interview room, but changed behavior in the therapy room does not always translate directly into changed behavior in the outside world. Its members are learning some of the language of health, and tolerance for ambiguity and self-ownership. There are many points during the interview which disrupt their routine pattern for thinking about themselves. There is something stable in the behavior of this family.

Readers may think of this family as being representative of a defiant, chaotic, toxic family and wonder how this experience translates into working with the different family scenarios (the egocentric family, or the overwhelmed family, or the apathetic family) described in Chapter 1. There is a good deal in here which is very essential and relevant to the problem of defiance. We maintain that all families are alike, in the sense that all football games are alike. Although they follow the same rules and keep score in a similar fashion, however, the style of play may vary. The pathology in this family has been particularly pornographic, and thus they are being more open about it. The egocentric family has similar dynamics. The mother is blamed for the trouble. The father tends to be protected by the children. This family has been fragmented and intruded on by the police and by other social agencies. Its members feel like they have little to lose. Families with more money and higher social standing are more concealed and therapy with them has more the feeling of a chess game. But we would emphasize that the dynamics are similar. We have highlighted points from this interview, however, additional meaning from the interview material is also plausible. If a family asks us to summarize an interview, we don't comply with the request. In a sense, they are asking us to tell them what has happened to them in therapy. It is best that they leave with their own experience rather than our experience.

8

Three-Generation Family Consultation

Having always believed strongly in the value of consultation in family therapy, we use it routinely. Consultation is most specifically useful when a therapeutic impasse is reached or when the therapist wants to expand the experiential context and enrich the therapeutic relationship by including extended family members. Consultation increases the likelihood that family therapy will move forward, and it maximizes opportunities for a collaborative relationship between the family and therapist. A consultation offers a pause and the possibility of a transformation in the therapy process. The therapy process is certain to become broader and more creative and to gain momentum when consultation becomes a routine part of ongoing treatment.

In the case of a therapeutic impasse, the therapist arranges for a trusted and like-minded colleague to be present, which provides an opportunity for the therapist to experience the family differently. Such a consultant is like a therapist to the therapeutic family (therapist plus family). Her presence enables the therapist to think more deeply and openly, to become more patient-like temporarily, and to appreciate her role in the therapeutic impasse. In this way, the therapist models for the family how to be vulnerable without being destroyed. Simultaneously, the interaction between consultant and therapist helps the family understand that the therapist does not know all, and that the process requires thinking. As the primary therapist listens to the consultant's investigations, she expands her experience with the persons who are being treated. This type of consultation has been explicated in a series of articles (Connell & Russell, 1986; Connell, Whitaker, Garfield, & Connell, 1990).

This chapter focuses on another form of consultation: a three-generation consultation. Extended family members are invited to attend a consultation when the goal is to gather more information (historic, symbolic, and nonverbal) and to create support for the therapeutic work in the extended family system (Keith,

1989). It is important to note that extended family members also serve as consultants who help the therapist help the family. They are not induced to be patients, nor are they expected to change but, instead, to contribute to the change process of the family members who are in treatment (Keith, 1994).

The extended family consultation is especially valuable when working with defiant families, as this work is a challenge to the skill and maturity of even the most seasoned therapist. It is not unusual to feel overwhelmed, cornered, and impotent with these families. They have an uncanny ability to neutralize or co-opt the therapist; they are crisis prone and habituated in their responses; and their interactions are charged with negative emotion. A consultation is warranted when an impasse is reached, the therapist dreads seeing the family, or when progress is thwarted by frequent crises. Members of defiant families often appear disconnected from each other, the community, and extended family. An extended family consultation implicitly challenges the perception that they are alone.

There are several functions served by a consultation. The primary function is to help resolve an impasse in the ongoing therapy process. An impasse involves deterioration in the therapeutic relationship and a slowing of the therapy process. The therapeutic relationship becomes dysfunctional as, to some degree, the family and the therapist withdraw involvement in the change process, preferring to maintain the status quo. Interactions become rigid and repetitive. There are two common causes of impasse. The most frequent type is created by the therapist's overinvolvement in the outcome of therapy. The therapist has a clear picture of what needs to happen in this family, but the family remains ambivalent about what to do. The family members either go underground and sabotage therapy or adapt to this overinvolvement by co-opting the therapist into telling them how they should lead their lives. Neither of these behaviors on the family's part moves therapy toward a successful resolution. A consultation in the case of a therapist-induced impasse is helpful to reactivate a systems perspective. The implication is that the tension and specific crises that arise around defiance push the therapist out of an ecosystemic awareness, which is crucial to working with defiance in families. The consultation restores the ecosystemic perspective.

Impasse may also be induced by the family's apathy or anxiety about change, conflicting messages from other professionals involved in the problem, or one family member's unilateral disengagement from the process. Fathers are notorious for wanting to turn the problem over to the therapist so they can get back to their real work. Consultation for impasse allows the therapist to observe the therapeutic process as the consultant guides the encounter. The therapist's perspective is expanded, allowing her a broadened experience of the family from her stance of participant observer. The consultation interview also helps to refocus the family's initiative. The goal of the consultation is to disrupt the impasse in the therapeutic process and to recognize the power of the therapeutic system.

For example, one family with several defiant children had pressured the therapist to see several of the older children in individual therapy. Three of the children were on probation, and probation officers were threatening to remove them from home. The therapist had reluctantly agreed to see the children individually but recognized immediately that the momentum necessary for family therapy was drained off in individual therapy. A consultation helped the therapist recognize that she had abandoned an ecosystemic perspective in an effort to help the adolescents. The therapist covertly sabotaged the therapeutic work in an effort to rescue the children from their crazy family life and from their predicament with probation. It is important to see how her caring helped create the impasse.

Another function of a consultation is to activate the family's perception of themselves as a unit with more capability as a team than as individuals. Even the family members at a distance are an organic part of the family unit. They need to be involved so that their concern for one another can become more effective. Defiant families often lack a coherent family identity. This identity either never develops in the early phases of partnering or is interrupted due to chaotic circumstances or constant crises. Through the extended family consultation, the family can experience a sense of unity, identity, and connection with the past. A premise in working with defiant families is that the ethical core of past generations is unavailable to the current generation. The nuclear family has not absorbed fundamental family principles, due either to poor relationships, faulty attachment, or insufficient resources so that survival is more important than growth. Extended family consultations can produce anxiety in the system because the encounter is unfamiliar. Under the stress of an extended family consultation, the contributions of aunts, uncles, cousins, and grandparents take on a significance, relevance, and incisiveness that are previously not apparent to the therapist.

The consultative process helps transcend the narrow reality of the identified problem. The family is placed in the context of previous generations and relationships and interactions are played out in the encounter. Attention is focused the perception of family problems, the strengths of the system, intergenerational issues, and family interaction. In this way, the family of the present is connected to the ethical core of the background family. Consultation does not lead to specific answers, rather it produces an experiential hologram that potentially activates an alternative experience which blends the family, its problems, and its subjective experiences. The consultation is not a diagnostic process. It is an affective experience that contributes to the momentum necessary for treatment. This affective experience includes not only the family but the therapist and consultant as well. The consultant is able to be more invasive, more directive, and more supportive of the therapist. This allows the therapy to get back on track.

It is not necessary to take a thorough intergenerational family history. The consultation is at best a sketch of scattered bits of information from three to four generations. The family interacts according to its tolerance of anxiety and its intuitive perception of what will be most valuable. The objective is an emotional contribution to the family in treatment, not a confessional ceremony within the family.

This chapter describes a consultation in a case in which an impasse reflects the family's symbolic struggle around issues of belonging. The therapist had been working with this family for about 18 months. He started by working with Mark, the father, in individual therapy regarding depression and PTSD. The therapist included Judy, the mother, in order to do some work on the marriage. All three boys, Greg, Doug, and Chris were in trouble at home, at school, and in the community. They had a few family sessions, but most were subgroup interviews. Mother continued in therapy when father went to Boston to seek treatment for his PTSD. He lived with his sister during treatment. Mother was going through a rebellious phase and was not doing much as a mother. She felt defeated by the children and abandoned by her husband. The adolescent sons were trying to escape the family. Greg had gone to live with mother's older sister. The next two adolescent sons expressed a desire to live with the maternal grandparents. No one wanted to belong to the family in its current state and the children harbored fantasies of life being better elsewhere. Mother had a male friend who lived with her and the children for a short period. The children hated him and she claimed she did not really care for him either. A consultation interview with the nuclear family occurred a few days prior to convening this extended family conference. Greg refused to attend the first interview. The mother's parents were enlisted to help understand the family's problem with identity. The father's parents were deceased. Whenever possible it is beneficial to include extended family members from both sides to help maintain balance and develop a fuller perspective of family life.

GETTING STARTED

Involving the extended family in a consultation is a reflective activity. The therapist enlists the help of a colleague in the process. There is no specific agenda beyond resolving the impasse or broadening and enriching the context of therapy. The therapeutic alliance between primary therapist and the family is grist for the therapy mill. The therapist takes a risk with the family by exposing their joint work in therapy to the scrutiny of a colleague. As stated earlier, the relationship between consultant and therapist should be a trusted, respectful relationship. The consultant is an adjunct to the therapist, not an ally to the family. The consultant's job is to help the therapist help the family.

The interview begins in a standard way: The loose agenda is to learn more about the family. As emphasized earlier, the grandparents are there to be consultants to the therapy project. They have come in to help, not to be patients themselves. It might be useful for family therapists to know that although we have been doing three-generational consultation interviews for at least 25 years, a certain amount of anticipatory anxiety is always present. One can never predict what the interview will be like.

The extended family interview begins with the therapist introducing the family to the consultant and then turning the interview over to the consultant. The consultant explains a bit of what to expect without going into such depth as to control the flow of the meeting. A rule of thumb is to start by involving the highest-ranking person, who is often the most emotionally distant. Usually that is the grandfather. If he is not addressed early, he is likely to stay back. In this interview, the grandfather was eager to talk and to tell his story. It is worth knowing that he was discharged from the hospital 24 hours earlier. He was in marginal heart failure and his digitalis medication had been adjusted. There was some question as to whether his health would allow him to attend.

The consultant begins by asking the older generation an open-ended question aimed at learning more about the family history. Asking the grandparents to talk about the families in which they grew up serves as a projective test. They are less likely to be defensive about this ancient history and more apt to talk about components of those families that relate to the family of the present.

Consultant: (*To Family*) So, Dr. Owen and I have been working like this for a long time. He's a family therapist and I'm a psychiatrist, and what we like to do in treatment is have the whole family come in because it helps us. We don't have a specific agenda that we need to get at, except to talk about the family.

(*To grandparents*) This goes for you, too. Anything you feel is important, feel free to talk about it. The way I like to start is to have you talk about the family you grew up in, what that family was like—your mother and father, your brother and sister.

The grandparents are free to talk about whatever they feel is important in their growing up. This stage of the interview takes on the quality and feel of a family reunion. The grandparents are guests who are invited to open the discussion and share their stories with the younger generations. The narrative is important because when the grandparents talk about their parents, it firmly grounds the family in a rich four-generational history. The consultant and therapist listen to the narrative, looking for patterns of health, belonging, and unity to aid the current generation. Themes of intergenerational conflict are noted, as are similarities and differences between the generations. Adult children and grandchildren have an opportunity to listen and learn from the older generation.

Grandfather: Well, I'm one of 10 kids. I grew up in the Depression. I grew up on a farm, though, so we never thought much about our being poor. We were, though. We worked for ten cents an hour, a dollar a day, farming around the countryside at different farms. I followed steam tractors around.

Grandmother: (*To grandfather*) I think they want to know about our family, not that one.

Consultant: No, I was thinking about the one he's talking about (*Points to grandfather*). Next, I'll ask you about yours, and then we'll move toward the present.

Grandfather: If you didn't work, you didn't eat. Anyway, there were six girls and four boys. At present, only two of the girls are left; all four of us boys are left. My brother joined the Army and went to the Pacific, specifically around the lower portion of it. Me, I joined the Navy and went straight across the Pacific.

Consultant: World War II?

Grandfather: World War II. I joined the Navy at 16. My first day at boot camp I was 17 years old. (*Consultant starts chuckling*) You want all this?

Consultant: Oh, I was just wondering if you were doing it to get away from your girlfriend or your mother.

Grandfather has a clear memory. He starts in with a story about the military, but the consultant attempts to make it part of the family story by wondering out loud who he was trying to get away from, his mother or his girlfriend. The question, posed with humor, is done to encourage him to include more levels in his talking about his family. War stories can be fun, but they tend to be impersonal, so the consultant interjects a personalizing question.

Grandfather: No, the 'Japs' bombed Pearl Harbor, and I just decided I was going after them. That's why I joined the Navy.

Consultant: Hmm, your parents must have been scared by it.

Grandfather: Well, they had two of us out there in the thick of it for 3½ years. We both had a lot of close calls. My first trip was to Bermuda and then I went to Casablanca. Then I had a trip back on the USS Iowa to Norfolk, headed down around the Panama Canal and up to San Diego. From there I went up to—oh, what do you call it?—Hawaii. Sorry, I had a couple of heart attacks; I don't talk quite right.

Consultant: You're doing a good job.

Grandfather: (*Laughs*) Then, from there I had to escort some troops up to . . . (*Begins listing Pacific Theater sites*)

Consultant: (*Interrupting*) Actually, let me steer you away from that and back to what your family was like.

At this point in the consultation, the consultant redirects the conversation back to grandfather's family life. He gently blocks grandmother's attempt to control the interview. The consultant is in charge of setting the tone and direction of the encounter. When discussion rambles into unproductive or distracting areas, closed-ended questions or suggestions redirect the conversation back to the territory the consultant is interested in learning more about.

Grandfather: We all got along really quite well. We were a big family, and we had to work. We had to cut wood for fuel to keep warm.

Consultant: You all grew up in this part of the country?

Grandfather: Well, in McKean, yeah. We had a big garden. My mother canned tons of food. We'd go into the woods and pick berries in the spring. In the fall, we'd go out and pick berries, mushrooms, and apples, what have you. My mother would can them all up. Of course, back in the beginning we didn't even have a washing machine. Mom would wash everything with a scrub board. We had no electricity or water in the house. You had to go out back and get water to bring in the house.

Consultant: Do you remember how you used to go about getting your parents mad at you?

Grandfather: (*Laughing*) Well, I'll tell you what—you didn't want my father mad at you because he would make you go and cut your own stick. If you didn't get a big enough stick he'd make you go back and get another one. He was pretty tough—a tough old guy. He grew up in the mountains. He was a tough old man. My mother was the most pleasant woman you ever met in your life.

The consultant is interested in the interactions among family members, particularly around managing conflict and issues of belonging. He wonders if grandfather's parents were mad at him. This is relevant because of the troubles in the present family. The children of the present make their parents angry; how did grandfather upset his parents? This is an example of the older generation talking about how tough Dad was. This continues to be a persistent theme. He is projecting the present onto themes from the past. The consultant's comments are a little off center, but playful and deepening. There is guidance in talking about the emotional infrastructure and looking for meaningful subtexts below the less personal surface adventures. His story is interesting but too general. The consultant does not ask whether grandfather's parents got angry at him, rather he assumes that this is a normal emotion and is more interested in how the anger was handled. The consultant is interested in the interactional nature of the relationships, particularly in the marital and parental relationships.

Consultant: Did your mom have any way of getting Dad straightened out when they fought with each other?

Grandfather: They didn't fight too much. Once a month he'd come home after having a little too much to drink with the guys, which he probably shouldn't have. He wasn't too bad that night—he was just kind of happy-go-lucky. The second night he'd be kind of nasty. He was never really nasty to us, we all got along. We had to get along.

Consultant: Did your mother boss him around?

Grandfather: No, he was the boss. (*To grandmother*) Wouldn't you say he was the boss, Mother?

Grandmother: Oh, yes.

Grandfather: (*Laughing*) Yeah. But, all us kids got along pretty well, really.

Consultant: Yeah. Do or die, I guess. (*The consultant is teasing grandfather, establishing his freedom to do that. No one else can.*)

Grandfather: Yeah, we all had to work like dogs. We'd work in the fields, and we had to go house-to-house to make enough money. To make enough money to buy school clothes we'd have to work all summer. You wouldn't draw your pay until the fall, and then you'd go and buy your own school clothes.

Consultant: Each kid?

Grandfather: Well, not later on. I'm the third one from the top. It's my brother Harold, then Grace and me, and then Don and Howard. . . . (*pauses, then to grandmother*) How am I doing?

Grandmother: Okay.

Consultant: So you were the third oldest? Maybe going into the Navy was easy compared to working at home.

Grandfather: Uh, yeah. You had a bathroom inside and electricity. I found a home. Of course, we had beans for breakfast every morning and sacks of Army rations. But I didn't scoff too much.

The consultant moves next to grandmother to hear the story of her growing up. He moves to her because he senses the children are getting a little restless. Also, grandfather is obviously into the idea of the meeting. He is not holding back or attempting to neutralize things, so he will probably continue to participate. On the other hand, his stories are not very emotionally compelling or touching. These are the boastful stories men are likely to tell. War stories tell of time and place, less of relationship or meaning. The encouraging thing is that he has had a life and he likes to talk about it.

Consultant: (*To grandmother*) So, how about your family?

Grandmother: Um, I was an only child, and my mother had it very rough. When she was 13, her mother died, and she was in charge of the house. She had to do the cooking, the cleaning, the raising of six kids. It was very difficult, and she didn't know that much about it.

Therapist: What a young age to be in charge.

Grandmother: She didn't know too terrible much about raising a baby when I come along, so I was an only child until I was about 14. My mother's brother died of leukemia, and before he died he begged her to come and get his two kids. So we adopted the girl and the boy, and things were kind of rough after that because I wasn't spoiled—they were. They got the best of everything because it was a responsibility to her brother, and they didn't turn out as good as me.

Mother: That's true.

Consultant: They're still spoiled, I suppose?

Grandmother: Well, one's dead. One blew his brains out, and the other we haven't had any contact with for over 14 years.

Consultant: How about your dad; what was he like?

Grandmother: Oh, he was great. He was great.

Grandfather: He was a fun guy. He was a bowler and a drinker. He drank lots of beer, but you never knew he was drunk. In fact, he wasn't drunk. One night he came home . . . (*to grandmother*) Is it all right if I tell this story?

Consultant: Sure, well, if she can stand it.

Therapist: (*Laughing*) I don't know, she looked a little disapproving when he started talking.

Consultant: You were awful polite listening to him talk.

Grandfather: Well, he was a great guy. I mean, he was a nice guy.

Consultant: Do you think he fell in love with your father before he fell in love with you?

Grandmother: It's a possibility.

Consultant: Yeah, he was looking for somebody to teach him how to have fun.

Grandfather interrupts to tell a story about grandmothers' father. The therapists redirect the discussion back to grandmother for two reasons. First, she is telling the story and we like to keep it flowing that way. Second, it is best if the grandparents talk about their own families separately without being interrupted. The discussion is deflected into exploring the nature of the grandparent's relationship—how they got together, their courtship, and their marital life. The consultant comments on the courtship, and introduces a component of a model for thinking about marriage. A young man often falls in love with a young woman's mother and then marries the daughter as a way to maintain the affair. In this case, grandfather had a tough, gruesome sounding background, and it would have been a blessing to find a father who was playful and occasionally sinful—someone to teach him how to have fun. So he marries the daughter in order to enjoy a healthier father-son relationship. This is part of the process of making the parents reflective and of inducing patienthood in them, but not in a confronting or upsetting way.

Grandmother: When we first met he wanted take me home from work, and I refused because in my group of girls you do not have anything to do with a service man—especially a sailor. I mean, that was as dangerous as it gets. I refused to let him take me home. Well, I get home on the bus and a car is in the driveway. I get inside, and my father informed me that I'm going out the next night with him. (*Grandfather laughs*) Well, I stood my ground and it didn't do me any good. So I called a girlfriend and said, 'to satisfy my father, will you go with me?' She said, 'Sure, the two of us can't get into no trouble.' That's the way it went.

Grandfather: Well, we went roller-skating over at Findlay Lake. On the way home, we had a good time. On the way home, it was raining like a son-of-a-gun. There were these two girls on the road hitch hiking, and I said, 'What the devil?' Anyway, I stopped to pick them up, and they said, 'Oh no, not another service man.' They'd been kicked out of the car because they wouldn't do what these two army guys had wanted, so I took them back to their home. (*To consultant*) Was that all right?

Consultant: That was all right.

Grandfather: Anyway, eventually we got married.

Grandmother: Sixteen months later.

Therapist: Huh.

Grandfather: We've been married 52 years.

Then comes the story of how they met, which somewhat confirms our idea, although it may have worked the other way. The father found him to be an appealing son. Grandmother is thinking of herself as a young woman here, and they are describing their awareness of sin and sex in the 1940s. She illustrates how she was clever and knew how to handle her father. We sense a candid, open quality about grandmother, which in many cases gives great permission to the family to be more open. Grandmother establishes ethical parameters with her stories. When grandfather asks, "Was that all right?" it reveals a side of him that does not show up in the transcript. He appears as a rough and tough man, but he does have a mildly dependent side, which appears in his transference to the consultant. He is about 15 years older than the consultant and has an affiliative quality. We learn that he has a bad temper, but, for the most part, is a good, and thoughtful man who wants his family restored.

The grandparents discuss some problems with their children in which the grandfather was more aggressive than normal. The consultant asks about conflict in the marital relationship. The tone of the encounter is important because it signals to the consultant the level and quality of involvement among family members.

Therapist: Did you ever unleash some of this . . . uh, fury on your wife?

Grandfather: Never, (*Begins laughing*) she was the aggressive one, not me. Let's see, she threw a pound of butter at me that splashed all over the walls. She threw a potty chair at me one time and busted it. (*Family is giggling*)

Grandmother: And he just said, 'Now, here it is. Fix it!'

Grandfather: No, I was never nasty to her.

Consultant: (*To grandmother*) So you were the captain of the ship, huh?

Grandmother: Well, I don't know.

Consultant: Are there any battles that you've won?

Grandfather: I don't know. (*Laughter*) (*To grandmother*) Was there?

Grandmother: I don't know.

Grandfather: She's pretty much the boss.

Consultant: Um hum.

Grandmother: Well, things work better that way. (*Judy, the mother, starts laughing*) See, she agrees.

This unleashes some talk about how grandfather disciplined the children. He is simultaneously embarrassed by and proud of his bad temper. The consultant asks about any change in grandfather's attitude toward discipline after his father was angry with him for being too mean, but receives no response. His question focusses on how change comes about in the background family, and while simultaneously encouraging them to look for points of change in the present. The family is enjoying the conversation. They are engaged in answering the consultant's questions as candidly as possible and defenses appear to be low. There are no tears and not too much bravado. Occasionally, there is even deeper reflection on events. Mother encourages her mother to tell a story about how she motivated her father to do things around the house.

Mother: Tell them the story about how you got Dad to fix the washer. This is how things went at our house!

Grandmother: Oh, that one, yeah. Well, he is an appliance repairman, and everybody's stuff gets fixed first. We wait. One time there was something wrong. We had a leak from our well and didn't have any water. Well, instead of fixing that, he's fixing everybody else's leaks. A woman called up on the phone, and my daughter answered, and the woman said, 'It's been terrible—we haven't had any water for two hours.' And she (*Pointing to Judy*) said, 'Try it for four days, sometimes, I am sick of taking a bath in a tea cup.' So there were six kids living in the house with all that laundry. Oh, he was perfectly willing to take it all up to the laundromat, but it didn't come back looking right. Some of it was actually ruined, and I wanted my washer fixed. So, I put signs up all over the house, 'I am a washer. Fix me.' That didn't do any good. Then all of the sudden, (*Leans back and moans*) he says, 'Oh my God! I forgot to send for my license. In a week I can't drive! Oh!' So he goes to the alderman, and they pulled some strings and sent it special delivery. That meant the mailbox lady brought it right to the house. Well, he's out on jobs, and the license plate arrives. So I hid it. (*Consultant starts laughing*) He comes home, 'Did the special delivery come?' 'What special delivery?' He says, 'My license.' I says, 'Oh yeah, that came.' He says, 'Well, where is it; where is it?' I told him, 'Well, you can have it just as soon as you fix the washer." (*Grandson is laughing*) So he screamed, 'What the hell are you talking about?' Well, he went through my drawers, his drawers, the cupboards. After about a half-hour, he went and got his toolbox and fixed the washer. When the first load was in, I went and gave him his license plate.

Consultant: Good story.

These are great stories about how grandmother got grandfather to fix some things around the house. They are examples of creative marital fighting. Grandmother fights with grandfather and gets somewhere. This has not happened with mother and father. Their battles with each other are often laid on the kids. They have shown little ownership of their troubles. Father has no capacity to think that way. Mother knows how to, but it is self-destructive to do so.

MIDDLE STAGE OF THE CONSULTATION

During the middle stage of the consultation, the discussion moves naturally to the next generation. The consultant includes the grandparents' perceptions of the family unit in treatment and the family they raised. The grandparents are still the focus of attention. The consultant asks about mother as a little girl, moving them toward the present, because it appears that there is not a great deal of perplexing conflict in the distant past. Because the current family is broken apart, and it is important to move to the relevance of the present. To give the children a chance to hear how mother was seen as a girl, the grandparents are asked to describe their daughter's growing up and later to describe the family group. Again, the focus is on perceptions (subjective reality), not the consensual reality of family life.

Consultant: So, how about your daughter—what was she like as a little girl?

Grandmother: I think she had two spankings, and I know one of them she didn't deserve—it was all my fault. (*Therapist laughs*)

Consultant: Wow.

Grandmother: She was fine. She was . . .

Consultant: (*Interrupts*) She wasn't good at doing wrong?

Grandmother: She did very little. She was very, very good.

Consultant: (*Interrupts*) Any stories about her?

Grandmother: (*Continues*) Until she became a teenager; then she got a little bit difficult.

Doug: Talk about her car.

Grandmother: (*Breaks out laughing*) Yeah, you'd holler up the stairs and say, 'Judy, come help me with supper.' She'd yell down, 'You want me to flunk chemistry, don't you?' would be the answer I got. Then later she was sorry she didn't know how to do nothing much.

Father: Her dad always took her out.

Grandmother: Yeah, he'd take her shopping for the perfect dress. 'I wouldn't be caught dead in that.' You know, she had her own taste, which was good taste, so we went along with it. No problems with her.

Consultant: How many kids?

Grandmother: Five.

Consultant: She's the oldest?

The consultant probes deeper to find out more about the family the grandparents raised. The boundary between generations is permeable, so that talking about one generation blends into talking about the next. This is crucial, as it palpates intergenerational patterning. The consultant and therapist get a sense of the emotional tone, parental expectations, and rules of the family. They also note the children's agreement or disagreement with what the grandparents expose. The quality of the extended family relationship appears in the therapy session. The grandchildren may hear for the first time what the parents were like as children. They become aware of intergenerational themes and similarities shared with their parents. The child who feels isolated from the family recognizes that Dad had similar experiences and that they are more similar than different. The estrangement decreases, even if for a brief instant. For this reason, it is important to ask about the patterns between the generations. Did the grandparents' child rearing differ from that of their parents? What were the healthy adaptations that they made in raising their children? How were the similarities and differences played out? Which parent was in charge of the children? How did they manage day-to-day living?

Consultant: What was your family like, the one you raised? Were you the kind of father your father was, or did you take lessons from your father-in-law?

Grandfather: Not quite as bad, but I disciplined them. They got spankings when they needed them. Sometimes, I guess I went a little overboard. (*Laughs*)

Grandmother: Yes.

Consultant: Well, you probably had to live up to your dad's standards.

Grandfather: Yes.

The idea here is that grandfather would have parented as he was parented. That question interferes with moralizing about the past and, instead, tells what happened, not what should or should not have happened. Our friend and colleague, Douglas Kramer says, "each family is its own masterpiece." The implication is that that there is a combination of balance and drama in each family that enables members to say, "this is us. There was pain and there were threads of glory. Some of it we got right and some of it went wrong."

During the middle stage, the consultant looks for connections between the generations. Families with the ability to share stories, have a sense of humor, and to be involved with each other are more likely to resolve differences in a healthy direction. They feel more hopeful. They can rely on the older generation for guidance, encouragement, and support. Families that remain disconnected, angry, bitter, and confrontational during the extended family interview are more challenging and disruptive during therapy. They are far more likely to remain stuck and to resist the therapist's efforts to intervene because their level of defense remains high. In this extended family interview, the adult generation and grandchildren get more involved. They encourage the grandparents to tell stories and appear to enjoy the reminiscing. For example:

Grandfather: She did tell her father a fib one time, though, about her leg. We talked about it yesterday or the day before. It was about when her dad was in the house.

Greg: Let's hear it, Grandma.

Grandmother goes on to elaborate about telling fibs and how she got her husband into trouble. As the family laughs, the consultant becomes aware of the cleverness of grandmother to get things done. She could be devious, but always with the goal of making family life better. Greg's acknowledgment of grandmother's courage and playfulness is a sign of health. There is evidence of relational reward. The present generation has not mastered grandmother's craftiness, but rather has attacked problems in such a manner that everyone loses face. They are brutal and unyielding toward one another. Giving in to the other's perception or goal is somehow considered dishonorable. Greg picks up on the previous story grandmother told when he says she should have hid his license plate in order to get him to fix the barn. It is apparent that the grandchildren are involved in the narrative to the point of utilizing the threads to weave new stories or solutions. The therapist broadens the context to include the current generation in the discussion.

Greg: You should have taken away his license plate and made him build a new barn. (*Laughter*)

Grandfather: All the kids seemed to gather at our place, and they just had a good time.

Therapist: Well, that's still going on in this family.

Grandfather: Yeah, I think—well, he is a real different type of kid (*Pointing his finger at Greg*)

Greg: Me? (*Mocking tone*) No!

Grandfather: (*Mimicking Greg's tone*) No!

Grandmother: Yeah, you run with some bad kids.

Consultant: Are you the oldest grandson in the family, Greg?

It is apparent throughout the interview that the grandparents are instrumentally involved in the extended family. The grandchildren either respect or fear grandfather's involvement. He is a tough old guy who does not back down. He is concerned about Greg's behavior and inserts himself when he feels it is necessary.

Consultant: (*To grandfather*) It sounds like you were pretty fierce when you were young. (*Grandfather shrugs*)

Doug: He still is. (*Laughing*)

Consultant: Is he? I figured you would have switched.

Grandfather: I've been known to.

Greg: A friend of mine pulled in to see me the other day and my grandfather told him he would drag him under his car if he continued to get me in trouble.

Grandfather: That is the kid he ran away to Florida with. I had just gone by the house and saw his white car sitting there. So I pulled in.

Greg: I said, 'Jodie you'd better leave because that is my grandfather.' So he pulled in and wouldn't let him back out. My grandfather read this kid the riot act. I was worried, sometimes my grandfather can lose it.

The consultant expands the focus to the generation in therapy by asking the grandparents their thoughts about this family. The question is framed in an open manner so they can elaborate on aspects of the family they feel are essential.

Consultant: What are your thoughts on this family?

Grandmother: I think they are coming along really good thanks to therapy. Greg is doing very well living with my older daughter. She's like an army sergeant.

Mother: She's a female drill instructor.

Consultant: Oh, is that right?

Greg: I've actually been grounded twice. (*When grandfather starts talking Greg touches Chris's face and Chris slaps him back*)

Grandfather: She has eight kids, she had four and has adopted four. She's done a pretty good job raising them. Her kids haven't been in trouble like these kids. These kids seem to like to be in trouble. That's why she had Greg move in with them. He's been giving his mother so much trouble since she and Mark split up. She was hoping to relieve some of the pressure.

Greg: I don't get in trouble anymore.

Grandfather: No, not anymore, but that's just recently.

The family, as we have heard about it, is a playful battle zone. There is a toughness in this family, which is different from what the therapist and consultant grew up with. The stories are appealing, but it is not clear what sort of healing or recovery could go on. What did they cry about? The therapists did not get into questioning them in this way, probably because they were concerned about the absence of a "we." In this interview they encounter a very palpable "we," yet it feels important to bring it to life in the session rather than to evaluate its quality in detail.

The family tells some stories about mothers's sister, Mary, comparing the two sisters. It is disappointing she didn't attend the interview. She sounds very different from mother. The therapists have not yet heard of Roxanne being mischievous, only that she was good. The family story gives the feeling that grandparents were more involved with the sister. Mother comes across in their stories as two dimensional and concealed or invisible. She is unassertive and does not show much of herself. Her voice is soft. She has been going through a period of silent defiance.

The objective at this point is to explore the older generation's perceptions of the problems the family is having and any thoughts they have about resolving issues among family members. There is an inquisitiveness about the family problems, but no desire on the consultant's part to expose the grandparents to negative feedback from the younger generations.

Consultant: Do you have any ideas as to why they like to get into trouble so much?

Grandmother: Greg likes to go along with the crowd.

Greg: How come it is always Greg, Grandma?

Grandmother: That is Greg's problem.

Grandfather: You're a follower and not a leader. And you have to go around with a lot of the wrong group.

Greg: The town rats.

Grandmother: There is nothing wrong with that, as long as it is the right crowd that knows the difference between right and wrong. And you do know.

Grandfather: I hate to say this, but a lot of the trouble was your father, I really do.

Grandmother: Well he was quite the troublemaker when he was growing up.

Grandfather: He's not anymore, but I think they learn trouble from their father. I get along with him, but a lot of the trouble is him. I have a feeling that's it.

The grandparents feel a lot of the problem is due to father's trauma in his own childhood and his subsequent trauma in Vietnam. So far father has remained outside the discussion, although clearly he is viewed as a central part of the problem. They are clear about including him. If father objected to the discussion, the consultant would neutralize the tension by stating that while this is helpful to his understanding of family life, it is not the definitive answer to what the problems are. It is imperative to keep tension low around the older generation as they are invited guests, not patients in the endeavor. The therapist wants them to leave feeling that they have been helpful. This is not necessary, however. Sometimes things heat up without benefit and the process can be painful. The consultant involves father at this point, so that he is not further alienated. His involvement is critical to the success of therapy.

Consultant: Mark, has he been like a father to you for all the years that you have been married?

Father: Yeah, he really has.

Consultant: I was thinking about the story about how they got together and wondering if the pattern will continue. Like I was teasing about the way you fell in love with her father first.

Grandmother: We liked him right away.

Grandfather: He stayed at our house for quite awhile while she was in college.

Grandmother: Yeah.

Grandfather: He used to beat on the wall, thinking he was still in Vietnam.

Consultant: Morse code?

Grandfather: No, that is when he was having trouble with flashbacks. That is when he was having a hard time—Vietnam, Laos, and his home life as a child. (*Greg laughs*) Right? (*Father nods in agreement*)

The discussion then wanders back to Greg. We inquire as to who Greg might be modeled after. This, again, is a standard and interesting question. It gives an idea as to where personalities come from. He might have been like grandmother's nasty stepbrother, but no, Greg is not nasty.

Consultant: Another thing I was wondering is if you think there were other Greg's in the family?

Greg: Another what?

Consultant: Do you think Greg is modeled after anybody?

Grandmother: No.

Consultant: Not one of your sons?

Grandfather: Another Greg?

Consultant: No, I was wondering if his personality matches anybody else's in the family. Either side. Like did either of you have a brother like him?

Grandfather: She had a nasty brother. (*Pointing to grandmother*)

Grandmother: Greg is not nasty.

Grandfather: No, not like that.

Grandmother: Nothing like that.

Consultant: I had a different fantasy then you, but that's okay.

The consultant has the idea that Greg might be like other personalities in the family from either the grandparents' or parents' generations. The family does not see the connection, so the consultant lets it drop by saying that he has another fantasy. During this type of interview the consultant suggests his hypotheses about the family. If the family picks them up and elaborates on them, this is beneficial, if not, they are just the consultant's free associations about the family. The goal is to expand perceptions through a language of inference, not to force ideas on the family. Then Greg says fairly honestly that he gets mad at mother, but he is not sure why. Some comparison of mother and her sister follows.

During the middle stage of the consultation, the family is likely to disclose information that has not yet been discussed within the family. The therapist and consultant note these issues but do not process them to the depth required for therapy to be successful. Instead, they pay attention to the family's emotional tone and interaction when these issues are raised. In the following example, the family has been talking about its odd sense of humor when the topic of conversation shifts without notice.

Grandfather: We had a babysitter that made some trouble, and we had no idea what was going on. I guess there was sexual crap, at least I think that there was.

Grandmother: I am not sure—I heard two different stories.

Grandfather: I think that's where our older kids got into problems.

Grandmother: I thought this was a great baby sitter. I would have the dishes done, and everything was all set for her to come. I would have supper in the oven and just tell her to turn the oven on at 4:00, or something like that. It would be all ready, and then off I'd go to work. For months—I don't know how long that was—everything appeared fine. I thought, 'Boy, we've never had a babysitter who left the house the way I left it.' Well, the first thing that got me suspicious was when I noticed the roast. 'What happened to the roast?' My oldest said, 'Oh, that's at the babysitter's house.' 'What's it doing there?' I said. Well, finally it came out. After I would go to work she would take the roast, or whatever I had in the oven, and pile the kids in the car and take them to her house. No wonder the house didn't get messed up. Well, I thought, I don't like that. That's why I have her come to the house—to our house, with their things, their clothes. At the same time, I answered the phone and it was the babysitter's mother. She said, 'Now, I hate to be the one to rat on my own daughter, but you'd better do something. She lives upstairs, she locks your baby in a bedroom, and off she goes. Then she picks up your older children from school, drops them off, and takes off again.' She said, 'They are not supervised or taken care of.' Well, the little one had been coming into our room every morning at like 4:00 crying about the big man, "the Big Man." (*Raising voice*) We had thought it was something on television and had tried to ask, but we couldn't get anything out of him but the big man. Well, of course, we fired her immediately, but we didn't know all of it. Well, the big man, it turned out, had been her brother. He would pick the baby up by the arm and throw him over onto a chair. I mean, anytime there had been a bruise or a scrape, she had been telling me he had fallen on this or that—and I had believed her! Oh, I wish that had never happened.

Consultant: (To mother) Do you remember that?

Mother: No, I wasn't involved with that, but my brother talks about that quite a bit. He was only 2 when that happened, but he still has nightmares about it. Usually when he's drunk he'll call up and tell me about all that stuff. I . . .

Grandmother: (*Interrupting*) But he won't tell me. I've asked him to tell me so I can understand, but he won't tell me.

Mother: He'll go on just crying as he tells me. He'll start crying and say that he wet the bed until he was 14 or 15 because of it, and that he still has nightmares.

Grandmother: I mean, here you are potty training a kid, and the kid is locked in a bedroom. What's a kid supposed to do?

Grandfather: I think that's all that was going on, hopefully.

Mother: No, there was more. He told me. I think that's the start of all his troubles.

Grandfather: We never knew about it at the time. We didn't know anything about it at all.

The subject of abuse is broached, then grandfather quickly changes the topic. They get into something else about mother's brother. When he was a child, something happened that involved a crazy babysitter. It sounds like sexual or physical abuse—a mystery that continues to be upsetting for grandmother. Mother is the one who provides comfort to her brother. It sounds like this was a painful time and it is still unfinished. In ongoing therapy, the therapist would come back to this subject to gather more information on how the family dealt with the issue and what the long-term ramifications of the abuse appear to be. Clearly, the current generation is at risk due to these issues. The therapist makes a mental note of the fact that the family really doesn't comprehend the significance of the disclosure. A common pattern within this family is to dance around ambiguous issues without really dealing with them. This is true with father's drug and alcohol use. Everyone in the family knows about this but tries to find ways to normalize or ignore the problem.

Grandfather: You haven't said anything, Mark. Don't you have anything to say?

Father: I'm just listening.

Grandfather: You're supposed to talk, too.

Father: I did my talking the other day.

Consultant: Anything you want to know?

Grandfather: (*To consultant*) Anything I want to know from you?

Consultant: Yes.

Grandfather: Yeah. He's (father) still smoking pot, and he said he got over that up in Boston.

Father: No, I didn't say I got over it

Grandfather: You told me you were totally over it!

Grandmother: (*Interrupting*) You told me you were totally done!

Father: Fine!

Doug: (*Laughing*) He probably was on it then.

Grandfather: Don't you think that if you used the medication you were supposed to use that you wouldn't have to use pot to keep yourself calm? When you went away, we found all of your pills underneath the couch. You just threw them away! You spent good money on them, and instead you smoke pot. The kids all know, which I think is lousy, because they have to put up with that and have to know that.

Greg: I know more of my friends whose parents smoke more weed than them.

Doug: Yeah, everybody has it.

Grandfather: I never smoked it in my life. I never smoked dope my whole life, and I don't see the need.

Father: That's a subject that's really hard. If I was to go the legal route and drink alcohol—as you know I am worse than I ever am when I drink alcohol. When I smoke pot I'm quiet, calm, and collected. I tried Valium, but it didn't do anything for me, did it?

Mother: No.

Father: What did Thorazine do for me? It made me like a zombie. What did Stelazine do for me? It made me like a zombie.

Consultant: Well, what you're saying is that you don't like the dishonesty. You feel like it gets in the way of being a dad.

Mother: It's not so much the pot as it is the fact that he lies about it.

Grandfather: Well, the thing that bothers me is the kids. It makes the kids think that they can do it.

Doug: Oh, I know I don't do it.

Grandfather: Well, as long as his smoking doesn't make the kids think it's okay. It's awful damn expensive, though.

Greg: When I was younger . . .

Father: I'm not smoking it like I used to. I had totally stopped. My anniversary started coming up here just recently and my therapy group started getting into some heavy stuff, so I started up again. I bought an eighth of an ounce when I first got up here, and I still have some left. I've only had maybe two or three bowls out of it. It isn't like I go home and smoke or stay stoned all day long, like I used to.

Greg: Yeah, he used to sit on the couch and smoke weed. We weren't allowed in the house.

(*Boys all begin talking at once. They refer to the parents describing marijuana use as 'coffee time.'*)

Greg: We used to come back in and be like, 'Whew, that's some coffee man.' (*Makes a fanning motion with his hand as if blowing away smoke*)

The consultant listens to the family's discussion about the drug use but again leaves it for the therapist to process in ongoing therapy. Grandfather comments on father, but father turns passive and backs out. Grandfather then parents him. When father alludes to the interview from "the other day," he is playing "boy" and defying his surrogate father. The consultant's question to grandfather supports his interaction with father. He is implying, "Go ahead and push him a little." A group dialogue about father's drug and alcohol use follows. An intervention by the therapists at this time would be an error. This is something one senses more than decides. The family is taking over and working on the problem. The therapist and consultant remain alert, listening in detail. It is not the time to challenge father to stop his use or to help him see the potential effect it has on his adolescent son's defiance. It is significant that the family feels comfortable enough to bring up the issue within the extended family interview. Clearly, the grandparents are worried about the effect on their grandchildren as well as their son-in-law's coping skills. It is inappropriate in an extended family interview to raise tensions within the treatment group. If information on *ongoing* physical or sexual abuse is disclosed, the consultant and therapist pursue this information because of mandated reporting requirements. It is more common for past abuses, rather than current problems, to be disclosed in extended family interview. Nonetheless, the consultant and therapist need to be prepared to handle tough predicaments, should they arise.

The parents discuss dilemmas they have with disciplining adolescent children. A common problem for parents is how to set and enforce limits. Most parents have difficulty tolerating being disliked by their children. There is a myth that it is not okay to have your children hate you and that somehow you have failed as a parent if this happens. The consultant takes on this challenge with mother.

Consultant: One thing I've figured out is that you can't be a success as a parent until you learn to enjoy being hated by your kids. (*Greg laughs*)

Mother: That they do.

Consultant: It sounds like that's hard for you—for anybody to be angry with you.

Mother: Yes, it is. I don't like being hated that much.

Grandmother: I don't think any of my kids ever hated me.

Consultant: Well, you missed out on it then.

Mother: No, she was perfect.

Grandfather: The kids got mad at me because I got rough a few times, but we all could get together and be a beautiful whole family.

Consultant: Well, you can get along beautifully even though you hate them.

Greg: That's kind of why, though, Mom. You can't handle it. You call Pop and everyone just shuts up.

Mother: That's true, whenever he's around.

Greg: You're just like, 'You all better shut up, or I'll call your grandfather.' I'm just like. (*Puts his hands up in the air*)

Mother: When you guys all got drunk that time, I brought you right to his house.

Consultant: I'm impressed.

Mother: Sometimes I worry that I'm the one who's caused his heart problems.

Chris: That was me and Doug, and we weren't even drunk.

Consultant: I don't know. My fantasy is that you're keeping him alive by giving him a reason to live.

Judy: (*To grandfather*) I make you feel needed?

Consultant: (*To grandfather*) You sound like you enjoy it.

Grandfather: Oh, yeah, we all . . .

(*Greg, Doug and Chris are all discussing the event where they had been drinking and drown out some of the conversation.*)

Consultant: If we could get all four parents mad at once, I bet they'd take care of business. (*Therapist laughs*)

The consultant advances the notion that it is healthy to be hated by your children. It is an indication that you are on the right track as a parent, especially with children who challenge the limits. The consultant speaks to the therapist, but he is giving mother the message that the children will not be grateful for having limits set. They will pressure her. This is an important issue, as it is dealing with the self—the importance of mother's self. At the same time it suggests something about the parenting role, and thus we are dealing with mother's personhood as well. Grandmother neutralizes the point by suggesting her children never hated her. The consultant tells her she missed out on the experience. That comment is also directed to mother. Still she seems to be in the role of child, not yet self-owning. If the consultant wanted to work with grandmother, he might have said, "You were never aware that your kids hated you." Grandfather supplied an explanation here, "The kids got mad at me . . . " Hatred is a common emotion in intimate relationships. Love and hate are a dialectical pairing. One can only have as much love as one has hatred. Being in danger of losing someone of great importance leads to hatred. The consultant points out that families can get along beautifully even though children hate their parents.

Mother does what most people in her shoes do: She calls for grandfather when things are out of hand. Including grandfather is a by-product of her husband being unable to fulfill the role of father. But the solution has a problem. It highlights her inability to deal with the children and collapses her into a generation with them, making them of equal rank. Mother has never been any good at being tough, partly because it seems to not be her manner. She is too apprehensive, and her personhood is too far in the background. It is not clear if father is a factor, but it seems likely his behavior says to the children, "You don't have to take her seriously." Here grandfather moves in to be mother's partner. He sounds rough and tough, but be reminded there was some question about whether this man was too ill to make it to the interview. The parental team is weak and ineffective. Rather than dealing with this issue directly, the consultant suggests that if the four adults took on the children as a team, they could take care of business much easier.

By this point it is clear that the older generation is doing its best to help the current generation emotionally and financially, almost to the point of detriment to themselves. They are fearful that if they pull back, the family will fail. The focus is shifted to the health in the family.

Therapist: So, in a way you guys are still around trying to raise this crowd.

Grandfather: Pretty much. I've been nervous. I've had prostrate cancer and two heart attacks. I've had a stroke, so, I've got problems. I'm still trying to keep up with this gang here. It's not easy.

Therapist: Yeah, they are a hard group to deal with.

Grandfather: It has a lot to do with why I'm feeling so worn down all the time. I've still got to watch the business so I can pay the bills.

Consultant: Oh, you've got to run a business.

Grandfather: Oh, yeah. I get $324 a month for Social Security, so I've got to run a business. Plus, we've had to help these guys out with about $17,000 to help pay stuff off. Our money is tight as the devil, and we still try to help these guys out—it's not easy. I can't hardly—lately, I've been so stressed out that I can't hardly walk. I try to walk, and my legs just give out on me. I think a lot of this stuff is tough.

Consultant: How long do you think you have left? Do you have any idea?

Grandfather: How long do I have left to live?

Consultant: Yeah.

Grandmother: A while.

Grandfather: Well, I think the fact that I never smoke or drank is going to help. I can't say I never drank, but it's been a long time.

(*Doug and Greg begin joking about grandfather having a couple of beers to help him get to sleep.*)

Greg: If anything, his drug problem is Tums.

Therapist: What do you think is right about the family? What keeps you so invested and loving? There's got to be something that you're seeing that you're caring for pretty deeply.

Grandfather: I love them all!

Therapist: What's to love?

Grandfather: Oh, I don't know. I do—I love every one of them. I know they fight, but . . .

Greg: (*Interrupting*) When we do stuff together it's the best.

Grandfather: Yes. When we go out hunting together. I bought them their rifles, and I buy the ammo and their licenses for them.

Greg: We just go into the woods and enjoy ourselves.

Grandfather: We go down to Garland, PA, and there are lots of big rocks down there. They climb all over them and bring friends with them. That was before all this. I'm kind of laid up now.

The therapist makes an important comment when he refers to them "raising this crowd,"which is also more evocative and colorful than "providing support in this time of pain." Grandfather then comments on his being self-sacrificial. The consultant poses the strong question "How long do you have left?" in response to the implication he might die soon. But grandfather avoids the question, as many do. Parents like to threaten with death or craziness, but when the therapist pushes either issue, they make it indefinite again. This is an important question with any extended family interview. Children begin to worry that the parents will die soon when the parents reach age 40. They may not speak about it and avoid the issue if raised, nevertheless, death has become part of the equation in the family's unconscious planning about the future. Grandfather does not have long to live, and all know it, despite what he says. The grandfather is tired of all the responsibility he has for the family. He would like his daughter and son-in-law to become more effective in their roles as parents so he could become the grandfather. Toward the end of the session, the therapist and consultant function more as a team. The therapist goes on to ask the family why they can't get their lives together.

The group anxiety must have been pushed by the question about how much time grandfather has to live, even though no one commented on it. The therapist moves in with the question about what is good about the group, as if to say, "lets get back to life and the future." The grandparents are relieved by his question and respond with an affirmation of love. The therapist makes one of those deliciously reversing questions, "What's to love?" This backs him out of the cheerleading seduction and reestablishes him as therapist. This is always important to do, especially after a therapist has been encouraging or reassuring. It makes them decide what to believe about themselves; it interferes with dependency, and perpetuates the process of the family's life belonging to the family.

Therapist: Yeah, well what do you guys think makes it so difficult to pull together as a family and figure out what you need to do?

Greg: I don't know. I don't really care is part of where I'm at.

Grandfather: (*Voice raised*) You what?

Greg: That's probably where I'm at. There's no way we're all going to get pulled back together as a family. That's just not going to happen. Mom and Dad are like—I don't know, how would you say it? After that happened, I don't really care to get back together. That broke everything up.

Consultant: (*To Greg*) You mean when they split up?

Greg: Yeah, since they ran away from each other. I was like, 'Huh?' and then it was like, 'Wow!'

Grandfather: Well, what did finally happen to get you guys like that?

Doug: All of the fighting and then Dad finally left. I don't think any of us were there.

Greg: I was definitely there. I got chased out of the house.

Doug: I was at a friend's house. Mom just came and got me.

Missy: Greg just grabbed me out of my room and we took off to the creek.

Mother: Oh, that was the day before. That was the day the police came.

Doug: Well, I was at a birthday party.

Greg: I was taking care of my sisters.

Therapist: So you just think it's been since your mom and dad split up?

Greg: Since they split up I'm thinking, 'what is there to put together?' You know.

Therapist: You just don't have much of a sense about what the family is about?

Greg: There is no base to put the family back together.

Therapist: Hmm.

Greg: I mean, relationshipwise it's all right, but it's never going to be the same, you know. It can't.

Mother: Even if we were to fix things between us?

Greg: Between you and Dad? Yeah, but with all the fighting and all.

Doug: That's why Dad could keep the place he has, you know, if he needs a time out.

Greg: It's like, if you guys get back together and there's a base. If you guys get back together and just start arguing, what's the point? What's the logic? You know you need to go step-by-step.

Grandfather: Right now seems to be working pretty decently.

Greg: I mean, because I caused a lot of problems. I raised a lot, I raised a lot of hell that didn't need to be raised. I don't even know why I did it.

Consultant: I have a theory that you might have just been drawing fire. If they could be mad at you then they might not be mad at each other.

Grandmother: Exactly. Very true. Yes.

Therapist: So you think that it's hopeless if they get back together, that it's inevitable.

Greg: I'm saying that that is just a base. That's something to start on, you know. That's something to start at, but if they get back together and it's just like it was before—what's the logic?

Therapist: Why bother?

Greg: Yeah, why bother?

Therapist: Do you think it has to be that way, or do you think that there is any hope?

Greg: Oh, I think there's hope, if they want there to be hope. If they want to try, if everybody wants to try, but all it takes is one person saying no.

Doug: If one person starts yelling, then everybody else is going to start yelling.

Greg: That's all it takes is one person. I'm not just talking about yelling, Doug, you know.

Therapist: What more do you mean?

Greg: I'm not just into yelling. It takes everybody as a team. In a family, everybody is connected. It's like one big circle. If one person doesn't want to do it, then that circle is broke. Do you know what I'm saying; do you understand?

Grandmother: Boy, he has brought an awful lot of sense out here today! Very good, Greg.

Therapist: So, you're only as strong as your weakest link.

Greg: (*Smiling*) That's too technical.

Grandfather: I did not realize how bad things had gotten.

Grandmother: No, we did not know. She . . .

Grandfather: (*Interrupting*) She never said anything. We didn't know what was going on.

Grandmother: (*Interrupting*) She never told us. I don't know what we would have done. I don't know if we could have done anything.

Grandfather: I don't know. I've heard the neighbors say. . .

Consultant: (Interrupting) You just told her about that spanking you gave her by mistake—she's earned it finally. (*Grandparents chuckle*)

Greg: I'm saying that when everybody else starts trying, that's when I'll try.

The children are now more involved in the interview, in doing something, and in thinking about fixing things. They are also concerned about what has happened. Greg is the most active, talking like a young cotherapist about the base being gone. This is very impressive, and it shows the need for defiance has diminished apparently. He is skeptical about the mother and father reunion, as is probably everyone in the room. It also seems that the therapist is now more active and the consultant has backed out. Was all of this stimulated by the question about grandfather's impending death? We believe it was. Greg says he created a lot of problems, then asks why he did it. The consultant answers from the metaphysical model of this book, making the idea explicit, "You did it to keep your parents from being so upset with one another. You did it so their war would not be so destructive."

We love that fact that grandmother gets it. She has been listening very carefully during the interview. This is a good prognostic sign. The grandparents endorse the therapist's work with the family wholeheartedly. This is one of the most important components of consultation interviews like this. The background family gives the therapist an endorsement, and at the same time, gives the treatment family permission to go ahead and change—an important benediction.

Greg is very poetic, developing his own metaphorical models. This is a signal of high-quality thinking by the family; it is non-concrete, parallel play in the family. If all are not into solving the problem, then the circle is broken. Grandmother gets it, loves it, and endorses Greg. It is very important that the scapegoat is appreciated when he speaks, if not by the family, then by the therapists, but best by the family. As Greg becomes more active, the grandparents become more reflective.

Why, at this point do they start to say that they did not realize how bad things had become? We don't know exactly what events the grandparents are referring to here. At this time, the consultant makes a primary process comment about how mother got a spanking when she did not deserve it, and that now she has earned it. He likes the grandparents' response and underscores it.

The consultant repeats his comment, again reversing the overt valence of the issue. Good for mother, the angelic little girl has finally earned her spanking. Being angelic is such a horrible burden. She has been being defiant in ways that are self-destructive but also give her a life. Mother's falling apart may be an attempt to pull the family together by making it necessary for them to take care of her. She and father are both abnegating their parental roles. She is also undermining the saint and sinner dichotomy that often develops in a marriage. This kind of characterization confuses how the children's defiance is seen and makes the parents' kids' anger more explicit.

In the next segment as the consultation reaches the end, the consultant has backed out and the therapist takes a more active role. At this point in the interview the children reveal that they meet during lunch at school. The consultant and therapist have no awareness of this covert "we-ness." This leads to the conclusion that the bickering among the children has served to support the parental split. Mother concludes that the children want them back together. The therapist questions her, "That's the message you get out of it?" She is oversimplifying, and in that sense, being dishonest when she hints she would do what the children want. Grandmother gives her permission not to do it that way. Greg clarifies that they should not do it as a means of social appropriateness, but that they had better be honest with themselves. Father joins in and sounds just like a mealymouthed drunk. He adapts to the discussion, but with only a pseudo-understanding of adaptation. He exhibits no sense of self-ownership or knowledge of how he has contributed to the problem, and thus stays a nobody. Then mother starts to talk like a drunk, but focusing on, "Poor me."

Doug is increasingly active, and makes his disappointment with mother explicit. He is father's partner. The consultant and therapist previously viewed him as the angriest of the children and the least seducible. Doug makes an interpretation of intent to mother. The consultant says that it sounds like they are just trying to understand something, not to lay blame. This is a good statement because it invites participation. Mother ends up crying. The consultant depathologizes crying by saying that it increases togetherness. He then gently tells father to quit being such a self-justifying jerk and suggests that if he could cry more with mother and with himself, it would help the pain for everyone.

Dr. Owen: Hmm. So you think the family is just so broken that the only way to grow into the kind of person you want to be is to just get away from it?

Greg: No, I think it can be fixed, but you need a base—somewhere to start from, you know.

Grandfather: You're getting along better now that you're . . .

Greg: (*Interrupting*) Yeah, I'm getting along with everybody now. Me and Doug used to wring each other's necks.

Doug: Now at lunch, we're always sitting there talking.

Greg: Now, I'll get out of chorus early to go see Doug, and I'll sit there and talk to him.

Doug: Lunch time is like our visiting time.

Greg: Right, and I get along with her now. (*Points to Missy*)

Therapist: Well, how does that make you feel about your family, about your parents?

Greg: Bad, man. It's like, what family? Now Grandma and Grandpa, I used to run to them, too.

Doug: I think I know what Greg's trying to say about base. (*Begins using blocks on the floor*) Like say here's Mom and Dad. (*Points to two blocks at the base of a tower*) Take one away, and everything crumbles. (*Blocks fall over*)

Greg: Yeah, there you go.

Therapist: (*To father and mother*) Well, what do you guys do with what the kids are saying right now?

Mother: I feel badly for things in the past, but there's nothing they can do to correct that. One thing it tells me is that what they want more than anything is for us two to get back together.

Therapist: That's the message you get out of it?

Greg: But you guys need to want to get back together, you know. You got to want to.

Grandmother: You can't just be what they want.

Greg: No, it's got to be done as a family, not just like, 'Hey, I'm saying that if you two get back together I'm going to be good.' No, it ain't just like that.

Mother: No, I mean that's what I'm hearing from you is that you wish we would get back together.

Therapist: That's what you're taking from their statement.

Greg: I'm saying that, but I'm not wishing that you guys would get back together and things could be like they were, because—no. If that even happens, I won't even say, 'See you.' I'll just go live on my own.

Therapist: What about you, Mark? You got any thoughts on what they're saying?

Father: I don't know. I have a lot of thoughts. I do hear in the background of it that they want for us to get back together.

Greg: But there's more to it than just getting back together, you know.

Father: I brushed it off from the two boys because I don't see Greg all that much now that he's away. With these boys I keep telling them, 'Well, what if I do come back? You know that some of the rules are going to have to change. That's just the way I am.' They just say that they would expect that, and that they would like some of the rules back or some of the rules to change.

Greg: It might kind of feel weird, though, seeing you two back together—seeing you both at the same time.

Doug: There are hardly any rules there. That's why everything is starting to fall apart. Everybody is just doing whatever they want.

Grandfather: Well the rules are there.

Father: No, there are rules there. It's just that nobody is following them.

Doug: Right, everybody is just doing whatever they want. What we need is somebody to enforce the rules.

Greg: So what if they hate you for a day or two, you know, so what.

Chris: I mean, Mom's at work, she's goes to the bar during the week, and she's upstairs in her room.

Mother: I'm downstairs watching TV with you kids a whole lot, too.

Greg: Yeah, but when Dad—the way it used to be was that we'd go on family drives and stuff. That just all crumbled, you know.

Chris: Yeah, we used to do all sorts of stuff.

Therapist: It's just the way you feel. Your mother's not available like that.

Chris: Yeah.

Greg: The last 2 months its just been like, 'Let's get together for the family argument.' You know?

Mother: I work long hours.

Chris: Well, it's fine when you're at work, but when you come home you're still not there. You go upstairs or you'll be like, 'All my friends at work are going to be at the bar, so I'm going to be at the bar.' And you're gone.

Mother: I do that once a week, on Tuesdays. Or Wednesdays, sometimes, instead of Tuesdays.

Chris: Then there's sometimes when I have to be somewhere, and Mom will be like, 'Well, I'm only going to be at work for 20 more minutes.' Then I'll call her 20 minutes later, and she's like, 'Well, I'm only going to be here 20 more minutes.' Twenty more minutes go by and I call. Then I end up missing out on wherever I was going to go. Like one time, all Jeff had to do was . . .

Greg: (*Interrupting*) You used to do that to me. You'd be at the bar and it was like, '15 minutes' then it was 2½ hours later you'd show up.

Chris: (*Continuing*) Remember that one time when it was me and Jeff on a school night?

Chris: (*Continuing*) Remember that one time Jeff wanted to stay the night? I tried to talk to you, and you just kept saying, 'Twenty more minutes. Twenty more minutes. Twenty more minutes.' Finally, I just said, 'Well, I'm just going to go stay at Jeff's house.' (*Other kids get up to help clean up the blocks Kelly had been playing with*)

Therapist: Uh huh. So you guys are just kind of more worried about your Mom when your Dad's not around. You're thinking she just needs someone to parent her?

Doug: Yeah, like the rules are there, but nobody really obeys them. We need someone to enforce them, and she can't.

Therapist: When you say nobody, are you including yourself or are you just trying to . . . ? (*Trails off*)

Doug: Yeah, I'm including myself, because why bother to follow the rules if nobody else will.

Chris: Hmm.

Doug: Nobody else will do it, so even if I obey them, nobody else is doing it. So what's the point?

Chris: We're not trying to put you down or anything, Mom.

Consultant: No, it doesn't sound like that. I think you're just trying to figure something out.

Chris: But then she ends up crying.

Consultant: That's okay if she cries. There's a lot to cry about. Sometimes it takes crying to get back together again. That's just more demanding. I sometimes think that's true for you, Dad. If you could cry more about this it wouldn't be . . .

TERMINATING THE CONSULTATION

The consultation ends with the consultant asking the family members if they have any further questions or points they would like to raise. He tells the family that he and the therapist will be discussing the interview and that they may ask about the discussion during their next appointment. The consultant turns the therapy process back to the therapist. This is a crucial move, as the consultant should not usurp the therapist's relationship with the family. The consultant is an ally to the therapist and functions in a step-parent role with the family.

Consultant: Is there anything else anyone would like to talk about before we stop? (*To the therapist*) Dr. Owen, do you have anything you would like to bring up? Did we miss anything you wanted to discuss?

Therapist: No, I feel like we covered a lot of ground today. I am pleased with everyone's willingness to say what was on their mind. I know that can be risky.

Consultant: Dr. Owen and I will talk about you after you leave. Feel free to ask about what we discussed if you would like. I think this family has a lot of strength and creativity. If you parents can become more of a team, I think the kids would calm down a bit. It is unsettling for kids to not know whether the parents will make it or not. I think that may have something to do with their acting out. Like I said earlier, I think they try to draw the fire toward them to calm things down between you two. It's only a hunch, I could be wrong.

Therapist: Okay, I think we better wrap it up. Remember, there's a 24-hour rule. No talking about what we talked about here for 24 hours. Just let it go and make your own sense of it.

The therapist hits the brakes appropriately and reminds them of the 24-hour rule. Not talking about the interview for the next 24 hours is important because silence interrupts the usual pattern of the family. If the discussion continues, it does so under the rules of the standard family structure. Therapists who focus on social adaptation would like for such a discussion to continue. Those who focus on personhood know that the self benefits from a period of contemplation on a new experience. For example, Greg and Chris have been articulate, making very strong contributions to healing during the interview. Father may be jealous and angry about what happened. If they continue talking after the interview, he may shut them down out of his feeling hurt by the interview. They are then obliged to feel hurt and act out, just like they did before the therapy session. In that way, change begun during therapy is neutralized.

Returning the direction of the therapy back to the therapist sends the implicit message that the family is in good hands. The consultation is ended on an optimistic note. Following the family interview, the consultant and therapist debrief. The consultant shares thoughts about the therapy relationship and observations about the family in treatment. Conducting family therapy is a highly unconscious process, one that is learned through countless interview experiences. It should be noted that the therapists never make a statement longer than a few sentences, with most being short comments. Many comments are in the name of stimulating meditation.

SUMMARY

An extended family consultation is a valuable tool when working with defiant families. It helps transcend the narrow reality of the identified problem as simply existing in one family member. As a reflective activity, it aides the therapeutic process in becoming unstuck by acknowledging the power of an extended family. Consultation explicitly reactivates a systems perspective and symbolically reminds both the therapist and the nuclear family that they are not alone in their therapeutic endeavor. The family is situated within the context of previous generations while the therapist is placed in alliance with a trusted colleague.

A therapist's work with almost any clinical problem, especially when an impasse arises, can benefit from a consultation interview with the extended family. The consultation interview is helpful in the following ways:

1. From a purely pragmatic view, it helps the family group to understand the practitioner's view of the problem and its implications. If powerful family members do not support a diagnosis and the subsequent treatment plan, chances are the practitioner's efforts will be stymied.
2. The interview gives the therapist a vast amount of information about the personal context in which the child lives, and helps the practitioner modulate the treatment appropriately. The therapist's in-depth understanding of the context can help to free the child for individual therapy.
3. The family can learn a great deal about themselves, about each family member, and about the group. When the interview does not have this implicitly therapeutic effect, it is probably because the family members are being overly cautious. It is not unusual for the parents of a disturbed child to feel cut off from their extended family. The consultation interview often restores relationships.
4. Something happens in these interviews. It is seldom clear what that "something" is, but as a result of it there is often a therapeutic shift in the family relationships, the triangular doctor-family-patient relationship or both. We believe the something that happens comes out of the family process, not out of maneuvering by the therapist.

Consultation does not lead to answers. Rather, it reactivates a process by broadening the context and adding emotional voltage as one means of helping the system remain personal and involved. A certain amount of anticipatory anxiety is always present, and one can never predict what the interview will be like. The interview frequently takes on the quality of a family reunion, but the family stories shared shed light on important symbolic themes and relationships. The profound effect of this sample interview was that the group spirit embodied in the family "we" was aroused. The sense of an expanded "we" that emerges as a result of the consultation interview becomes a crucial part of the therapeutic process as it continues.

9

Termination:
A Restless Farewell

Termination is an integral part of the therapy process and it raises a number of interesting issues. One issue relates to the length of time required by any therapeutic process. Families in treatment attend and average of 10 to 12 therapy sessions, based on the experience of our professional practices. A significant number of families struggling with defiance come one to three times, and then fail to return for a variety of reasons. Other families, like the one in Chapters 7 and 8, may continue in therapy for a year or two. The total number of therapy sessions is not a measure of its success or failure.

This chapter examines termination in relation to when it occurs in the therapeutic process. Three categories of time frames are useful to consider. The first involves termination earlier in the process, which might even be considered a failure to begin. The second invovles termination after the establishment of a relationship and approximately 5 to 12 session. In the third category termination comes after a longer term relationship has been established in the range of 15 or more sessions.

TERMINATION AT THE BEGINNING

Oddly, the issue of termination in family therapy is most important at the beginning of therapy, when the implicit therapeutic contract is being negotiated. Therapy is most helpful when the family is invested. Defiant families are resistant about attending therapy and are equally hesitant to embrace new ideas. For example, "We were blaming the school and the neighbors and his screwy friends, but we have met the enemy and it is us, is a difficult notion for them to accept. They tend to more readily embrace the idea that the school, probation officer, or other community representative is forcing them to come. More commonly, the disaffected father is participating at his wife's insistence. One way to clarify a family's investment is to ask at the end of the first session, "Do you want to come back?" rather than simply making another appointment.

Termination is a part of therapy in the way that death is a part of life. "In order to stay alive," Plato suggested, "it is important to practice dying." Life is enriched through encounters with death. Likewise, in order for therapy be effective and alive, it is important to consider termination. In the beginning of therapy, every interview should be treated as if it will be the last. The fact that a family comes to one interview, does not imply there will be another. Especially in the early interviews, we always ask the question of whether or not they want to return. This encourages the therapist to strive to provide the family with a significant experience in each interview.

Ending is considered in the first session when the therapist asks, "Do you want to come back?" and is prepared for the fact they may not want to come back. This is an existential component of family therapy. Families may think psychotherapy is like going to see their medical doctor, where they deposit their pain, and the practitioner works on it while they wait for results. Experimental family therapy does not work unless the family members realize they are in charge of their lives and the therapist is simply a consultant. When the question, "Do you want to come back?" is followed by "Are you getting anything out of this?," we are making it explicit that working on their troubles is up to them. They are also invited to comment on the relationship with the therapist. Defiant families often act as if someone is making them come, even when this is not so. It is crucial to test a family's investment and to make it clear that therapy is something they are electing to do. In cases of ambivalent responses, the therapist may go so far as to hint that they are not adequate to the task, and that they don't have what it takes to be good mental patients.

A combination of firmness and playfulness is useful when working on the issue of whether or not a family should return. The therapist pushes the family members to be explicit about who wants to come back. Sometimes mother wants to come back, but father is ambivalent. His ambivalence or indifference—the equivalent of "no"—interferes with a successful therapy outcome. An available technique is to take a vote in the family as to who is for and who is against coming back. "I don't care," counts as "no" and one "no" is worth two "yes's." The justification for this way of counting the vote is that psychotherapy can be very effective if the participants are invested in getting somewhere, but it can be rendered useless by those who do not value it. Thus, the "no's" have more weight. The therapist must accept the family's vote. An example might be that mother and son want to return, father says "no," and daughter "doesn't care." That puts the vote at two "no's" and two "yes's," or, according to this value system, four against and two in favor. Father and daughter win. The therapist leans back and says "Good luck," and lets them go without an appointment. The mother is discouraged, and says to the therapist, "What are we going to do now?" The therapist replies, "I think you have to learn to follow your husband's lead. If he does not want to do this, he must have a better idea. So turn the problem over to him." Now the problem belongs to the two who do not want to attend therapy. This interaction may sound aloof, but it is very important that a therapist assess the family's investment before investing himself. If a therapist can learn to take this position, he will be surprised by its effectiveness. The therapist's willingness to let the family go obviously raises the members' anxiety about their own problems.

If they can't decide about returning, the therapist can suggest that they talk about it at dinner the following day and call if they want to continue. This is especially important to do at the end of the first session. The driving force for the encounter must be the family's investment, not the therapist's anxiety about the problem.

Case Example: Pressuring a Disaffected Father

Dr. B. was chairman of orthopedic surgery at a private hospital. He was a well-dressed, handsome, quick-witted man who was good at men's club, locker room, and surgical scrub room repartee. He and his dispirited wife had an angry compliant son, age 17, an angry defiant son, age 13, and an angry 8-year-old daughter, who had not decided how compliant she would be. Father was cheerful, mother was depressed, and all three children were angry. During the interview father stayed outside the emotional stream of the family, remaining a clinical observer. He said he thought his wife's depression was a "protracted postpartum depression—twelve years is a long time to suffer, can you imagine?" There was a sliver of the supercilious in his remark. A wire-fine stiletto slipped between his wife's ribs, with a smirk at the therapist that said, "What are you going to do about that one, if you were smart enough to catch it?" The end of the interview approached.

Therapist: (*Smiling, and speaking directly to Dr. B.*) So do you want to do this again?

Father: (*Glancing at his wife*) Do you want to come back?

Mother: Of course!

Therapist: (*To father*) I was asking *you* what you wanted to do. You need to decide what you want to do for yourself. It feels like you are arranging to be here because she wants you here, so you don't have to take this seriously. And you shouldn't come back to be a nice guy. You should come back because you want something from it.

They did come back and when Dr. B. began to speak more personally about his concerns and his smirk disappeared, mother's depression began to fade and his children's constant anger melted. What is significant in this example is that the therapist explicitly forced him to make a decision, and was fully prepared for the possibility that they would not continue.

Case Example: Recognizing the Limits of Therapy

The D. family consisted of mother and daughter, Morgan age 15, a talented equestrian. She was close to her father who died unexpectedly when she was 12. Morgan became increasingly angry when she started high school. She and her mother engaged in daily screaming matches. Morgan threatened to hurt her mother when she was upset. Morgan pushed all limits—she came home later than asked, refused to do anything around the house, and challenged anything her mother suggested. She had seen several therapists with no change. The first interview had hardly started when Morgan began screaming at mother that therapy would do "no damn good!" She didn't care what anyone thought about her, and her mother could "go to hell" before she would cooperate. "Besides," she told her mother, "I hear this therapist is an incompetent jerk, anyway." At this point Morgan stormed out of the office, slamming the door and swearing as she left the building. The mother looked sheepish as she said, "See what I'm up against? I don't know what to do with her." The therapist and Mrs. D. continued the session. Mrs. D. decided that forcing Morgan to attend more therapy would be pointless. Perhaps she should come alone to figure out how to manage as a parent of an "out-of-control" adolescent.

Therapist: So, do you want to set another time?

Mother: Should I come?

Therapist: (Smiling) It would be best if you came with Morgan, but I can stand it if you come alone.

Mother: I would like to think about it. Is that okay?

Therapist: Of course it's okay. You need to decide if therapy can be useful for you.

She didn't reschedule, but the therapist believed they got something they needed. This was a therapeutic interaction. The therapist's presence contaminated the situation so that while Morgan was being her usual impossible self, mother, who at home was inclined to be reactive and vengeful, was able to remain nonanxious and in the correct generation. In a family with fundamentally good health, this one interview was sufficient. It would have been pleasing to go further. In this kind of situation, it is not unusual for a family to return some months later.

For better or worse, the family members are in charge of their lives. A family may pull out of therapy rather than expose the high-school principal father's indifference or if mother's abusive rages are exposed. A family may sacrifice the son in order to protect someone they regard as more valuable, in much the same way that the bishop is sacrificed to protect the king in chess. The family members do what they believe is best for the family, but it can look very distorted from outside. Again, it is the therapist's job to let them go.

It is important for the therapist to pay attention to his intuition and the family's nonverbal behavior. If they seem disinterested, he should be sure to ask if they want to return. Suppose that 20 minutes into the third interview someone says he isn't sure why they are coming. The therapist might say, "That's a good question. Were you thinking you should quit?" He says, "Yes, we were thinking about canceling." The therapist responds, "So, why don't we stop?" then is quiet, expecting them to leave. No one says anything. The therapist asks, "How long do you plan to be here?" "We've only been here 20 minutes," responds the mother. "I know, but you said you wanted to quit. If you don't know why you are coming, I think you should probably pretend you didn't come. So let's quit," continues the therapsit. This is a dance aimed at clarifying the group's investment in staying. It establishes anxiety about therapy, not just to make people anxious, but to increase the likelihood that the therapy will succeed. Occasionally a family will get up and leave at this point, but in most cases a discussion erupts amongst the family members about what they want. The family discussion may identify who is against therapy and why. Or discuss what they should do if not this. The reason for participation is often reset.

TERMINATION AFTER THERAPEUTIC ENGAGEMENT

With families who come to 5–12 sessions there is some success in developing the ability to look at family process as the problem, some changes are made, and a relationship is formed between therapist and family members. There is overall improvement, but ending is earlier than expected. The family is like an adolescent deciding to leave home and the therapist is like the parent who feels it is too soon. Ultimately the *family* decides when to leave therapy.

A variety of scenarios are possible for an adolescent's departure from the family: from mutually gratifying graduation rituals to a disturbing denunciation of all family values. Exiting through defiance may be painful for both parties, yet it may serve the health of both generations. Other adolescents, who launch with less conflict and more appreciation of what they have received, feel free to enter and exit as needed. Family therapy endings are similar. In individual therapy, the therapist and patient "work through" the ending of the relationship and termination may be planned over several sessions. In family therapy, the ending is like an adolescent deciding to leave home. When family members decide to go, it is best for the therapist not to interfere with their decision. Leaving, of course, means they are on their own. Their lives belong to them. When the therapist attempts to hold on too long by suggesting additional issues for them to work on, he steals authority from the family.

More often than not, endings seem premature to therapists. However, termination occurs when family members decide they are ready to take back responsibility for their own living. The therapist who lets a family go, rather than trying to sell it on the idea of continuing, is supporting the family's initiative toward their own ideas about solving life's problems. Their flight into health is respected. However, the therapist should not hesitate to state his honest response to their decision to end. Appropriate statements would include, "I'm going to miss you," or "I think it's too early, but you have to learn that for yourself," or "I think there is a lot more to talk about, but you have to decide about when to end." Defiant families are both tough and smart. Toughness and directness are easier for them to deal with.

Sometimes a family leaves too soon. The flight into health stalls and they fall in the dirt. For example, after five sessions the child goes back to school. Some of the tension in the family drops, and the parents decide they don't need to come back. The child doesn't complain, but within 3 weeks he stops doing his homework again, won't get up in the morning, or provides a new surprise for the family. The child is saying, "I needed more of this and you double crossed me by not sticking with it." In order to be honest with the family about his suspicion that they are backing out too soon, the therapist might say, "We will be worrying," or "I have had the feeling there is something you have needed to talk about but wanted to get out of here before it comes up."

There is a kind of change that occurs at this point in which the family may learn to set limits or how to apply pressure, but the members have not been able to develop a way to respond with flexibility. They have learned how to use the brake and the accelerator, but they have not learned how to use the clutch. They don't know how to shift gears when the terrain changes.

With a famiy who is ending therapy prematurely, it may be useful for the therapist to predict potential problems. He might say, "I know things are on level ground right now, but I don't think it will last. I hope I'm wrong, but usually things go haywire a few months down the road. If that happens, feel free to give me a call. I'll be here at least five years." The issue of termination with a defiant family can create uneasiness if the child is creating problems with the community. Rather than saying, "I would feel better if you came back five more times," it is better not to make them stay only to make him feel better. Unless the therapist is clear about his motivation, a more respectvul comment might be, "It is hard for me to figure out why you are ending right now. The only way it makes sense to me is if you have decided that staying hopeless is more comfortable." In this way, the therapist owns his concern and ambivalence.

Premature endings may be handled with humor. The therapist might say to the family, "You know, everyone who comes here gets a lifetime membership. You can reactivate it at anytime. If I don't hear from you in the next 5 years, why don't you drop me a line and let me know how everyone is doing." The family is not made to feel inadequate or incompetent for deciding to end. Rather, the therapist acknowledges his investment by saying implicitly, "Let me know how things go. I care about your future." The goal is to symbolically invade the family's infrastructure as they leave.

This also implies welcoming these families back whenever they initiate contact in the future. "You know if you hadn't quit 2 years ago, you wouldn't be in this mess," and other judgmental statements do not serve the reactivated relationship well. Families move at different speeds. One pattern that evolves in working with families and defiance is for the family to come for five sessions, end for 4 months, come back for eight sessions, end for 6 more months, then return for two sessions. After that, they may not see them again.

Successful therapy is based on the caring of the therapist and family for one another. It is often tempting to encourage a family to stay longer to help them become more like the therapist, especially when a positive relationship has developed. When a family captures a therapist's creativity and investment, it may be more difficult to let go and return to working with strangers. For the therapist, there is a sense of loss, coupled with excitement over family progress at the time of termination. With successful termination, the family leaves with the feeling that they are in charge of their lives. The therapist reinforces this value by insisting he takes 3% credit for anything that goes right or anything that goes wrong in treatment. The message is: "I believe I had an effect, but most of the credit for changing belongs to you," or "I'm partially to blame—but you have to live with the failure, not me." It is more pleasurable to work with families once there is an established relationship and the struggles of the initial stage have produced a valued therapeutic alliance. However, this is unusual with defiant families because the possibility of a new crisis is always in the background. The stakes are high for this group. They have much to gain if they can learn to lower their defenses and engage therapeutically. Yet these families are more likely to fade out as patients when their anxiety is reduced, but before the problem is actually solved. Although the problem is engaged during therapy, it is resolved later in their daily living.

Entering a therapeutic relationship is not an easy undertaking. A therapist can represent a danger, not only in the guilt that may be induced by having the need to meet with a therapist, but also the problems created by the feeling of being cared for. When we are angry we are clearer about who we are, but if we are in love or feel loved we can be confused. That confusion can lead to painful feelings. For example, in the context of a caring relationship, grief about loss in an earlier relationship may emerge. Therapy occurs in what Winnicott (1971) referred to as a "transitional zone of experience" in which inner and outer reality are merged. The zone is usually soothing, but it can be painful initially.

Case Example: The Adverse Effect of Caring

The C. family, consisted of mother and four children, ages 12, 11, 8, and 6. Mr. C. was in jail for sexual abuse of the 12-year-old son and 11-year-old-daughter. Following the abuse, the 12-year-old was diagnosed with conduct disorder and attention deficit hyperactivity disorder, and placed in a very effective day treatment program which required the family to participate weekly in an on-site family therapy program. Mother became anxious about running out of Ritalin and called the center eight times in 2 days. The physician was not at the clinic on the morning of the first day, however, the prescription was written by the end of the day. At a metalevel, her frequent calls suggested anxiety about getting her needs met by the day treatment center which could imply a concern that the people in the treatment program did not care sufficiently. In the therapy session, the therapist discussed the situation with mother. The therapist said, "It left me worried that you thought we didn't care enough about you; that somehow we didn't take you seriously. Just so you know, we do care. We want this to work out well." "Oh, I know," responded the mother. Surprisingly, they never came back and ultimately Bob had to be dropped from the program because his family would not participate. Our understanding of what happened was that while mother was upset and concerned that her son wouldn't get his Ritalin, the prospect of being taken seriously made her even more anxious. This was a family who had a lot of previous treatment that made little difference. It was her expectation, perhaps her desire, that nothing change too much. If she felt cared for, she might have feelings she did not like to have. She might have to make decisions she didn't want to make. Being cared for may seem a burden, and it has reciprocal demands. She did not want to shoulder the burden. If the family preserves the fantasy that the therapist doesn't care, they don't have to get better. The moral is: Caring is a drug with side effects. While it is usually helpful, sometimes it has adverse side effects.

Termination is not always a final ending. The door is open for return, should it be warranted. Families often return with a deeper commitments.

Case Example: Success in Therapy is not Always Evident

A young mother made an appointment for her family due to behavioral concerns with the two middle children, who were in grades 1 and 2. Both children were unmanageable at home and at school. The two elfin terrorists were suspended on numerous occasions. The parents were estranged, and father turned down the therapist's invitation to attend. When the family (mother and four children) arrived, the therapist recognized the mother as Tracy M., a former patient who had been wildly defiant and difficult as an adolescent. In fact, looking back, she was one of the therapy cases the therapist considered a failure. As the session began, the young mother explained that she wanted to get help for her kids earlier than her mother got it for her. In fact, her worst nightmare was a repeat of her adolescence. She wanted to avoid this at all costs. As Tracy brought the therapist up-to-date, she described the previous therapeutic relationship in much fonder terms than the therapist recalled. What she had found helpful was the therapist's honesty and willingness to stick with her despite her defiance. This part of the story highlights the belief that it is important for the therapist to be honest, see around the defiance, and respect the person, as opposed to pressuring the defiant adolescent to mind her manners. The process had a long-lasting benefit that had not been obvious at termination. She was bringing her children to the same therapist because she trusted the therapeutic process. She hoped she could use her experience as an adolescent to short-circuit her children's behavioral problems.

The question of termination may be raised by either the family or the therapist. Periodically, it is important for the therapist to check on the progress and viability of the therapy system by saying, "Are you still getting something out of this?" or, "It sounds like you've come as far as you would like to. Perhaps you ought to give up for a while and see if you've gotten somewhere." or, "You have raised the idea that you are really wasting your time coming here. Maybe you aren't ready to do what is necessary or maybe you've decided things aren't so bad. Either way, let's talk about stopping." The point is *they* are taking the break, not the therapist. The ensuing discussion may lead to recommitment to therapy or to ending; either way is preferable to limping along.

Often a family ends therapy before the therapist anticipates ending. The members have learned to apply the brakes in family living. Prior to therapy, the family was careening out of control and defiance was running the household. The safety of being able to apply the brakes and slow the conflict down is a blessing. Often, this level of symptom relief is all the family is looking for, or all they are capable of at the time. A defiant family will frequently pull together in four or five sessions. The parents are happy with the aroma of progress and will opt to terminate. The therapist senses that although daily interaction is less destructive, there is no qualitative shift in family interaction. Such a family may experience a honeymoon period that collapses 2 months later. What we hope for prior to termination is that the family members not only be able to apply the brakes and use the accelerator in their lives, but that they learn to shift gears as well. Shifting gears allows them to interact with more flexibility and with the energy required to maintain intimacy. Learning to live at different speeds broadens their options.

Case Example: Anticipating Relapse

The S. family had a defiant adolescent daughter, Nikki, who was drinking, skipping school, and fighting with her parents. They ended therapy when she began attending school regularly. They were pleased with the emergence of a new ability to talk rationally with one another. The therapist cautioned them that this probably would not last, but wished them luck anyway. The therapist said, "I have a worry that you've figured out how to use the brakes and the accelerator, but you still don't know how to shift gears. I'm worried that Nikki still doesn't trust you and you are only pretending to trust her. Of course you can leave, but remember, you have a lifetime membership here which you can reactivate anytime." Three months later mother called, frantic because the problems with Nikki were beginning all over. She was caught with marijuana, became truant again, and her grades plummeted. When they returned to therapy, father indicated he was upset by Nikki's behavior, but even more by the way mother reacted to it. It was interesting that in the earlier sessions the issue of the mother-daughter relationship had never come up. We believe it was because the family wanted to be repaired but without upsetting mother. The family was seen for 8 more months for 22 sessions. There were two problems: Mother was furious about many things in her relationships with her daughter and her husband; and Nikki had discovered the fun of being a naughty girl and was reluctant to give it up.

A defiant family often has a flight into health that it mistakes for problem resolution. At the beginning of the flight, the therapist may be apprehensive but must face the fact that the future is unknown. There is a broad area of overlap between symptom resolution and a qualitative shift in family interaction. A family may be willing to risk that things are better rather than face the upheaval they envision with continued therapy. Additionally, they are pressured by the adolescent's promise that things will change if he will only be given a chance to prove himself. Family therapy often has the quality of guerrilla warfare without a coup. It is important to remember that the seeds of change are in place. The therapeutic guerrillas create an uproar, so that a perturbed system can find new options.

Defiant family members are likely to change their minds midway into therapy. At the beginning they cooperate because they are dependent. As therapy progresses, they become aware of the many issues percolating in the family. Because of their apprehensiveness, parents may opt for a change in strategy, usually by requesting individual therapy for the defiant family member. Many parents want the child under control, but not at the expense of their busy schedules or at the risk of having to address their disappointment in the marriage. Individual therapy offers an out for them. "It's not us, it's him," they safely contend.

Case Example: A Case for Individual Therapy

The W. family attended several family therapy sessions. Bill, age 17, was truant, abusing drugs and alcohol, belligerent to his parents and siblings, and recently threatened suicide. He attended sessions but was uncooperative, negative, and threatening. His parents had difficulty getting him to attend. Father was involved, but ineffective. Mother was withdrawn and bewildered. In the second session, Bill and his 15-year-old sister talked about their worry over mother's alcohol use. Father supported the confrontation but chose to stay silent. The whole family came to the third session a week later, but Bill and his sister were silent. It seemed that they had decided at home that it would be too frightening to move ahead. Only father and Bill came to the fourth and last session. Father had heard of another therapist who had a reputation for being successful with defiant adolescents and decided to schedule an individual appointment for Bill. It would be easier to have him in individual therapy due to everyone's complicated schedules. The daughters were complaining about missing work and social activities. Besides, Bill said he'd rather have individual therapy. It was none of his family's business what his problems were. The therapist said, "I have a different view of what has happened. I think that you all have had a look at the problem, and it scared you. I think you're scared you can't fix it. And Bill thinks he should remain the family problem. So, good luck. I will be worrying. I sure as hell couldn't stand to live like you characters do."

Four months later father called to reschedule. He was discouraged that things had not improved and the family was in more disarray than ever. There was a lull in the chaos, but it did not last long. Mother promised to stop drinking but failed. Bill broke into grandmother's house to steal liquor and $20. Bill's new therapist did not respond to phone calls. This was an interesting series of events. Mother's drinking was exposed for the first time in the second interview. By the fourth interview, the family was frustrated that, though mother took responsibility for her drinking and was essentially trying to stop, family interaction was unchanged. The drinking was not the problem. It was a symptom of the emotional emptiness of the family. They were frustrated and Bill continued to be defiant. They decided to neutralize the family treatment and pursue individual therapy for their son. When that didn't work, they returned with more investment in the family and more sense of ownership of their problems.

LEAVING AN ESTABLISHED RELATIONSHIP: TECHNIQUES FOR TERMINATION

This section we will talk about the smoother ending that occurs with the family who is ambivalent about ending and leaving the therapeutic home they have experienced as soothing. Relevant techniques for this type of ending include highlighting changes, commenting on strengths and resources, highlighting negative ambivalence, and asking for feedback from the family. The gains made in therapy are solidified in the process of termination. The family and therapist review the progress made over the course of the relationship by highlighting changes the group has made. The therapist asks family members what changes they feel have been significant for them. Identifying positive changes is a healthy sign for the family. Members are aware of the road they have traveled toward healthy interactions. For example, father may say, "I can see how my kids were upset by the way I was working so much and being irritable all the time."

Another technique is to ask for feedback about what has been helpful to the family's growth. Giving feedback to the therapist encourages the peer relationship that has evolved through the therapy process. A family who is capable of talking directly about what was helpful or bothersome in the relationship suggest higher self-esteem and an ability to value their opinions. Asking for feedback also says to the family that the therapist believes their opinion is significant. It reemphasizes that mutual growth can take place during the therapeutic process. Inevitably the family will want to say how much they appreciate the therapist. It is important to accept their appreciation, but also to open the door to honest critique as well. He may say, "Thanks for your kindness. Of course no romance is all goodness. How do you think I let you down?" This is a very difficult question to deal with but it is very important to the health of the therapy process.

Case Example: Highlighting Changes: Some Clinical Illustrations

The L. family had been in therapy for a year, attending biweekly sessions. The marital relationship had evolved to a point that a viable team emerged. The three adolescent sons had histories of delinquency, drug and alcohol use, truancy, and theft. When therapy began, the family was one of the most dysfunctional and chaotic families the therapist had worked with. The degree of conflict and misbehavior was overwhelming. At the beginning, crises were regular, family conflict was out of control, and the parents abdicated their roles and responsibility in favor of self-medication with marijuana. The younger children were at the mercy of the older siblings. As termination approached, the family was asked what changes they felt were most helpful in uniting the members. Mother said, "I used to call you whenever there was a family crisis. Now I talk to my husband about it and we decide how to handle things." This change sounds so simple, but relying on another family member was a monumental milestone for this group. Self-reliance had increased dramatically. The therapist shifted to an adjunct position in the family sessions and termination soon followed.

The therapist can also serve as a role model by giving the family appropriate negative feedback. For example, the M. family, though very chaotic, did well in therapy, and it was time to stop. The therapist said to father, who was a lawyer, "You know, when you first came I didn't trust you for a minute. I thought you were just a high-quality con man who had made it." This kind of interaction gives the family freedom to be less adoring of the therapist.

In the termination process with the M. family, father said, "I was relieved that we didn't rattle you when you initially saw us. I was afraid we were the craziest family you had ever seen, but you didn't make us feel weird, no matter what we told you. That gave me some hope that maybe one day we could get our act together." Father was also able to talk about what he found bothersome in therapy. He felt in the initial stage that his wife was more supported by the therapist than he was. It made him angry because he knew they were equally at fault for their parenting problems. He felt good that he could share this perception with the therapist.

Identifying strengths and resources is helpful to future life struggles. Re-empowering the family at the close of therapy by summarizing both individual and family strengths is a positive ending maneuver. The therapist stresses that the family is responsible for its own destiny. When the G. family terminated, the therapist acknowledged not only the family's strengths, but also discussed his pleasure at the growth 16-year-old Chris exhibited. Chris experienced academic failure in high school, but over the past 6 months he not only attended school but received mostly C averages. As the family was leaving the session, the therapist gave Chris a hardy handshake saying, "I always knew you had it in you!" Chris acknowledged by saying, "Yeah, I've even surprised myself. Thanks for the vote of confidence."

It helps to be able to identify microchanges. This helps the family refine their expectations. As mentioned earlier, change is made up of small shifts. The golfer is able to get more power out of his swing if he keeps his left arm straight. He can also straighten out his drives if he moves his right foot about 2 inches. Small changes directly impact the game.

The termination phase represents a return to reality. Successful therapy changes a family's relationship to reality. It creates a transitional zone of reality in which the inner world and the outer world are blended, and there is a walking backward into the future. Living in the transitional zone is accompanied by a tension of creativity. The measure of health is related to the family's ability to be soothed by being there. Healthy families are enriched by the experience. It feels good. In the A. family, father liked it. Mother, on the other hand, could not stand therapy. The 17-year-old son responded to mother's tension because he was more like her. He felt and complied with her limiting metaphorolytic pressure. More belligerent families feel the entry into the transitional zone as tension-filled. They may run from therapy in order to reestablish a familiar relationship to reality. There is something strange about clinical work where the patient is a family system. Family systems do not become dependent in the way individuals do. Sometimes at the termination of therapy the therapist is left with the feeling, "What happened?" This is the point at which the family takes back the responsibility for its own life.

With the advent of managed care, termination may be predetermined. Both the family and the therapist know in advance they have a finite number of sessions. In this case, termination may be premature, with the family ending before they would normally choose to stop. These endings can leave everyone, including the therapist, feeling as though they have unfinished business or unmet goals. The fact that sessions are numbered, should not change how therapy is done with defiant families. The same techniques and relationship focus apply. Our work with defiant families rarely exceeds 15 sessions, which may be spaced out after the therapist gets to know the family to give them time to tackle issues at home. Limiting the number of sessions may motivate the family to take initiative quicker than they would normally. Motivated families work best within these confines. Resistant families can be more difficult to engage when sessions are limited.

SUMMARY

Termination is an integral part of the therapy process. It can take many forms. Consideration of termination is present in all phases of the therapeutic process. Talking about termination is probably most crucial at the beginning of therapy. Defiant families are noted for abrupt endings or opting for symptom relief. The therapist cues into the family's ambivalence about ending, often heightening the tension, predicting problems, or agreeing that the family has come as far as they want. Coaxing a family to stay with false promises of more progress is antitherapeutic. Families get what they need from therapy: When they are ready to take responsibility for their living, it is time to end.

References

American Psychiatric Association. (1994). *Diagnostic and statistical manual of mental disorders, fourth edition*. Washington, DC: Author.

Bateson, G. (1979). *Mind and nature: A necessary unity*. New York: Dutton.

Bateson, G. (1972). *Steps to an ecology of the mind: Collected essays in anthropology, psychiatry, evolution and epistemology*. San Francisco: Chandler.

Bateson, G., & Bateson, M. (1987). *Angels fear*. New York: Macmillan.

Brown, N. O. (1966). *Love's body*. New York: Random House.

Camus, A. (1955). *The myth of Sisyphus and other essays* (J. O'Brien, Trans.). New York: Alfred A. Knopf. (Original work published 1942)

Castaneda, C. (1987). *The power of silence*. New York: Simon & Schuster, Inc.

Chodorow, N. (1978). *The reproduction of mothering*. Berkley: University of California Press.

Connell, G., Mitten, T., & Whitaker, C. (1993). Reshaping family symbols: A symbolic-experiential perspective. *Journal of Marital and Family Therapy, 19,* 243–251.

Connell, G., Whitaker, C., Garfield, R., & Connell, L. (1990). The process of in-therapy consultation: A symbolic-experiential perspective. *Journal of Strategic and Systemic Therapies, 9,* 1, 32–38.

Connell, G., & Russell, L. (1986). In-therapy consultation: A supervision and therapy technique of symbolic-experiential therapy. *American Journal of Family Therapy, 12,* 313–323.

Eco, U. (1982). *The aesthetics of chaosmos: The middle ages of James Joyce* (E. Esrock, Trans.). Cambridge, MA: Harvard University Press.

Gibran, K. (1923). *The prophet*. New York: Alfred A. Knopf, Inc.

Green, M., & Solnit, A. (1964). Reactions to the threatened loss of a child: A vulnerable child syndrome, pediatric management of the dying child, Part III. *Pediatrics, 34,* 58–66.

Hillman, J. (1996). *The soul's code: In search of character and calling*. New York: Warner Books, Inc.

Hooks, B. (1995). *Art on my mind: Visual politics*. New York: The New Press.

Jaffe, R., & Whitaker, C. *Parallel play*. Unpublished manuscript.

Jung, C. G. (1996). *The spirit in man, art and literature* (R. F. C. Hull, Trans.). Bollingen foundation XX, Princeton, NJ: Princeton University Press.

Keith. D. (1994). The family origin as therapeutic consultant to the family. In M. Andolfi and R. Haber (Eds.) *Please help me with the family*. New York: Brunner/Mazel.

Keith, D. (1989). The family's own system: The symbolic context of health. In L. Combrinck-Graham (Ed.), *Children in family contexts*. New York: Guilford Press.

Keith, D. (1986). The self in family therapy: A field guide. *Journal of Psychotherapy and the Family, 3,* 61–70.

Keith, D. (1996). The growing edge in psychotherapy: Healing and play. Lecture presented at The Growing Edge, a tribute to the ideas and work of Carl Whitaker. Rome, Italy.

Keith, N. (1992). *Integrating therapeutic play into family therapy*. Unpublished manuscript.

Kundera, M. (1993). *Art of the novel* (Linda Asher, Trans.). New York: Harper & Rowe.

Partridge, E. (1966). *Origins, a short etymological dictionary of modern english* (4th ed.). New York: Macmillan.

Pruett, K. (1997). How men and children affect each other's development. *Zero to Three, 18,* 1, 3–11.

Whitaker, C. (1971). Process techniques of family therapy. Lecture presented at the Family Therapy Conference. Montreal, Canada.

Whitaker, C. & Keith, D. (1981). Symbolic-experiential family therapy. In A. Gurman & D. Kniskern (Eds.), *The handbook of family therapy* (pp. 187–225). New York: Brunner/Mazel.

Whitaker, C. (1989). Personal communication.

Whitaker, C. (1986). Family therapy consultation as invasion. In L. Wynne, S, McDaniel, & T. Weber (Eds.), *Systems consultation: A new perspective for family therapy* (pp. 80–86). New York: Guilford Press.

Winnicott, D. (1971). *Playing and reality*. New York: Basic Books.

Index

For Product Safety Concerns and Information please contact our EU
representative GPSR@taylorandfrancis.com
Taylor & Francis Verlag GmbH, Kaufingerstraße 24, 80331 München, Germany

www.ingramcontent.com/pod-product-compliance
Ingram Content Group UK Ltd.
Pitfield, Milton Keynes, MK11 3LW, UK
UKHW022118190926
475702UK00013B/1512

* 9 7 8 0 4 1 5 7 6 3 3 1 8 *